Somerset Mapped

Cartography in the County through the Centuries

Emma Down and Adrian Webb

Somerset Archaeological
& Natural History Society

SOMERSET ARCHAEOLOGICAL AND NATURAL HISTORY SOCIETY
in association with
HALSGROVE PUBLISHING

HALSGROVE

First published in Great Britain in 2016
© Somerset Archaeological and Natural History Society (SANHS), 2016
The text is the copyright © of the authors.
The images and text are from the collection of the SANHS unless otherwise stated in round brackets at the end of the caption.

*The Somerset Archaeological and Natural History Society (SANHS) was founded in 1849
and purchased Taunton Castle in 1874 which has been the home of the Society ever since.
The Society is a registered charity who have been publishing and preserving Somerset's heritage since 1849.*

*The views expressed in this volume are those of the author and not those of the
Somerset Archaeological and Natural History Society.*

British Library Cataloguing-in-Publication Data
A CIP record for this title is available from the British Library

ISBN 978 0 85704 287 3

HALSGROVE
Halsgrove House,
Ryelands Business Park, Bagley Road,
Wellington, Somerset TA21 9PZ
Tel: 01823 653777   Fax: 01823 216796
email: sales@halsgrove.com

Part of the Halsgrove group of companies
Information on all Halsgrove titles is
available at: www.halsgrove.com

Printed and bound in China by Everbest Printing Investment Ltd

*This book is dedicated to
Keith Needell (1927–2011)*

Contents

Foreword

Ever since I was a teenager I have been fascinated by maps: the challenge of trying to locate an extract from a current OS map in a Geography exam; the huge excitement of the arrival on approval of a genuine old map from a trusting dealer; the creation of a map to illustrate a route taken and a journey observed.

The concept of a collection of maps of part or all of a single county covering such a long and significant period of time is a happy one, not simply because it enables us to compare the skills of so many cartographers, or to enjoy the curiosities that some of them produced, but collectively, because maps offer us so much more than a depiction of their time. Many are serious records of the past, for they name hills and rivers, towns and villages pointing to settlement centuries before. Some had contemporary purposes, conveying political or ecclesiastical power, supporting legal claims, delineating possession, guiding the serious traveller. And there are a few, some the most fascinating, that look to the future, illustrating in a traditional way what the landscape might be in years to come.

Together, within the compass of a single county, such maps, and others drawn for special purposes, offer a history of our county not through the wordy descriptions of historians but by line and symbol, careful lettering and sometimes flamboyant cartouche that are the creations of the cartographer.

I am very happy to commend this book.

Robert Dunning

Editorial

In order to add clarity to the presentation of the maps in this volume, text shown within square brackets has been added by the editors. Dates in the titles of maps shown in round brackets are the dates when the maps were published, often many years later in the case of many of the early maps in chapters one and two. Foreign language material and the titles of publications, including printed maps, are given in italic text. Written quotations are shown in single quotation marks, whereas quotes from spoken words are shown in double quotes. Each map is cited in full at the end of the text. From chapter two each opening of this book follows the same format: on the left-hand page is a description of the story behind the map, plan or chart and on the right-hand side is a reproduction of all or part of that piece of cartographic history. In some instances the pages which follow on have also been used to show further reproductions.

Acknowledgements

Numerous people have kindly answered questions or provided information for this volume, including Lesley Aitchison, Phillip Ashford, Peter Barber formerly of the British Library Map Library, Dr Joe Bettey, Stephen Bird, Daniel Brown of Bath in Time, Dr Andrew Butcher, Robin Cloke, Jennifer Ebrey, Ann-Marie Fitzsimmons, David Hart, Ian Hodge, Professor Simon Keynes, Andy King, Colin Lewis, Hilary Marshall, Nick Millea, Map Librarian at the Bodleian Library, Rose Mitchell, Principal Map Specialist at The National Archive, Brian Murless, Frances Neale, Mike Nolan, Chris Preston, Naomi van Loo of New College Library, Margaret Webb, Kevin Welch, Andy White, Dr Julia Wood of Wells City Archive, and Jenny Wraight of the Admiralty Library. Special thanks go to Liz Grant, Jane du Gruchy, Tom Mayberry, Mervyn Richens, Dr Janet Tall, and the staff at the Somerset Heritage Centre for their help and support. Also to Barry Lane of the Wells and Mendip Museum for supplying numerous images and Nathan Webb for his I.T. expertise. Of particular note is the Herculean effort David Bromwich made using his encyclopaedic knowledge of the contents of the Somerset Archaeological and Natural History Society's (SANHS) library to locate numerous maps, some of which are unique to the Society's collection.

The authors are especially grateful to Dr Robert Dunning for writing the foreword and for his comments on the text, as well as to Steven Pugsley of Halsgrove and his team. This volume would not have come into print without the generous support of the Wyndham Trust Taunton and of the Fairfield Trust, who are the main sponsors. Without the kindness and vision of Dr Dunning and Lady Gass this volume would have been greatly reduced and compromised, fortunately this is not the case.

Introduction

This volume is a study of maps of Somerset over a 600-year period. It is not exclusively about county maps but about maps compiled for widely differing purposes. Some of them cover the whole county, some only small parts of it, some are extracts from regional or national maps. Others are part of national mapping schemes such as those of the Ordnance Survey and maps produced under the Tithe Commutation Act of 1836. Thomas Chubb, in his work on the printed maps of the county published in 1914, wrote that 'down to 1782 cartographers compiled their maps of Somersetshire mainly from those of Saxton and Speed.'[1] Many exceptions to this statement have been included in this volume; equally, many county maps have been omitted because they were derivatives. It has not always been possible to show a complete map, but extracts have been made to give a flavour of the maker's style and choice of content. Important national mapping schemes also find a place, such as William Smith's Elizabethan survey of cities and Captain Greenvile Collins' survey of the coast.

This book is not a carto-bibliography of the kind Chubb compiled. In its time that was a landmark publication. The author worked in the Map Room of the British Museum and provided a chronological catalogue of county maps and a comprehensive index of compilers, engravers and publishers. This volume contains maps of all periods. Some were issued in atlases, some folded for the popular market, some resulting from legal proceedings, some emanating from parliamentary legislation. Several capture a brief moment in British history, while others show a whole epoch of human activity. They were produced for varying purposes, some thematic, others very practical, occasionally as secondary to advertising or entertainment.

The purpose of this volume is to bring examples of Somerset's unique history to light with the aid of maps and to explain something about their makers and how they portrayed the ancient county. To achieve this, maps such as the Revd H.M. Scarth's of Roman Somerset, published in 1878, has been included to illustrate the Roman period (see page 8-9). This methodology has been applied to the first chapter, which covers the period from the Bronze Age to the end of the fifteenth century. A chronological arrangement has been applied throughout.

The earliest mapping

The first contemporary map to be included is the anonymous 'Gough map' of the fourteenth century (see pages 22-5). A century earlier, a map drawn c. 1250 by the chronicler Matthew Paris names Somerset as south of Devon and Dorset and mentions Bath, Wells, Glastonbury and, in one version, Montacute.[2] In a more sparse depiction of the British Isles in another map, Paris does not even mention the county, but Bristol and Lundy are shown.[3] A diagram of the Heptarchy naturally includes Wessex.[4] Other pre-Reformation maps of Great Britain show Bath and Glastonbury, but notably not Wells.[5] Gerald of Wales named the Severn as *Sabrina*[6] and Hereford Cathedral's famous *Mappa Mundi* of c. 1300 shows *Sabina* [sic], Bath and Glastonbury.[7] The Evesham world map of c. 1390 names Bath, Bridgwater, Minehead, Glastonbury and Wells, the three ecclesiastical centres obviously familiar to its monastic source.[8]

Somerset places also feature in depictions other than maps. A drawing made between 1031 and 1046 appears to show the consecration of the first cathedral at Wells in 909.[9] The walled city of Bath appears in a copy of Geoffrey of Monmouth's *Historia Regum Britanniae* of the first quarter of the fourteenth century.[10] A more fanciful image of the city is found in *Elmham's Chronicle* of about 1416 where it is portrayed beneath King Bladud;[11] and another possible image is in a Book of Hours of 1445-6 that once belonged to John Beaufort, duke of Somerset. There the city is shown dominated by the cathedral priory, the river flowing outside its walls, and its meadows grazed by sheep.[12] A depiction of another kind, on a seal, was in use at Bridgwater in the fourteenth century and appears to show both the bridge that was so important to the town and the two gatehouses which guarded the entrance to its castle.[13]

Seal of the Community of Bridgwater attached to a document dated May 1343. (SHC, DD/S/WH/61)

A depiction which is almost a map is a bird's-eye view of the precincts of Wells from the market place (see page 22). It was drawn between 1463 and 1466 by a distinguished cleric, Thomas Chaundler, a native of Wells, as one of the illustrations for his book in praise of Bishop William of Wykeham. Featured are the two stone gateways, the Penniless Porch and the Bishop's Eye, leading respectively to the cathedral and the Bishop's Palace. Two stone and timber-framed buildings in front of the precinct wall between the two gateways might represent the 'New Works' Bishop Thomas Bekynton had built on the north side of the market place, and perhaps the dwellings in Sadler Street where Chaundler's family lived.[14]

Mapping Somerset: county maps

More detailed and comprehensive maps of Somerset first appeared in the sixteenth century. The *Anglia Figura* of *c.* 1537,[15] the most important manuscript map of Britain created during Henry VIII's reign, shares many similarities with the Gough map in terms of the places marked (though not named). It includes Bath, which is not on the earlier map, and Watchet, which modern scholars have identified as Cleeve Abbey. It omits Bruton and Frome, perhaps through lack of space, but names Crewkerne, Glastonbury, Taunton, Uphill and Wells. Sebastian Munster's 1554 edition of *Geographica*, printed and thus assumed to be of potential use to travellers, contains a map of the British Isles, but its simplistic depiction only allowed room for Bridgwater, the 'Holms' and Bristol, with the county name shown as 'Somset', missing the contraction probably indicating an engraver's error.[16] George Lily (*fl.* 1528-1559) in *Britanniae insulae quae nunc Angliae et Scotia regna continent cum Hibernia adiacente nova descriptio* of 1546 named Bath, Chard, Ilchester and Wells, *Sabrina* and the two 'Holms'.[17]

Possibly in the early 1560s Lawrence Nowell drew a map entitled 'A General Description of England and Ireland' where he named over a dozen Somerset places.[18] It is thought Nowell's map was used as the basis of Gerard Mercator's map of England, Scotland and Ireland published in 1564 (see pages 40-1).[19] Mercator named 21

towns or villages, the River Tone, Athelney island and Mendip hill and his spelling of a few presents problems: 'Bauell' is Banwell, 'Comage' is Combwich, but where are 'Towen' between Watchet and Bridgwater and 'Tabuton' to the south of Wells? The first may simply record a tower and may perhaps refer to Stogursey; the second may be a copying mistake from an unknown source and suggests Bruton.

Humphrey Lhuyd's map of England and Wales, published in 1573 by Abraham Ortelius,[20] was heavily based on Mercator's 1564 map, as he copied the latter's 'Bauell' and 'Comage', for example.[21] There is also a similarity to George Lily's work in the inclusion of Chard and Ilchester, though Lhuyd's place-name spellings are his own and he named the rivers Avon and Ivel. The Quantocks are depicted but not named, the Mendips are entirely omitted, but an unnamed range of hills appears between Ilminster and Selwood. Nevertheless,

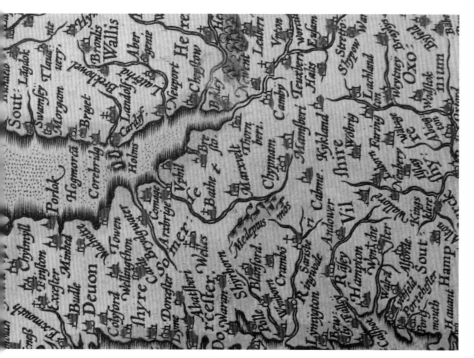

Abraham Ortelius' map of England showing the county of Somerset with the Mendip Hills drawn too far to the east. (A. Ortelius, *Theatrum orbis terrarum* (London, 1606) (Admiralty Library)).

this is the first example since the Gough map to name such a large and significant number of Somerset place-names on one map. Ortelius also published his own map of King James's kingdom in 1606 which portrayed the Mendip hills running from a position south-east of Bath to the south of Chippenham in Wiltshire.[22] All these maps predate the small-scale county maps whose first appearance in the second half of the sixteenth century marks what has been called the first age of mapping.[23]

The work of Christopher Saxton (*c.* 1540-*c.* 1610) and John Norden (*c.* 1547-1625) heralded that first age. In 1575 Saxton produced the first detailed map solely of Somerset[24] (see pages 44-7). Norden is thought to have been born in the county, but produced no map of it, although he made surveys of Crown lands with his son, also John.[25] During his time the work of the surveyor began to include maps alongside surveys, perambulations and evidences, and some examples of such maps have survived for the county. Among them is one of Black Down on the Mendip Hills in the 1550s[26] (see pages 36-9) and another of some disputed land in Compton Martin in the 1570s[27] (see pages 48-51). Both maps show thumb-nail-size drawings of churches, although only Compton Martin's is shown with any accuracy. Because of their age and content, both maps are of national importance. A survey of Bath and the surrounding area by Henry Savile is another rare survival. Thought to have been surveyed *c.* 1600, it was published in 1610 by John Speed in his *The theatre of the Empire of Great Britaine*[28] (see pages 56-7).

The first thematic map to be published was produced by Jodocus Hondius (1563-1612) in 1589-90. It shows a number of places in each county, but Wells is the only one named in Somerset.[29] Another rare early survival is the map of the county printed on a playing card by William Bowes in 1590.[30] The use of playing cards in Somerset is documented from the time Raffe Bowes and Thomas Beddingfield esquires were granted a patent for importing playing cards for 12 years from 1571.[31] A game of cards was played at Keynsham for three to four hours in February 1607/8,[32] and the game was unlawfully played at Easter 1608 at Middlezoy and possibly Othery.[33] In 1612, or earlier, John Perce of Midsomer

Norton, tailor, was accused of overcharging in his alehouse, allowing drinking and card playing on Sunday, selling drink in the churchyard, playing tables and cards for money,[34] and in 1617 Mark Hurford of Wellington, cutler, was accused of being generally abusive, drunk and guilty of playing cards.[35] An example of this early card, the three of diamonds, is in the collections of the Somerset Archaeological and Natural History Society and is thought to be dated to around 1620,[36] and a more simpler card, the 10 of diamonds, printed before 1616, is amongst the muniments formerly at Nettlecombe Court.[37] Several other cards showing the county were produced in the seventeenth and eighteenth centuries.[38]

The three of diamonds published in 1676 by William Redmayne in his pack of 52 cards known as a Recreative pastime by card-play; geographical, chronological and historiographical, of England and Wales. The reverse of the card is blank. (SANHS).

County maps continued to be produced for another four centuries, but the seventeenth century saw many new ones, not merely re-workings. William Hole's maps in *Polyolbion* (see pages 58-61) show rivers as the most important features of the landscape. Land improvement lay behind the map of Sedgemoor by Richard Newcourt (d. 1679) published in 1662; and the strip road maps of John Ogilby (1600-1676), produced in 1675 (see pages 78-9), were a landmark in map publishing. They are also the best evidence of popular map use. The map of Bath and surrounding area by Joseph Gilmore (d. ?1723) (see pages 86-7), first published in 1694, puts the city in its topographical context.

The seventeenth century saw much map recycling, when already-published maps were issued in new formats. One, engraved by Wenceslaus Hollar (1607-1677) and published in 1644, is known as the 'Quartermaster's Map' from the title page of the volume: *The kingdome of England, & principality of Wales, exactly described whith every sheere, & the small townes in every one of them, in six mappes, portable for every mans pocket, … useful for all commanders for quarteringe of souldiers, & all sorts of persons, that would be informed, where the armies be, never so commodiously drawne before this.* Somerset appeared on the fifth sheet, folded many times over.[39] The maps were derived from Saxton's great wall map[40] and they were subsequently re-issued with an amended title page omitting any mention of the conflict.[41]

An extract from Hollar's map of Somerset published in 1644. (*The Kingdome of England, & Principality of Wales …* (London, 1644) (Admiralty Library))

For Somerset the eighteenth century was a golden age of cartography, with a rich variety of maps, charts and surveys and a greater change in cartographic styles than in any other period. A genre of circular maps was established where a map is portrayed within a circle covering all or part of the county. Charles Western's

circular map of *The roads of England according to Mr Ogilby's survey*, published in 1713 (see pages 98-9) is an early example of a national map showing Somerset's roads. It was followed by Thomas Thorpe's *An actual survey of the city of Bath ... and of five miles round*, published in 1742 (see pages 106-09). Perhaps this last metaphorically opened the flood gates, as a similar scheme centred on Bristol, published in 1769 (see pages 116-19), was followed by a much smaller version of Thorpe's 1742 map, published in 1771.[42]
A circular map centred on Taunton, using revised work of Day and Masters and published in 1791, had a new inset map of Taunton (see pages 130-3).

The way in which county maps were presented had been challenged at the beginning of the eighteenth century by Herman Moll. His use of illustrations of some of the county's better known antiquities was an imaginative way of giving maps a further dimension (see pages 96-7). It was a dimension lacking in his competitors' work and meant that his product, although it contained nothing new geographically, had a unique selling point, giving Moll the edge in the face of growing competition. Moll, who described himself as a geographer, also engraved a volume of 62 maps entitled *Atlas Minor*, one of which covers the south of England including Somerset. The engraver added the legend 'This Map has been Copied four times very confused and Scandalously'; unlawful copying was evidently rife. All the maps in the atlas were clearly engraved and the title-page illustrated the tools of the map maker's trade, some of which had changed very little for centuries.

The eighteenth century also saw the first attempt since Christopher Saxton to map all, or significant parts of the county in great detail. John Strachey, F.R.S., of Sutton Court, Bishop's Sutton, produced a map based on his own observations. His 1736 map, although on a scale which did not allow the luxury of field boundaries, showed lime kilns, beacons, bridges, a Roman mount, a well, a ford, windmills, battle sites, a decoy, a single tree, posts on a race course, forts, coal works, lead mines, the 'Wedding' at Stanton Drew, 'Holloway's Pavilion' and a building with an inn sign. Insets allowed greater detail for Bath, Ilchester and Wells. Strachey's plan

of Wells, significantly different from that of William Simes published in the year before, includes an impressive amount of detail.

Between Monkton Combe and Widcombe a building is shown with a sign board. To the north is 'The Race' with the word 'Course' omitted. (Strachey's Map of Somerset / SANHS.)

Strachey's map was produced not in Somerset but in London, where the map trade was based. It was published by John Senex, F.R.S. (1678-1740), engraver and seller of maps and globes and one of the leading cartographers of the day, though Strachey himself marketed his map through a local network of friends and acquaintances (see pages 102-05). His sales were far less than Thomas Thorpe achieved with his Bath map in 1742 (see pages 106-09). Following Thorpe, Benjamin Donne produced, in 1769, a map of Bristol and an area 11 miles around (see pages 116-19), and together with Thorpe thus mapped a considerable area of north Somerset. Both maps were attractively presented in circular format.

Rather more utilitarian was the county map of Day and Masters of 1782 (see pages 124-7) which, together with Thorpe's and Donne's productions, was a landmark scheme. All three were produced when map publishing and selling were becoming integrated. At the same time there had grown an insatiable appetite for maps, resulting in much reprinting and copying. The copying was not always faithful, and re-working was designed to imply something new. At the same time there was a substantial increase in thematic mapping, more maps of engineering schemes, more accurate hydrographic charts, and bird's-eye views. Benjamin Donne's map of the Western Circuit of 1784 (see pages 128-9), a similar version by William Tunnicliff accompanied by a survey and map of the county (see pages 134-7), William White's soil map (see page 143) and the canal maps of Robert Whitworth, William Smith and John Rennie (see below) are examples of the thematic mapping of Somerset. As for more accurate navigational charts, which had far more practical applications as well as implications for human life than land maps, two charts published in the 1770s replaced information that was over 70 years out of date.[43] An unusual approach to mapping, returning back to the early 'views' of the sixteenth century, is George Bickham's birds-eye view of the county published between 1749 and 1754.[44]

At the end of the eighteenth century, maps with a purely educational purpose began to appear. John Aikin published *England delineated; or, a geographical description of every county in England and Wales: with a concise account of all its products, natural and artificial. For the use of young persons.* His stated aim was 'to make my young countrymen better acquainted than they are usually found to be with their native land'. The first edition of 1788 had no county maps, but they were included for the second edition of 1790. The work was published by Joseph Johnson, but the maps are unsigned. There were four later editions of the book with the maps, and one without. The Somerset map is fairly simple and does not have a scale, which for educational purposes would not have helped young Georgian children realise how big the county was. The map is quite small, measuring 130 x 94mm. Aikin lived in Great Yarmouth and had to rely on existing works for his information. His description of Somerset contained information of the county's location, its hills, rivers, manufacturing and historical events. He gave a substantial amount of information on the ports and harbours on the coast, as well as details concerning Bristol, which might reflect his maritime interests.[45]

During the nineteenth century Somerset was mapped in a wide array of styles and themes: from games such as those produced by Robert Rowe in 1805 (see pages 146-7) and Edward Wallis (see pages 164-5) to more serious maps of the administrative areas of the

county of 1868 (see pages 178-9) and 1888. Somewhere in between appeared maps showing the location of meeting-places of hunts (see pages 166-7) and those used by cyclists (see pages 184-6). A map showing the results of the censuses from 1801 and 1831 was published in 1833 and contained details of population, baptisms, marriages and burials arranged by hundreds. Others showing literacy rates and population figures were produced in the 1840s.

Aikin's outline map of the county of Somerset published to accompany his *England delineated* in 1790. (Adrian Webb collection.)

The literacy maps show that Somerset was one of the most illiterate counties as indicated by those who could sign their names at marriage.[46] Changes in Parliamentary electoral procedures and arrangements in the nineteenth century required maps showing electoral divisions and polling places.[47]

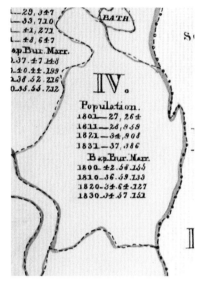

An extract from the 1833 statistical map for the hundreds of Frome, Kilmersdon, Mells and Leigh, and Wellow. (SANHS, Tite Collection.)

The use of circular maps continued with one of the smallest depictions of the county, at least since the playing card map, appeared within a double circle in 1803 in John Luffman's *A new pocket atlas and geography of England and Wales* (see dust jacket).[48] William Smith's *Fossilogical map of the county five miles round Bath* was published in 1811 (see pages 150-1). This was ground-breaking for its content and was pirated by the Reverend Richard Warner who had also published Smith's 'Table of Strata' in his *History of Bath* without acknowledgement.[49] Following the publication of the Ordnance Survey maps of the county, several new circular maps appeared based upon them. Two examples are Lander's *Electoral district map of the city and county of Bristol* published in *The new Bristol guide* in 1842; and Thomas Clark and Robert Down's 1853 map of the area *Five miles round Bridgwater.*

The twentieth century saw many more publications combining maps and advertisements (see pages 196-201) and there was one planned map designed by the Somerset Resorts' Association deliberately to omit all potential members (Keynsham Rural District Council was one) who did not pay a subscription.[50] Advertisements were often very colourful, but were unable to match the mapping resulting from the various regional reports in the 1920s and 1930s (see pages 202-09) and the numerous geological maps such as those by Horace B. Woodward in his *Geological atlas of Great Britain and Ireland*, published by Edward Stanford in four editions in two decades from the early 1900s. With the introduction of the Land Utilisation mapping (see pages 212-15) and the 'GSGS'

series by the Geographical Section, General Staff, War Office and Ordnance Survey, colour on topographical maps became more commonplace (see pages 220-3). The 1920s also saw the introduction of map-making in schools. The 'Mapograph', patent number 241,595 issued in 1924, had one roller covering the Bristol Channel and the West of England. It was the idea of A.T. King and B. Simons and was produced by the Mapograph Co. Ltd. of 110 High Road, Chiswick. The Mapograph was used in the teaching of geography into the 1970s.[51]

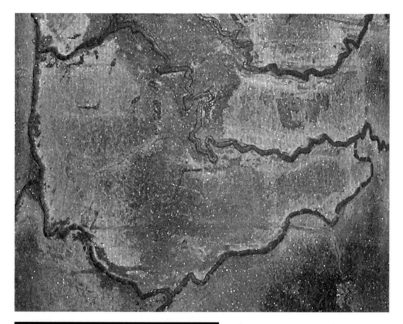

Above: The outline of the county boundary for Somerset which is in reverse. When ink was applied to the roller, and rolled across a piece of paper, the image would appear the 'right way reading'. (Adrian Webb collection.)

Left: The end view of map roller.

In face of the threat of war a large contingent of cartographers working in the Admiralty's Hydrographic Department took over the Royal School at Bath and later in the war moved to Ensleigh, on the outskirts of the city. In June 1941 the Department started printing maps and charts at Creechbarrow House, on the edge of Taunton, among them half a dozen covering the Bristol Channel and Somerset coast in some detail. There were special charts for submariners,[52] three charts showing mined and searched channels for parts of the Bristol Channel which were overprints of the standard navigational charts,[53] and others showing minefields[54] and wrecks.[55] In addition to these, the region featured on general charts and diagrams showing administrative limits,[56] Royal Naval shore signal and shore wireless transmission stations[57] and operational charts designed for planning purposes.[58] The most notable production was a suite of charts supplied for Operation Overlord and the D-Day landings. Also during the war maps were maintained to show the location of enemy bombs dropped on Bath and Weston-super-Mare.[59]

A printing press being operated by Mr Jack Cooney at the Hydrographic Supplies Establishment, or Creechbarrow House in Taunton pulling impressions from a copper plate, *c.*1950. (Reproduced with permission of the United Kingdom Hydrographic Office.)

Mapping the transformation of Somerset: roads

Gradually improving transport links was one of the factors in the growth of Somerset's population and later its industry and tourism. Maps showing the county's roads, accompanied by details of distances, can be traced back to the Gough map of the 1360s (see pages 22-5). Distances from 'All ye high wayes from any towne or citie, in England, to the citie of London' were included in Franke Adams' *Writing tables ...* published in London in 1581[60] and in 1625 John Norden wrote a guide for travellers showing distances between cities and shire towns.[61] Neither work contained a map of Somerset, though Norden's went on to be reproduced with a thumb-nail-sized map of the county and was later improved during the Civil War[62] (see pages 178-9). John Adams' *Index Villaris* (1680) includes distances between hundreds of town and cities in England and Wales, with their latitude and longitude; 34 Somerset places were named (see pages 80-1).

Jacob van Langeren's thumbnail map of Somerset, 1635. (Private collection.)

Following Ogilby's landmark publication (see pages 78-9), the flood-gates opened for variations of his work. John Seller's *A new map of the roads of England*, published in London *c.* 1690, based on Ogilby's maps, shows the worst depiction of Somerset of its age: the road from Bristol to Huntspill heads in a westerly direction towards Wales. To make matters worse, Seller failed to included a county boundary between Somerset and Gloucestershire, leaving any traveller using his map in a state of confusion.[63]

A much improved version of Seller's map was produced by George Willdey in 1713 (see pages 98-9) which has been described as 'outstanding'.[64] Strachey in 1736 (see page 102-5), Thorpe in 1742

(see pages 106-9), Donne in 1769 (see pages 116-19) and Day and Masters in 1782 (see pages 124-7) all showed road layouts more accurately than Ogilby. To supplement such works Edward Ward, bookseller of Bristol,[65] published a distance diagram from Bristol on a schematic map containing a panel with post times in and out by C. Douglas in 1737.[66] Ward, who was responsible for starting the *Bristol Mercury* in 1746 and the *Bristol Weekly Intelligencer* in 1748, met the demand for such maps, a business continued by another Bristol man, William Matthews, a printer and bookseller.[67]

Matthews' map was published from his Broad Mead premises in Bristol in 1791.[68] The maps of Ward and Matthews are very rare. As time went on cartographers became more imaginative. James Baker's *The imperial guide with picturesque plans,* published in 1802, included a map of the great post road from Thatcham to Frome. It included a bird's-eye view of Frome,[69] one in a series of views of prominent towns paralleled in medieval itineraries. Specific stretches of roads, notably turnpike roads, were not usually printed, but many examples survive in the records of the county Quarter

An extract from *Mathews's map of the roads and distance in measured miles from the city of Bristol, to all the cities & chief towns in England & Wales. From the latest survey's* published in Bristol in 1791. (Adrian Webb collection.)

The title and cartouche showing the cliffs dwarfing the River Avon.
(Adrian Webb collection)

Sessions[70] and also among the archive of Bennett and Co., land agents and surveyors of Bruton.[71] An example of a printed map covering a whole turnpike district can be found on pages 190-1.

When specialist maps for cyclists started to appear in the later nineteenth century they were copies of existing mapping series, but cleverly packaged to make them attractive to feed the demand of a growing pastime (see pages 204-6). Many local businesses saw an opportunity, among them Pople and Churchill, booksellers,

stationers and printers of Burnham-on-Sea, who published a *New touring, cycling, and driving road map for forty miles about* shortly after 1909. The map put Burnham at the centre of a series of one-mile circles on a map of half an inch to a mile scale, and also included detailed hydrography for the adjacent waters of the Bristol Channel (see pages 190-1).[72] A similar idea of circular lines for distances was used on Oliver's *Road map showing a radius of 80 miles from Bristol* of the 1960s, showing the whole of Somerset with lines at 20-mile intervals.[73]

One of the biggest developments in road mapping was the publication of the 'Rapid Route Indicator' in the late 1920s. J.E. Thompson took out a patent in 1928 for a paper system that showed the direction, route and distance of a destination. The rotary ring (2 on diagram) was pivoted on the map to be used at (5) bearing the names of various destinations, any one of which could thus be brought into radial alignment with a corresponding stationary line (10) bearing the names of places en route and their distances. The indicator might be pinned at any departure point on a map and a compass (12) used for even greater accuracy. (see pages 200-01).

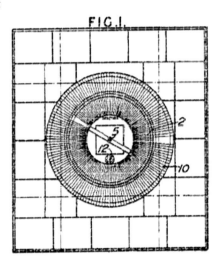

A reproduction of the patent drawing for the Rapid Route Indicator.
(Private collection.)

Mapping the transformation of Somerset: canals and railways

An early, large-scale scheme of canalization was proposed by Francis Matthews to Oliver Cromwell to make a navigable passage from Bristol to London, connecting with Salisbury and the sea at

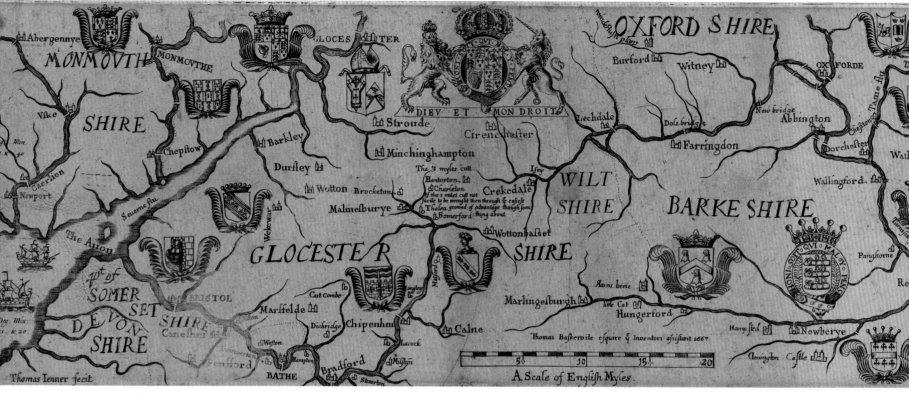

An extract from an early scheme of canalization proposed by Francis Matthews and published in 1668. (Bristol Museum, J1127)

Christchurch. The Lord Protector's death halted any progress, but Matthews did not give up and proposed it again, this time to the Attorney-General.[74] A map showing the scheme was published in 1668[75] and had the canal been completed, the implications for the development of north-east Somerset would have been brought forward by over a century. Sixty years later a scheme to improve the navigation of the Parrett was published which included cutting through the peninsula at the river mouth.[76] Many other regional maps survive to show the proliferation of proposals, some of which came to pass. Of this generation of schemes was Robert Whitworth's 1769 survey of an 'intended navigable canal' from Langport to Axmouth in Devon.[77] It was followed, for example, by William Smith's *Plan of the proposed deviations of the Somersetshire Coal Canal* of 1793 (see pages 138-9), Masters' *Plan of the navigation from Ilchester to Langport* and John Rennie's *Plan of the proposed Grand Western Canal*

from Topsham in the county of Devon to Taunton in the county of Somerset (see page 140-1), all products of the need for improved transportation.

On the eve of the great outburst of railway mania one obscure but abortive scheme had implications for Somerset. A bill first read in 1836 for making a harbour and breakwater at Tremoutha Haven in Cornwall and building a railway from there to Launceston, contained a map of the South West, showing two other proposed railways. One ran from Bristol to Exeter, the other from Bath to Weymouth, both sweeping through Somerset. The map was printed by C. Ingrey, lithographer of the Strand, London. The full scheme offered safety to ships using the Bristol Channel 'often compelled to put back by contrary winds to King-Road' and other harbours.[78] The proposed railways through Somerset shown on the map would

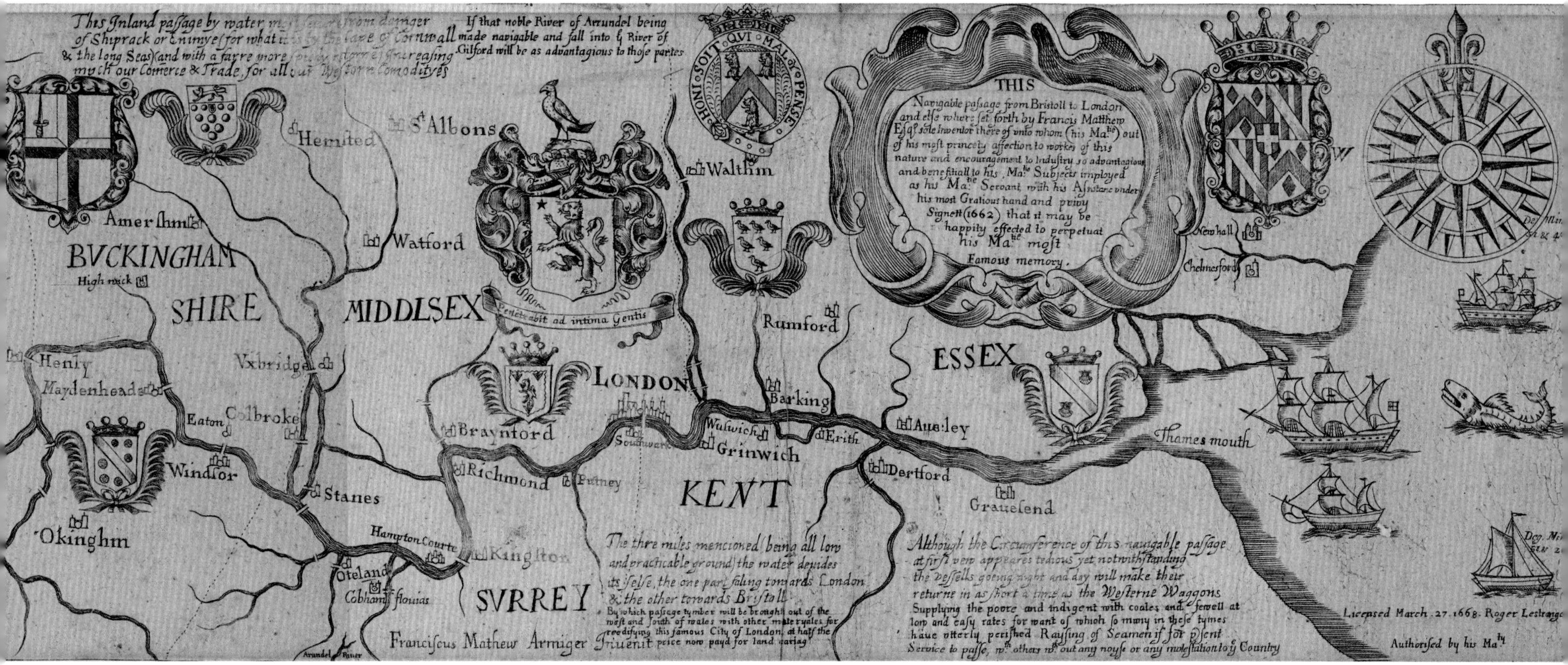

have joined the south coast of England with the River Avon, and hence to the Bristol Channel, something that all the canal schemes failed to do. A map[79] showing many of those schemes was produced by the antiquarian, writer on heraldry and popular map-maker Thomas Moule (1784-1851) in the late 1830s.

Local map collections

Significant private collections of predominantly printed maps of Somerset and its regions have made their way into the public domain. Bath Central Library has three. One was formed by Robert Edward Myhill Peach (1821-1899), a Lincolnshire native who lived in Bath for over fifty years and accumulated a number of maps amongst his collection of approximately 1,000 volumes that was purchased to form Bath Public Library.[80] C.P. Russell, clerk to the Rectory of Bath and librarian to the Bath Literary and Scientific Institution, put together a collection of maps and plans of the city from 1572 contained in two large folio volumes.[81] John James Chapman (1790-1867) also left three volumes of maps.[82] The antiquarian George Weare Braikenridge (1775-1856), F.G.S., F.S.A., owned a graingerized copy of William Barrett's *History and Antiquities of the City of Bristol* (Bristol 1789) which contains numerous maps.[83]

Almost from its inception in 1849 the Somersetshire Archaeological and Natural History Society collected maps of all types, both printed and manuscript. One significant part was reported on in 1927 by H.R. Phipps, detailing how the Society had acquired over 60 copy tithe maps, made about 1843, mainly from parishes in West Somerset, along with manuscript drafts of apportionment

 *Somerset Mapped*

books made between 1838 and 1870. Many of the maps in the collection are lithographed or are tracings ranging from large coloured copies to small rough drafts.[84] The total has grown to well over 1,000 manuscript items including examples dating back to the sixteenth century. In addition it includes hundreds of printed maps and plans in atlases, guide books, reports and volumes of transactions in their library. One particular volume was given to the Society by Charles Tite (1842-1933),[85] a newspaper proprietor, and contains some unique manuscript and printed items, some of which are reproduced in this volume.

An extract from the south-west sheet of Thomas Moule's Map of the inland navigation of England & Wales showing the canalization schemes in Somerset in the late 1830s (London, 1837-1839). (Adrian Webb collection.)

Further reading

The late Keith Needell (1927–2011), to whom we dedicate this volume, started collecting Somerset maps in the 1950s and working upon an improved version of Chubb in the 1990s. To do so he included in his own publications, where possible, a mixture of black and white, and colour illustrations. Many of these illustrations came from his own collection and some of the navigational charts were reproduced in volume 97 of the Somerset Record Society's series.[86] Needell, who undertook voluntary work at the British Museum, knew that undertaking such a task was not going to be achieved over-night. He therefore decided to split his research into different biblio-graphies, that is volumes covering county maps (in two volumes), the city of Bath, roads and the Bristol Channel. The volumes Needell produced were only issued to a very limited audience and published privately, which were supplemented with additional pages when new information was added. Sadly this project was not completed but nevertheless they are works of great value to anyone studying Somerset maps, produced by someone with a passionate interest in the county's cartographic heritage. The volumes are:

Printed maps and plans of the city of Bath 1588-1860 (London, 2001), 160 pages;
Printed maps of Somersetshire 1575-1860, 2 volumes (London, 2001), 568 pages;
Printed maps of Somersetshire roads 1675-1842 (London, 2002), 94 pages;
Maps and charts of the Somerset coast with the Bristol Channel 1583-1860 (London, 2002), 148 pages.

In addition to his cartobibliographies there have been numerous works on individual map makers and cartographers, as well as the publication of great scholarly projects on aspects of the history of cartography. Volumes such as that produced by Williams and Worms of *British map engravers*,[87] which should be referred to for further information on many of the engravers mentioned in our volume. The Tooley / Scott *Dictionary of mapmakers* (in four volumes),[88] Bendall's *Dictionary of land surveyors* (in two volumes)[89] and the *Oxford Dictionary of National Biography*[90] all contain information on many of the mapmakers mentioned in this volume. Catherine Delano-Smith's and Professor Roger Kain's landmark volume on *English maps: a history* (London, 1999) has been a guiding force for this volume and should be referred to for further reading. Their volume provides the national context for many of the maps reproduced in our volume and how they have interacted with society in England and elsewhere. A vast amount of information on the history of virtually every aspect of maps and mapmaking can be found on the 'Map History' website.[91]

Reproductions

Many friends, both old and new, have kindly let us reproduce maps from their collections, including Richard and Diane Charlton, Ian and Angela Coleby, Hilary Marshall, Adrian Seville and David Worthy. Specific acknowledgements include the image of Wells which is reproduced by permission of the Warden and Fellows of New College, Oxford. The photograph of J.W. Gough is reproduced by kind permission of the Provost and Fellows of Oriel College, Oxford. The image of Charles Western's road maps is reproduced with permission of Bonhams Auctioneers. The image of the map of Mendip of *c.*1590 is reproduced with permission of the Wells and Mendip Museum. The image of *The West Country revealed*, published in *Farmers Weekly* in 1958, is reproduced with permission of Farmers Weekly. Documents held at the Somerset Heritage Centre are reproduced with permission of the South West Heritage Trust. Other images are reproduced with grateful thanks to (in no particular order) the following institutions: Bibliothèque Nationale de France, The National Archive [of England and Wales], the British Library and the Bodleian Library. Many images have been used under the Creative Commons license.

References

[1] T. Chubb, *A descriptive list of the printed maps of Somersetshire 1575-1914* (Taunton, 1914), xi.

[2] All four places are marked in British Library (B.L.) Cott. Jul. D vii. Montacute is omitted in B.L. Cott. Claud. D vi f. 12v.

[3] B.L. Royal 14 c vii, f. 5v.

[4] Ibid. Cott. Claud. D vi f. 10v.

[5] Ibid. Harl. MS 1808 f. 9v: map of Britain *c.* 1400.

[6] Dublin, National Library of Ireland MS 700: late 12th century.

[7] Hereford Cathedral Library.

[8] London. College of Arms, MS Muniments 18/19, map of the world *c.* 1390; P Barber, 'The Evesham world map: a late medieval English view of God and the world', *Imago Mundi: The International Journal for the History of Cartography*, 47:1, 13-33.

[9] Rouen, Bibliotheque Municipale, MS 0368 f. 2v: Lanalet Pontifical.

[10] B.L. Royal 13 A iii.

[11] Ibid. Cott. Claud. E iv. Bladud was the mythical founder of Bath.

[12] New York, Pierpont Morgan Library MS 893; S Bird, 'The earliest map of Bath' in *Bath History* I (Bath 1986), 128-49.

[13] SHC DD/S/WH 61. I am very grateful to Dr Andrew Butcher for this information.

[14] Oxford, New College MS C 288; M.B. Goldie ed., *Middle English literature: a historical sourcebook* (Oxford 2003) 149. For Chaundeler's house, which he bequeathed to Winchester College, see Winchester College deeds, Wells no 15.

[15] B.L. Cott. Aug. I i 9.

[16] S Munster, *Das Engelland mit dem anstossenden Reich/Schotland* in *Geographica* (Basle 1554).

[17] B.L. K Top V 2: G. Lily, *Britanniae insulae quae nunc Angliae et Scotia regna continent cum Hibernia adiacente nova descriptio* (1546).

[18] Ibid. Add MS 62540: Lawrence Nowell, *A General Description of England and Ireland* (1564).

[19] Ibid. Maps 183 r 2 (facsimile), plates 5 and 6: G Mercator, *Angliae, Scotiae & Hiberniae nova descriptio* (Duisburg 1564).

[20] Ibid. Maps C 2 c 10: Map of England and Wales in *Angliae Regni Florentissimi Nova Descriptio Auctore Humfredo Lhuyd Denbygiense* (Antwerp 1573).

[21] Ibid. Maps 183 r 2: Mercator, *Angliae Scotiae & Hibernia nova descriptio*.

[22] A. Ortelius, *Theatrum orbis terrarum ... The theatre of the whole World* (London 1606).

[23] C. Delano-Smith and R.J.P. Kain, *English maps: a history* (London 1999), 51.

[24] K. Needell, *Printed maps of Somersetshire 1575-1860* , 2 volumes (London 2001), 394-9.

[25] *The Manors of Norton St Philip and Hinton Charterhouse 1535-1691*, ed. C.J. Brett (Somerset Record Society xciii, 2007), passim.

[26] Wells Museum. See *Proceedings of the Wells Natural History and Archaeological Society* (1911).

[27] S.H.C. DD/SPY 110. I am grateful to David Hart and Frances Neale for their comments about this important map.

[28] J. Manco, 'Henry Savile's map of Bath' in *Proceedings of the Somerset Archaeological and Natural History Society* 136 (1992), 127-39.

[29] G. Schilder, 'An unrecorded set of thematic maps by Hondius' in *The Map Collector* 59 (Spring 1992), 44-7.

[30] Needell, *Printed maps of Somersetshire*, 84-7.

[31] J. Ames, *Typographical antiquities: an historical account of printing in England . . .* (London 1790), 1628; S.H.C., DD\WO/35/21/1 Letters testimonial by William Jones for the Bishop of Bath and Wells concerning the replies of Polidore Helytree to the libel of not observing the articles of his dispensation, refusing to wear certain vestments and playing at cards and dice, 22 March 1572/3.

[32] S.H.C., Q/SR/3/17 examination, 17 February 1607/08.

[33] S.H.C., Q/SR/3/103 information, 1608.

[34] S.H.C., Q/SR/15/75 Presentments, 18 April 1612.

[35] S.H.C., Q/SR/27/178 Articles of misdemeanour, 1617.

[36] S.H.C., DD/SAS/G169/1 playing card, *c.*1620.

[37] S.H.C., DD/WP/55/5/18 playing card, pre 1616.

[38] Needell, *Printed maps of Somersetshire*, 268-9, 292-6, 366-7.

[39] The volume was sold by Thomas Jenner at the south entrance of the Exchange, London.

[40] Delano-Smith and Kain, *English maps*, 76.

[41] Ex inf. Jenny Wraight, Admiralty Librarian, 15 September 2015.

[42] K. Needell, *Printed maps and plans of the city of Bath 1588-1860* (London 2001), 56.

[43] A.J. Webb, *Maritime surveys, charts and sailing directions of the Somerset coast, circa 1350-1824* (Somerset Record Society 97, 2014) 144-6, 172.

[44] Needell, *Printed maps of Somersetshire*, 516-17; and ibid. *appendix 2, the coast of Somerset and the Bristol Channel* (London 1993), 9.

[45] J. Aikin, *England delineated; or, a geographical description of every county in England and Wales: with a concise account of all its products, natural and artificial. For the use of young persons* (London, 1790), 323-39.

[46] Delano-Smith and Kain, *English maps*, 236-7.

[47] S. Lewis, *View of the representative history of England* (London, 1840), plate LXXIV.

[48] Needell, *Printed maps of Somersetshire*, 283.

[49] S. Winchester, *The map that changed the World: a tale of rocks, ruin and*

redemption (London 2002), 152.

[50] *Bath Chronicle and Weekly Gazette*, 19 January 1929.

[51] B.C. Wallis, *The teaching of Geography* (Cambridge 2013).

[52] Taunton, U(nited) K(ingdom) H(ydrographic) O(ffice), OCB Y121.

[53] Ibid. OCB MO1152, MO1176, MO1179.

[54] Ibid. OCB Z27B.

[55] Ibid. OCB MISC320.

[56] Ibid. OCBY7.

[57] Ibid. OCB F08.

[58] Ibid. OCB MISC245.

[59] Bath, Bath and North-East Somerset Record Office, 0146; S.H.C., DD/Va.b.

[60] F. Adams, *Writing tables with a kalendar for xxiii yeres, with other necessary rules …* (London 1581).

[61] J. Norden, *England, an intended guyde, for English travailers, shewing in generall, how far one citie, & many shire-townes in England, are distant from other together, with the shires in perticuler: and the cheife townes in every of them, with a generall table, of the most principal townes in Wales* (London 1625).

[62] See Needell, *Printed maps of Somersetshire*, 260-1.

[63] B.L. Maps 1205(2): J. Seller, *A new map of the roads of England* (London *c.* 1690).

[64] Delano-Smith and Kain, *English maps*, 168.

[65] British Book Trade Index, entry for Edward Ward, http://www.bbti.bham.ac.uk/Details.htm?TraderID=72941, accessed 25 September 2015.

[66] http://www.oldmaps.com/maps/England-Wales/Plan-Shewing-Direct-Roads-City-Bristol-by-C-Douglas-circa-1737-id130857.htm.

[67] British Book Trade Index, entry for William Matthews, http://www.bbti.bham.ac.uk?Deatils.htm?TraderID=46106, accessed 25 September 2015.

[68] W. Matthews, *Matthews's map of the roads and distance in measured miles from the city of Bristol, to all the cities & chief towns in England & Wales. From the latest survey's* (Bristol 1791).

[69] K. Needell, *Printed maps of Somersetshire roads 1675-1842* (London 2002), 8-9.

[70] S.H.C. Q/RUp contains examples dating between 1810 and 1871.

[71] Ibid. DD/BT contains examples from between 1780 and 1869.

[72] Private collection.

[73] *Oliver's tourist road guide and map for motorist and cyclist shewing routes and distances from Bristol* (Worcester *c.* 1963).

[74] *Calendar of State Papers, Domestic Series, of the reign of Charles II, 1661-2,* preserved in the State Paper Department of Her Majesty's Pubic Record Office, ed. M.A.E. Green (London 1861), 306-7.

[75] Bristol Museum, J1127: F. Matthews, *This navigable passage from Bristoll to London and elsewhere, set forth by Francis Matthews esq, sole inventor thereof* (1668).

[76] Webb, *Maritime surveys*, 142-3, and facsimile 9.

[77] S.H.C., DD/CM/133: *A plan of the intended navigable canal from Langport in the county of Somerset, to the English Channel, near Axmouth in the county of Devon. Survey'd in October 1769 by Robt. Whitworth.* It was engraved by William Darling of Newport Street, London.

[78] A proof copy of the proposed scheme is held at the U.K.H.O., L510: *England Folio 2, Prospectus of a company, to be incorporated by act of Parliament, for the construction of a new harbour, in the Bristol Channel, … and a railway from thence to Launceston, in the county of Cornwall* (n.d.).

[79] T. Moule, *Map of the inland navigation of England and Wales* (London 1837-9), engraved by James Bingley.

[80] Bath Central Library, loose insert dated 1898 in Peach's copy of his *Historic houses of Bath* (2 vols. Bath 1883-4).

[81] http://isuu.com/bathintime/docs/russell_i_album?e=4325875/8331623.

[82] *The Magazine of the Survey of Old Bath and Its Associates* 6 (November 1996).

[83] Ex inf Jane Bradley, Bristol Central Library.

[84] H.R. Phipps, 'Tithe maps, chiefly West Somerset' in *Proceedings of the Somersetshire Archaeological and Natural History Society* 72 (1927).

[85] http://www.yeovilhistory.info/tite-charles.htm, accessed 5 September 2015.

[86] Webb, *Maritime surveys*, passim.

[87] L. Worms and A. Baynton-Williams, *British map engravers : a dictionary of engravers, lithographers and their principal employers to 1850* (London, 2011).

[88] V. Scott, ed., *Tooley's dictionary of mapmakers revised edition vol. 1: A-D* (Tring, 1999); V. Scott, ed., *Tooley's dictionary of mapmakers revised edition vol. 2: E-J* (Riverside, CT, 2001); V. Scott, ed., *Tooley's dictionary of mapmakers revised edition vol. 2: K-P* (Riverside, CT, 2003); V. Scott, ed., *Tooley's dictionary of mapmakers revised edition vol. 4: Q-Z* (Riverside, CT, 2004).

[89] S. Bendall, *Dictionary of land surveyors and local map-makers of Great Britain and Ireland 1530-1850, 2 volumes, 2nd ed.* (London, 1997).

[90] Oxford University Press, Oxford Dictionary of National Biography (Oxford, 2004). Updated entries can be accessed at http://www.oxforddnb.com/ but a subscription is needed.

[91] http://www.maphistory.info/.

Select Bibliography

A.J. van der Aa, *Biographical dictionary of the Netherlands. Part II* (Haarlem, 1865).

Abercrombie and B.F. Brueton, *Bristol & Bath regional planning scheme* (London, 1930).

T.D. Acland and W. Sturge, *The farming of Somersetshire* (London, 1851).

J. Aikin, *England delineated; or, a geographical description of every county in England and Wales: with a concise account of all its products, natural and artificial. For the use of young persons* (London, 1788).

G.A. Aitken, *The life of Richard Steele* (London, 1889).

J.R. Akerman ed., *Cartographies of travel and navigation* (Chicago, 2006).

G. Allen and R.J.E. Bush, *Book of Wellington* (Buckingham, 1981).

Anon, 'Edmund Hobhouse (1817-1904): obituary' in *PSANHS* 50 (1904), 113.

P. Ashford, 'Exmoor historical update' in *Exmoor Review* 47 (2006), 58-60.

A. Ashley, *The mariner's mirror . . . of Navigation* (London, 1588).

M. Aston, ed., *Aspects of the Medieval landscape of Somerset* (Taunton, 1988).

E. Baigent, 'Adams, John (b. before 1670,d. 1738), cartographer' at http://www.oxforddnb.com/view/article/119?docPos=4 (accessed: 07/12/2015).

W.G.V. Balchin, 'United Kingdom geographers in the Second World War: a report' in The Geographical Journal, 153:2 (July, 1987).

P. Barber 'The Evesham world map: A late medieval English view of god and the world' in *Imago Mundi: The International Journal for the History of Cartography*, 47:1 (1995), 13-33.

P. Barber, *King Henry's map of the British Isles* (London, 2009).

K. Barker and R.J.P. Kain, ed, *Maps and history in south-west England* (Exeter, 1991).

W. Barrett, *The history and antiquities of the City of Bristol* (Bristol, 1789).

E H. Bates, 'Five-hide-unit in the Somerset Domesday' in *PSANHS* 45 (1899), 51-107.

G. Beech and R. Mitchell, *Maps for family and local history* (London, 2004).

S. Bendall, *Dictionary of land surveyors and local map-makers of Great Britain and Ireland 1530-1850 II*, 2nd ed. (London, 1997).

J.B. Bentley and B.J. Murless, *Somerset roads – the legacy of turnpikes* (Taunton, 1985).

J.B. Bentley and B.J. Murless, *Somerset roads – the legacy of turnpikes – phase 2 – Eastern Somerset* (Taunton, 1987).

J. Billingsley, *General view of the Agriculture in the county of Somerset; with observations on the means of its improvement* (London, 1794).J. Blaeu, *Atlas novus* (Amsterdam, 1648).

S. Bird, 'The earliest map of Bath' in *Bath History* 1 (1986), 128-49.

Boundary Commissioners for England and Wales, *Report of the Boundary Commissioners for England and Wales* (London, 1868).

G. Braun, *Civitates Orbis Terrarum* 3 (Cologne, 1581).

G. Brown, *Richmont Castle, East Harptree an analytical earthwork survey* (Portsmouth, 2008).

E. Bowen, *An improved map of the county of Somerset* (London, 1750).

E. Bowen, *The Royal English atlas* (London, 1762).

S. Brown, *Dictionary of twentieth-century British philosophers* (London, 2005).

C.A. Buchanan, 'The Langport, Somerton and Castle Cary Turnpike Trust' in *Journal of the Somerset Industrial Archaeology Society* 2 (1977).

D. Buisseret, ed, *Monarchs, ministers, and maps: the emergence of cartography as a tool of government in Early Modern Europe* (Chicago, 1992).

I. Burrow, *Hillfort and hill-top settlement in Somerset in the first to eighth centuries A.D.*, BAR British Series no.91 (Oxford, 1981).

E. Burt, 'W.A.E. Ussher: an insight into his life and character' in *Geoscience in South-West England* 13 (2013), 165-171.

R.J.E. Bush, *Book of Taunton* (Buckingham, 1977).

J. Caley, *Valor ecclesiasticus temp. Henr. VIII*, 6 volumes (London, 1810-1834).

J.W. Carleton, ed, *The Sporting Review* (London, 1842).

C.E.H. Chadwick Healey, ed., *Bellum Civile. Hopton's narrative of his campaign in the west (1642-1644) and other papers*, S.R.S. 18 (1902).

T. Chubb, *A descriptive list of the printed maps of Somersetshire, 1575-1914* (Taunton, 1914).

G. Clifton, *Dictionary of scientific instrument makers* (London, 1996).

Captain G. Collins, *Great Britain's coasting pilot* (London, 1693).

Revd J. Collinson, *History and antiquities of the county of Somerset*, 3 volumes (Bath, 1791).

T. Cox, *Magna Britannia antiqua & nova: or, a new and exact, comprehensive survey of the ancient and present state of Great-Britain*, 6 volumes (London, 1738).

F.A. Crisp, *Abstracts of Somersetshire wills, etc., copied from the manuscript collections of the late Rev. Frederick Brown*, 6 volumes (London, 1887-1890).

W. Dampier, *et al*, *A collection of voyages* (London, 1729).

Lt-Cdr A.C.F. David, 'Lieutenant Murdoch Mackenzie and his survey of the Bristol Channel and the south coast of England' in *Cartographic Journal* 40:1 (June 2003), 69-78.

Lt-Cdr A.C.F. David, 'Collins, Mackenzie and the hydrographic surveys of the Somerset coast' in A.J. Webb, ed., *A maritime history of Somerset volume one: trade and commerce* (Taunton, 2010), 93-106.

J.B. Davidson, 'Notes on part of the county boundary between Somerset and

Devon' in *PSANHS* 28:2 (1882), 1-27.

J.B. Davidson, 'Charters of King Ine' in *PSANHS* 30 (1884), 1-31.

B. Donn, Master of the Mathematical Academy, Bristol, *The description and use of four new instruments, viz. First. The variation and tide instrument. Second. A lunar instrument for shewing the places of sun and moon; also for finding the time of high-water at any time and place, both on common and new principles; to which is added, a nautical pocket piece. Third. The improved analemma, for solving the common problems of the celestial globe. Fourth. The panorganon for solving those of the terrestrial globe; being very useful to young students in geography* (Bristol, *c.*1772).

B. Donne, *An enlarged syllabus of a course of lectures in experimental philosophy; as usually exhibited on a proper apparatus, by Benjamin Donn, teacher of the mathematics* (Bristol, 1780).

B. and H. Donne, Teachers of Mathematics and Natural Philosophy, *A map of the Western Circuit of England : containing the countries of Cornwall, Devon, Dorset Somersat, Wilts & Hants : geo-hydrographically delineated on a scale of an inch to a mile* (Bristol, 1784).

B. Donne, Teacher of the Mathematics, and Lecturer in Experimental Philosophy, at Bristol, *The British mariner's assistant: containing forty tables, adapted to the several purposes of trigonometry and navigation. To which are prefixed an essay on logarithms, and navigation epitomized; containing rules for solving the most necessary problems, with the method of finding the latitude at sea, by observations taken either before or after Noon. Also a more accurate method of finding the time of high water than any other hitherto published, &c.*, second edition with additions (London, 1785).

M. Drayton, *Poly-Olbion* (London, 1612).

W. Dugdale, *Monasticon Anglicanum: a history of the abbies and other monasteries, hospitals, frieries, and cathedral and collegiate churches, with their Dependencies, in England and Wales*, 3 volumes (London, 1655-1673).

W. Dugdale, *The history of imbanking and drayning of divers fenns and marshes both in foreign parts and in this kingdom and of the improvements thereby* (London, 1662).

R.W. Dunning, *Somerset monasteries* (Stroud, 2001).

C.W. Dymond, *Worlebury: an ancient stronghold in the county of Somerset* (Bristol, 1902).

A. Ereira, 'A Scot's atlas of England and Wales: Ogilby, Ogilvie and Britannia' in *CAIRT* 27 (July 2015), 5-6.

F.L. Fagan, *A descriptive catalogue of the engraved works of William Faithorne* (London, 1888).

A. Fea, *King Monmouth, being a history of the career of James Scott, "The Protestant Duke", 1649-1685* (London, 1902).

H.B. Fordham, *Road books and itineraries of Great Britain 1570-1850* (Cambridge, 1924).

E. and S. George, eds, *Bristol probate inventories part 1: 1542-1650*, B.R.S. 54 (2002).

E. and S. George, eds, *Bristol probate inventories part 2: 1657-1689*, B.R.S. 57 (2005).

E. and S. George, eds, *Bristol probate inventories part 3: 1690-1804*, B.R.S. 60 (2008).

J. Gillmore, *A letter to a member of parliament, concerning Dagenham-Breach: occasion'd by the late ruin of the works there* (London, 1718).

M.B. Goldie, ed, *Middle English literature: a historical sourcebook* (Oxford, 2003).

J.W. Gough, 'Witham Carthusians on Mendip' in *PSANHS* 74 (1928), 87-101.

J.W. Gough, *Mendip mining laws and forest bounds*, S.R.S. 45 (1931).

I.E. Gray, 'Ferdinando Stratford of Gloucestershire' in *Transactions of the Bristol and Gloucestershire Archaeological Society* 67 (1946-1948), 412-15.

E. Green, *The preparations in Somerset against the Spanish Armada, A.D. 1558-1588* (London, 1888).

E. Green, 'The earliest map of Bath' in *Proceedings of the Bath Natural History and Antiquarian Field Club*, 6 (1889), 58-74.

E. Green, *Bibliotheca Somersetensis : a catalogue of books, pamphlets, single sheets, and . . . in some way connected with the county of Somerset, 3 volumes* (Taunton, 1902).

C. and G. Greenwood, *Somersetshire delineated: a topographical description of the county of Somerset* (London, 1822).

C. and G. Greenwood, *Atlas of the counties of England* (London, 1834).

J.B. Harley, *The historian's guide to Ordnance Survey maps* (London, 1964).

J.B. Harley and Y. O'Donoghue, *The old series Ordnance Survey maps of England and Wales* II (Lympne Castle, 1977).

J.B. Harley and R.W. Dunning, *Somerset maps Day & Masters 1783 Greenwood 1822*, S.R.S. 76 (1981).

J.H. Harvey, ed., *William Worcestre intineraries* (Oxford, 1969).

P.D.A. Harvey, *The history of topographical maps symbols, pictures and surveys* (London, 1980).

P.D.A. Harvey, *Maps in Tudor England* (London, 1993).

D. Hart *et al*, *Compton Martin Tudor map* (Compton Martin, 2013).

E. Heawood, 'John Adams and His Map of England' in *The Geographical Journal* 79:1 (1932), 37-44.

Rt Revd Bishop Hobhouse, 'On a map of Mendip' in *PSANHS* 41 (1895), 65-72.

Rt Revd Bishop Hobhouse, *Map of Somerset shewing the chief estates as recorded in Domesday Book, A.D. 1086* in *PSANHS* 35 (1889).

D. Hodson, *County atlases of the British Isles*, 3 volumes (Welwyn, 1983-1985).

W. Hughes, *The Sporting Review* (London, 1842).

W. Hunt, *The Somerset Diocese, Bath and Wells* (London, 1885).

E.M. Jacobs, 'Lucas Jansz Waghnaer Van Enckhuysen (1533/4-1606): his impact on maritime cartography' in *Bulletin Ligue des Bibliothèques Européennes de Recherche*, 28 (1986).

T. Jenner, *A direction for the English traviller* (London, 1643).

T. Jenner, *A book of the names of all the hundreds contained in the shires of the Kingdom of England* (London, 1644).

T. Jenner, *A book of the names of all parishes, market towns, villages, hamlets, and smallest places, in England and Wales* (London, 1657).

The Very Reverend Jex-Blake, D.D., Dean of Wells 'The Battle of Lansdown, July 5, 1643' in *PSANHS* 41 (1895), 38-46.

D. Kingsley, *Printed maps of Sussex, 1575-1900*, Sussex Record Society 72 (1982).

C. Koeman, *The history of Lucas Janszoon Waghenaer and his Spieghel Der Zeevaerdt* (Lausanne, 1964).

B. Lane, *The Knights Templar in Blagdon*, Charterhouse Environment Research Team (Wells, 2008).

J. Latimer, *Annals of Bristol, eighteenth century* (Bristol, 1893).

R. Locke, 'On the improvement of meadow land, Burnham, 16th February 1789' in *Letters and papers on agriculture, planting, &c selected from the correspondence-book of the society instituted at Bath, for the encouragement of agriculture, arts, manufacturers, and commerce within the counties of Somerset, Wilts, Gloucester, and Dorset and the city and county of Bristol* V (Bath, 1795), 180-201.

H.C.M. Lyte, 'Edward Bates Harbin' in *PSANHS* 64 (1918), 92-5.

E.T. Macdermot, *The history of the Forest of Exmoor* (Taunton, 1911).

A.F. Major and Revd C.W. Whistler, *The early wars of Wessex* (Cambridge, 1913).

A.F. Major, 'The Rev. Charles Watts Whistler' in *PSANHS* 59 (1913), 100-102.

J. Manco, 'Henry Savile's map of Bath' in *PSANHS*, 136 (1992), 127-39.

P. McGrath, *The Merchant Venturers of Bristol : a history of the Society of Merchant Venturers of the city of Bristol from its origin to the present day* (Bristol, 1975).

H. Moll, *Fifty six maps new and accurate maps of Great Britain* (London, 1708).

R. Morden, *Britannia* (London, 1695).

R. Morden, *The new description & state of England* (London, 1701).

M.C. Morison, 'The Duc de Choiseul and the invasion of England, 1768-1770' in *Transactions of the Royal Historical Society, Third Series*, 4 (1910), 86.

S. Munster, *Geographica* (Basle, 1554).

F. Neale, ed., *William Worcestre: the topography of medieval Bristol*, B.R.S. 51 (2000).

K. Needell, *Printed maps and plans of the city of Bath 1588-1860* (London, 2001).

K. Needell, *Printed maps of Somersetshire 1575-1860*, 2 volumes (London, 2001).

K. Needell, *Printed maps of Somersetshire roads 1675-1842* (London, 2002).

K. Needell, *Maps and charts of the Somerset coast with the Bristol Channel 1583-1860* (London, 2002).

J. Norden, *England, an intended guide for English travellers* (London, 1625).

J. Ogilby, *Iliad* (London, 1660).

J. Ogilby, *Britannia* (London, 1675).

R.R. Oliver, 'The Ordnance Survey: a quick guide for historians' in *The Historian*, 30 (1991), 16-19.

J. Owen, *Britannia depicta* (London, 1720).

Oxford University Press, *Oxford Dictionary of National Biography* (Oxford, 2004).

M.S. Pedley, *The commerce of Cartography* (Chicago, 2005).

Revd W. Phelps, *The history and antiquities of Somersetshire*, 2 volumes (London, 1836).

Revd W. Phelps, *Observations on the great marshes and turbaries of the county of Somerset: with suggestions for their improvement by rendering the drainage of the moors and lowlands bordering on the rivers Parret, Ivel, Ile, and the Tone, more perfect and effectual* (Dorchester, 1836).

C. Pooley, *Stone crosses of Somerset* (London, 1877).

M.H. Porter, 'Boevey, James (1622–1696), merchant and philosopher' at http://www.oxforddnb.com (last accessed: 29/11/2015).

W. Ravenhill, 'Benjamin Donn, 1729-98: map-maker and master of mechanics' in *Transactions of the Devonshire Association for the Advancement of Science, Literature and Art* 97 (1965), 179-93.

W. Ravenhill, 'John Adams, His Map of England, Its Projection, and His Index Villaris of 1680' in The Geographical Journal 144:3 (1978), 424-37.

W. Ravenhill, 'The marine cartography of South-West England from Elizabethan to modern times' in *The new maritime history of Devon* I (Exeter, 1992), 155-62.

W. Ravenhill, *Christopher Saxton's 16th century maps: the counties of England and Wales* (Shrewsbury, 1992).

M.R. Ravenhill and M.M. Rowe, *Devon maps and map-makers: manuscript maps before 1840*, 2 volumes, Devon and Cornwall Record Society New Series 43 and 45 (2002).

E.J. Rawle's *Annals of the ancient Royal Forest of Exmoor* (Taunton, 1893).

S. Redgrave, *Dictionary of artists of the English School* (London, 1874).

G. Roberts, *The life, progresses, and rebellion of James, Duke of Monmouth, &c.*, 2 volumes (London, 1844).

A.H.W. Robinson, *Marine cartography in Britain: a history of the sea chart to 1855* (Leicester, 1962).

H.J. Rose, *A new general biographical dictionary*, 1 (London, 1857).

G. Rowley, *British fire insurance plans* (Old Hatfield, 1984).

The Royal Society, *Philosophical Transactions*, 1719 and 1725.

J. Rutter's, *Delineations of the north western division of the county of Somerset, and of its antediluvian bone caverns, with a geological sketch of the district* (London, 1829).

H. Saint George Gray, 'Albany F. Major' in PSANHS 71 (1925), 109-110.

J. Savage, *History of the Hundred of Carhampton* (Bristol, 1830).

J.H. Savory, 'Mendip mappe Ashweek Court Rolls' in *Proceedings of the Wells Natural History and Archaeological Society* (Wells, 1911).

Revd H.M. Scarth, 'Roman Somerset' in *Somerset Archaeological and Natural History Society Proceedings* 24 (1878), 1-21.

G. Schilder, 'An unrecorded set of thematic maps by Hondius' in *The Map Collector* 59 (Spring 1992), 44-7.

V. Scott, ed., *Tooley's dictionary of mapmakers revised edition vol. 1: A-D* (Tring, 1999); *vol. 2: E-J* (Riverside, CT, 2001); *vol. 3: K-P* (Riverside, CT, 2003); *vol. 4: Q-Z* (Riverside, CT, 2004).

W.A. Seaby, 'The Iron Age Hillfort on Ham Hill' in *Archaeological Journal* 107 (1950), 90-1.

W.A. Seaby, 'Coinage from Ham Hill in the County Museum, Taunton' in *PSANHS* 95 (1950), 143-58.

A. Seville, 'The game of goose and its influence on cartographical race games' in *IMCOS Journal* 115 (Winter 2008), 51-7.

W.A. Seymour, *A history of the Ordnance Survey* (Folkestone, 1980).

R. Shirley, *Maps in the atlases of the British Library a descriptive catalogue c.AD850-1800* (London, 2004).

B. Short, *Land and society in Edwardian Britain* (Cambridge, 1997).

B. Short, C. Watkins, W. Foot and P. Kinsman, *The National Farm Survey 1941-1943 state surveillance and the countryside in England and Wales in the Second World War* (Wallingford, 2001).

R.A. Skelton, *Lucas Jansz Waghenaer thresoor der zeevaert Leyden 1592* (Amsterdam, 1965).

R.A. Skelton and P.D.A. Harvey, *Local maps and plans from Medieval England* (Oxford, 1986).

R.A. Skelton, *County atlases of the British Isles 1579-1850* (London, 1970).

D.K. Smith, *The cartographic imagination in Early Modern England: re-writing the World in Marlowe, Spenser, Raleigh and Marvell* (Farnham, 2008).

J. Speed, *The theatre of the Empire of Great Britaine* (London, 1610).

J. Speed, *A collection of maps of England* (London, 1610).

J. Speed, *Prospect of the most famous parts of the World* (London, 1627).

J. Speed, *England fully described* (London, 1713).

J. Speed, *English atlas* (London, 1770).

L.D. Stamp and T. Stuart-Menteath, *The land of Britain. Part 86 Somerset* (London, 1938).

Sir R. Steele and J. Gillmore, *An account of the Fish-Pool* (London, 1718).

J. Strachey, *Somersetshire survey'd and protracted by Mr. Strachy* (London, 1736).

W. Stukeley, *Itinerarium curiosum: or, An account of the antiquities, and remarkable curiosities in nature or art, observed in travels through Great Britain*, volume 1 (London, 1724).

E.G.R. Taylor, ed., *A brief summe of geographie by Roger Barlow* (London, 1932).

E.G.R. Taylor, 'Robert Hooke and the Cartographical Projects of the Late Seventeenth Century (1666-1696)' in *The Geographical Journal* 90:6 (1937), 529-40.

E.G.R. Taylor, 'Notes on John Adams and Contemporary Map Makers' in *The Geographical Journal* 97: 3 (1941), 182-4.

R. Taylor and L.J. Schaaf, *Impressed by light: British photographs from paper negatives, 1840-1860* (New York, 2007).

W. Harding Thompson, *Somerset regional report a survey and plan prepared for the Somerset County Council* (London, 1934).

J. Toulmin, *The history of the town of Taunton, in the county of Somerset* (Taunton, 1791).

W. Tunnicliff, *Topographical survey of the counties of Hants, Wilts, Dorset, Somerset, Devon, and Cornwall, commonly called the Western Circuit* (Salisbury, 1791).

S. Tyacke, *London map-sellers 1660-1720 . . .* (London, 1978).

B. Tyson, 'John Adam's Cartographic Correspondence to Sir Daniel Fleming of Rydal Hall, Cumbria, 1676-1687' in *The Geographical Journal* 151:1 (1985), 21-39.

J. Vanes, ed., *The ledger of John Smythe, 1538-1550*, B.R.S. 28 (1975).

L.J. Waghenaer, *Spieghel der Zeevaerdt* (Amsterdam, 1589).

B.C. Wallis, *The teaching of Geography* (Cambridge, 2013).

P.J. Wallis, *An index of British mathematicians: a check-list part 2 1701-1760* (Newcastle-upon-Tyne, 1976).

F.M. Ward, *Supplement to Collinson's History of Somerset {by} Richard Locke 18th century antiquary, surveyor and agriculturist extracted from Locke's survey with a short biography* (Taunton, 1939).

R. Warner, *A new guide to Bath* (Bath, 1811).

F. Warre, 'Castle Neroche' in *PSANHS* 5 (1854), 29-48.

F.W. Weaver, ed., *Somerset Medieval wills (third series), 1531-1558*, Somerset Record Society 21 (1905).

A.J. Webb, 'Drainage, navigation and civil engineering: Straightening the River Parrett in 1568' in A.J. Webb, ed., *A maritime history of Somerset, volume one: trade and commerce* (Taunton, 2010), 28-43.

A.J. Webb, 'Lieutenant Colonel Paule St de Beville in Somerset, 1768' in *S.D.N.Q.* (2011), 34-8.

A.J. Webb, *Charts and sailing directions of the Somerset coast c.1350-1824*, S.R.S. 97 (2014).

E. Weller, *Weekly dispatch atlas* (London, 1860).

P. Whitfield, *The mapmakers: a history of Stanfords* (London, 2003).

H.B. Woodward, *The history of the Geological Society of London* (London, 1907).

L. Worms and A. Baynton-Williams, *British map engravers : a dictionary of engravers, lithographers and their principal employers to 1850* (London, 2011).

R.W.M. Wright, *A descriptive list of the published plans of the City of Bath and its environs* (Bath, 1925).

Newspapers

Bath Chronicle and Weekly Gazette; *Bristol Mercury*; *Derbyshire Advertiser and Journal*; *Illustrated London News*; *The Ipswich Journal*; *Morning Chronicle*; *Morning Post*; *Salisbury and Winchester Journal*; *Sherborne Mercury*; *Somerset County Gazette*; *Taunton Courier*; *Taunton Courier, and Western Advertiser*; *The Times*; *Western Daily Press*; *Western Gazette*.

Series

Volumes in the following series of publications have been consulted:
Bath History; *History of Cartography*; *Imago Mundi*; *The Map Collector*; *Victoria County History of Somerset*; *Proceedings of the Somersetshire Archaeological and Natural History Society*; *Somerset Record Society*; *Notes and Queries for Somerset and Dorset*.

Websites

British Book Trade Index, www..bham.ac.uk

Gough map, www.goughmap.org

Mendip Cave Registry Archive, www.mcra.org.uk/registry

Oxford Dictionary of National Biography, www.oxforddnb.com

William Smith's maps, www.strata-smith.com

CHAPTER ONE

Pre 1500

The Stone Age

The Stanton Drew stone circles have long been thought to have been associated with druids and are surrounded by much myth and legend. In 1664, following the Restoration, the antiquarian John Aubrey (1626-1697) took an interest in the stones and recorded them during his visit. In the following century, another antiquarian, William Stukeley (1687-1765) visited the site and published his findings in 1724. Interest in the stones grew and in 1740 the site was surveyed and mapped by John Wood, the elder (1704-1754) of Bath. Wood put forward the theory that the stones were laid out on the Pythagorean planetary system, and thought it was used as the Druids' 'University'.

Such was the interest in the Stanton Drew stones that Benjamin Donn (1729-1787), the celebrated map maker, mathematician and amateur hydrographer of Bristol, included a plan of the site in his *Map of the country 11 miles round the city of Bristol*. Donn's map was drawn to a scale of 4.4 inches to 2 statute miles. He dedicated his map to the Right Worshipful Thomas Harris esquire, Mayor, and to the 'worshipful the Recorder and Aldermen, The Sheriffs and Common Council', and also to the 'Worshipful S. Munckley Esq, Master, the Wardens, Assistants and Commonality of the Society of Merchants, Venturers of the said City: and the other Subscribers'. Donn's map may not have been a commercial success, as he was trying to sell copies off cheaply in Bath in 1773 at half a guinea in sheets, or coloured on canvas at 16*s* 6*d*.

The Stanton Drew stone circles, referred to by Donn as 'The Wedding', included the Great Circle, measuring 113 metres in diameter, which is the second largest stone circle in Great Britain. Experts believe it was constructed between 3000 and 2000 BC and is one of the largest Neolithic monuments to have been built. It was made a scheduled monument in 1982.

As can be seen on Donn's plan, the Great Circle was once surrounded by a ditch and is accompanied by smaller stone circles to the north east and south west. The group of three stones, known as The Cove, can be found in the garden of the local pub. Slightly further from the Great Circle is a single stone, known as Hautville's Quoit. Some of the stones are still vertical, but the ravages of time have taken their toll on one of the most important pre-historic sites in the ancient county of Somerset.

The days when stones were visible in Mr Fowler's orchard and in Pidgeon House Close may be long gone, but Donn's plan records them for posterity. Shortly after his plan was published another antiquarian, the Reverend John Collinson, published his *History and antiquities of the county of Somerset,* in which he wrote:

> The common people call this relique The Wedding, from a tradition that as a woman was going along to be married, she and all her attendants were at once converted into stones, and that it is an impiety to attempt reckoning their number.

Opposite: Right - An extract showing the stone circles from Donn's *Map of the country 11 miles round the city of Bristol.* (UKHO, D832/1-4 shelf D).
Top left - A plan of Stanton Drew from John Rutter's *Delineations of the north western division of the county of Somerset* (London, 1829), 208. Bottom left - An extract from an illustration in William Stukeley's *Itinerarium curiosum: or, An account of the antiquities, and remarkable curiosities in nature or art, observed in travels through Great Britain* showing some of the stones being viewed by two men in the early 1720s. (London, 1724). (SANHS.)

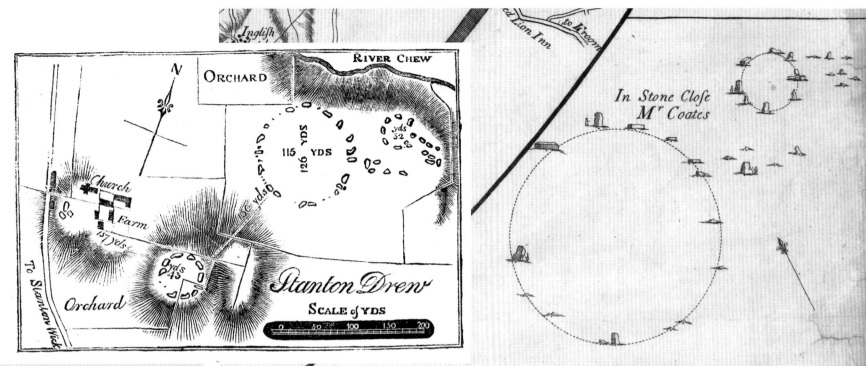

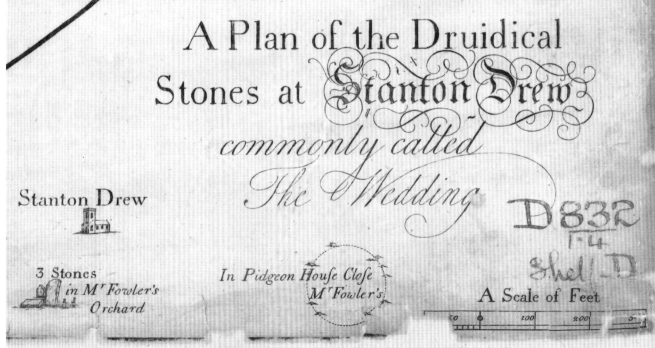

A Plan of the Druidical Stones at *Stanton Drew* commonly called *The Wedding*

Stanton Drew

3 Stones in Mr Fowler's Orchard

In Pidgeon House Close Mr Fowler's

In Stone Close Mr Coates

A Scale of Feet

D832
I·4

Shelf D

3

The Bronze Age

Hamdon Hill, or Ham Hill, is an iconic landmark in south Somerset. Looking out from the hill top it is clear why it held such a strategic position during the Bronze Age through to Roman times. The site is much more well-known for its Iron Age and Roman occupation, from which much evidence has been unearthed. Described as one of the largest contour hill forts in Great Britain, it has yielded hoards of coins as well as evidence for a twleve-room Roman villa.

Recent excavations identified prehistoric activity, the interior and entrance to a rectilinear enclosure of a Middle-to Late-Iron Age date, as well as evidence of a structure associated with Late Bronze Age pottery, suggesting an earlier phase of occupation. A ditched field system from the Middle Bronze Age with evidence for continued management and alteration was also identified.

The Reverend William Phelps F.S.A. (1776-1856) of Meare and Bicknoller, reproduced a map of the earthworks at Hambdon Hill in the first volume of his *The history and antiquities of Somersetshire*, published in 1836. Phelps described it as 'Hamdon camp' and reprinted an account of it written by Sir Richard Colt Hoare, Bart. (1758-1838), who stated 'The earth-works which surround the hill are the most extensive I have ever met with, being in circumference three miles; and the area comprehends above two hundred acres'. This account had been published by the Society of Antiquaries and Phelps relied heavily on Hoare's expertise in this area.

Above: A Bronze Age gold torc, belonging to the Somerset Archaeological and Natural History Society, found in 1909 by Henry Cole, a gardener working on Hendford Hill, Yeovil. The torc, despite being dipped in car battery acid to clean it when first found, is in near perfect condition. The torc dates from about 1300–1100 BC and is thought to be the finest piece of Bronze Age gold ever found in Somerset. The torc is on display in Taunton Castle, in a permanent exhibition in the Museum of Somerset. (SANHS.)

Opposite: A survey of the ancient camp on Hamdon Hill. (Adrian Webb collection.)

Source: W. Phelps, *The history and antiquities of Somersetshire volume 1* (London, 1836), opp. p.120. Original size: 250 x 193mm.

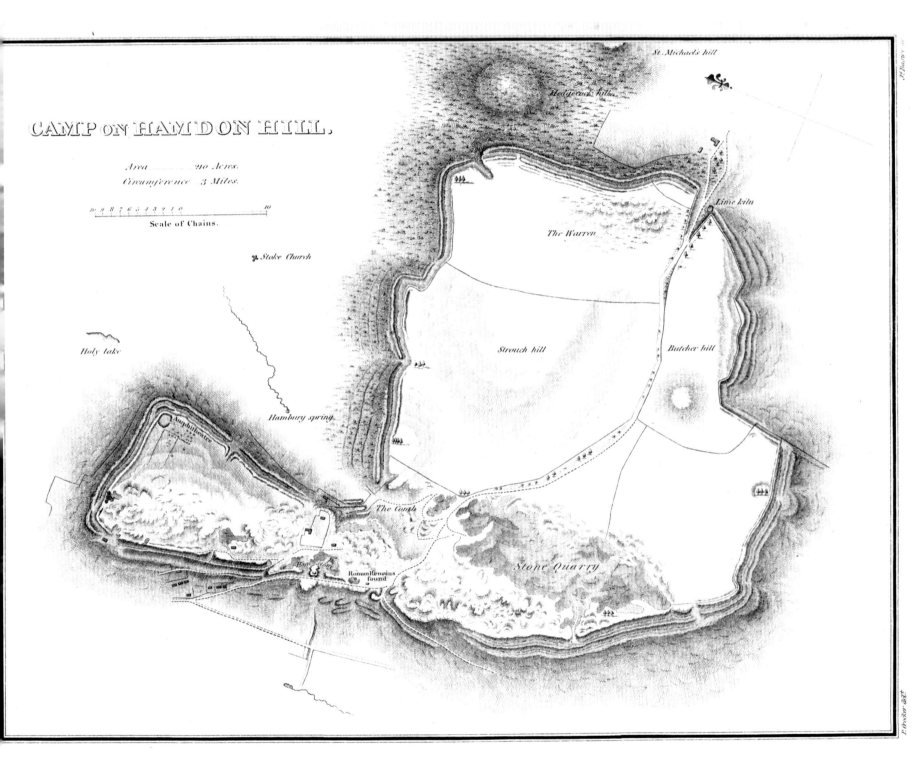

CAMP ON HAMDON HILL.

Area _____ 210 Acres.
Circumference 3 Miles.

10 9 8 7 6 5 4 3 2 1 0   10
Scale of Chains.

St. Michael's hill

Hedgecock hill

Lime kiln

The Warren

Stoke Church

Holy lake

Strouch hill

Butcher hill

Hambury spring

Amphitheatre

The Comb

Stone Quarry

Roman Remains
found

5

The Iron Age

Somerset has many outstanding Iron Age sites, such as the Glastonbury Lake Villages, round houses at Shepton Mallet and burial pits at Bleadon. Hill forts are far more visible, such as the one at Worlebury which lies in the parishes of Kewstoke, Weston St John's and Worle. A map of Worlebury appeared in John Rutter's *Delineations of the north western division of the county of Somerset, and of its antediluvian bone caverns, with a geological sketch of the district* (London, 1829), in which he described Worlebury Camp:

> Worle-hill is an isolated ridge, about three miles long, but not more than a furlong in breadth, and includes a view of not less than 30 churches from its elevated summit.

Another version of Rutter's map, albeit with a little more detail, appeared shortly afterwards in 1836 in Phelps's *History and antiquities of Somersetshire*. Phelps described the geography of the site but it was not until the 1850s that the first organised archaeological work took place when 93 pits and part of the ruined walls were excavated by the Reverend Francis Warre, E.M. Atkins, D. Tomkins, Reverend H.G. Tomkins, Dr Pring and Dr Thurnam.

In 1886 the archaeological work undertaken by Charles William Dymond M.Inst.C.E., Hon. F.S.A. (Scot) (1832-1915) was published as *Worlebury: an ancient stronghold in the county of Somerset*. He included illustrations of his discoveries (right), an artist's impression of the whole area without any tree coverage, as well as numerous cross-sections from the site. His 'Index - Plan' (a section of which is reproduced opposite) cleverly showed both the topography of the site and the location of his finds, including 'mines', rock pits and the extent of the remains found in 1852.

Source: C.W. Dymond, *Worlebury: an ancient stronghold in the county of Somerset* (1886). Original size of the whole map: 358 x 243mm.

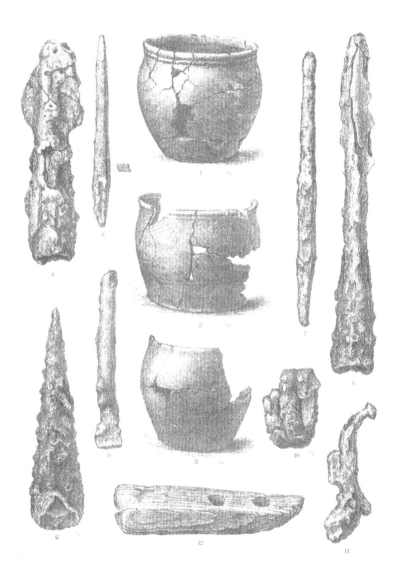

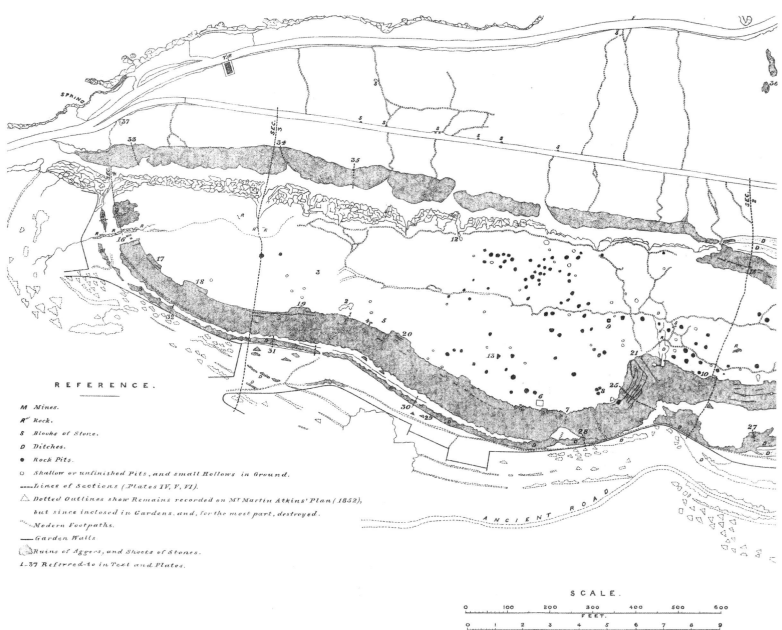

REFERENCE.

M   Mines.

R   Rock.

S   Blocks of Stone.

D   Ditches.

●   Rock Pits.

○   Shallow or unfinished Pits, and small Hollows in Ground.

---- Lines of Sections (Plates IV, V, VI).

△   Dotted Outlines show Remains recorded on Mr Martin Atkins' Plan (1852),
      but since inclosed in Gardens, and, for the most part, destroyed.

      Modern Footpaths.

____ Garden Walls

      Ruins of Aggers, and Sheets of Stones.

1-37 Referred-to in Text and Plates.

C.W. DYMOND, F.S.A., DEL.T.

SCALE.

0   100   200   300   400   500   600
                      FEET.

0   1   2   3   4   5   6   7   8   9
                      CHAINS.

7

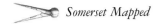

Roman Somerset

The Roman occupation of Britain left a long lasting mark on the Somerset landscape, not only Roman roads but the remains of industrial workings at Charterhouse and coastal defences. Men such as Stukeley, the Reverend John Skinner (1772-1839) of Camerton, Phelps, and the Reverend Harry Mengden Scarth (1814-1890) studied Roman Somerset. Scarth, who held the rectory of Bathwick with Woolley from 1841 to 1871, and Wrington from 1871 until his death, drew a map of Roman Somerset (reproduced opposite).

Scarth's publishing record was prolific. He contributed 20 papers (over a period of 30 years) to the Somerset Archaeological and Natural History Society which were published in their *Proceedings*. He also wrote two major works, *Aquae Solis; or, notices of Roman Bath* and a volume published by the Society for the Promotion of Christian Knowledge on *Roman Britain*.

His map of Roman Somerset was published folded (twice) in order to fit in to the 1878 edition of the *Somerset Archaeological and Natural History Society Proceedings*. The map itself was prepared by William Bidgood (1840-1900), who served as the Society's Museum Curator and Assistant Secretary. As well as including Roman sites and remains, Scarth included British ones as well.

Opposite: Extracts from *Roman Somerset*. Source: Revd H.M. Scarth, 'Roman Somerset' in *Somerset Archaeological and Natural History Society Proceedings* 24 (1878), 1-21. Original size of the complete map: 422 x 297mm.

Right: An extract from Day and Masters' map of Somerset of 1782 showing the 'Old Roman Fosse'. (SANHS.)

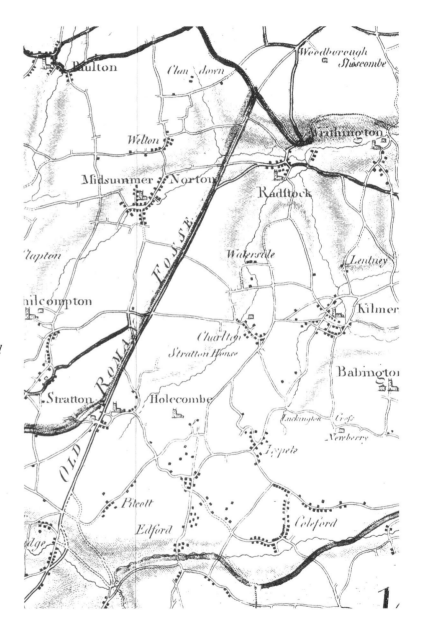

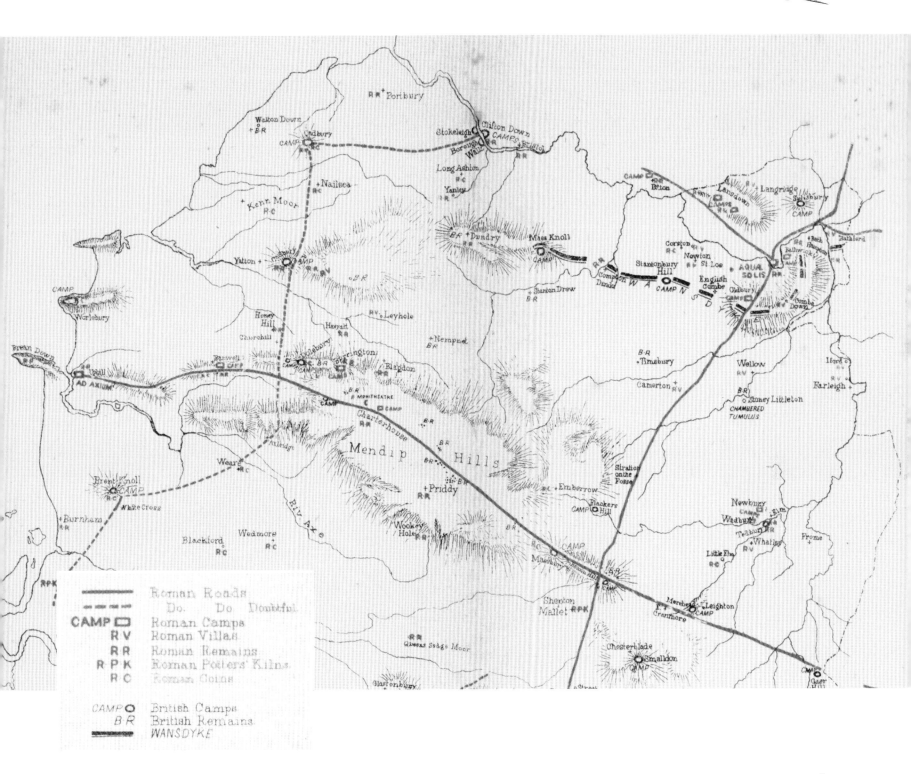

Mid-Somerset illustrating the Saxon conquest, probable Danish settlements and King Alfred's Campaign from Athelney
Albany F. Major and the Reverend C.W. Whistler
Seventh century to 878 (1913)

A lbany Featherstonehaugh Major (1859-1925), in collaboration with the Reverend Charles Watts Whistler M.R.C.S., L.S.A. (1856-1913), pictured right, wrote *The early wars of Wessex* published by Cambridge University Press in 1913. This volume contained two large maps, one covering *The boundaries and principal earthworks, etc, of Dorset, Somerset and adjoining portions of Hants, Wilts and Devon* and the other of mid-Somerset is reproduced opposite. The map of mid-Somerset was hand drawn and not engraved and thus looks amateurish in places. It was based on maps by Whistler which appeared in *Folk-Lore* volume XIX in 1908 and *The Antiquary* for October 1911. The authors pointed out that 'the boundary lines in this map marking stages of the Anglo-Saxon advance are of course only approximate, as the records on which they are based are very meagre'.

Major and Whistler were both active members of the Somerset Archaeological and Natural History Society. Major was well known for his field archaeology and had three papers published in the Society's *Proceedings*. Whistler was known in Somerset for his work upon the early history of the county and its folk-lore. He accepted the living of Stockland Bristol in 1895, serving until 1909. He was also an accomplished artist and craftsman.

———— ✺ ————

Opposite: A reduction of Whistler's map of *Mid-Somerset illustrating the Saxon conquest, probable Danish settlements and King Alfred's campaign from Athelney.*

Source: A.F. Major & C.W. Whistler, *The early wars of Wessex* (Cambridge, 1913). Original size: 513 x 401mm.

The Reverend Charles Watts Whistler (SANHS).

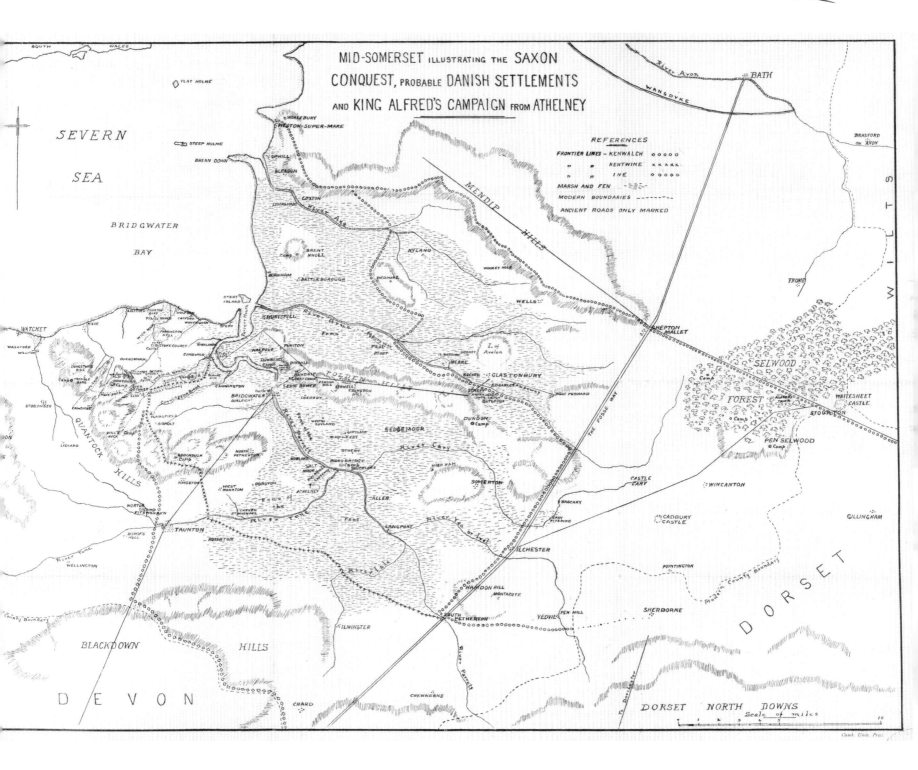

MID-SOMERSET ILLUSTRATING THE SAXON
CONQUEST, PROBABLE DANISH SETTLEMENTS
AND KING ALFRED'S CAMPAIGN FROM ATHELNEY

REFERENCES

FRONTIER LINES — KENWALCH ooooo
" " KENTWINE xxxxx
" " INE ooooo
MARSH AND FEN
MODERN BOUNDARIES
ANCIENT ROADS ONLY MARKED

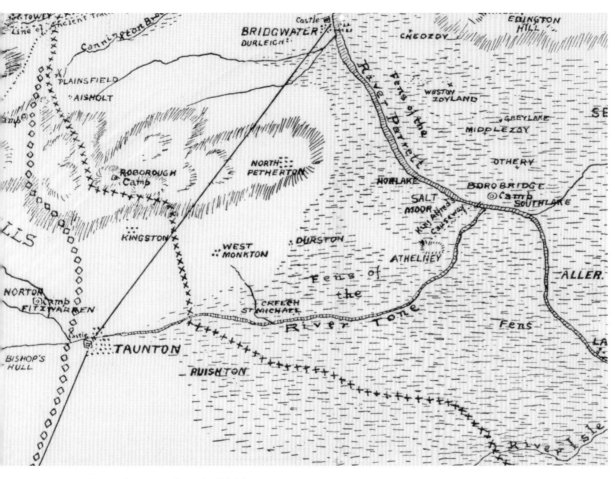

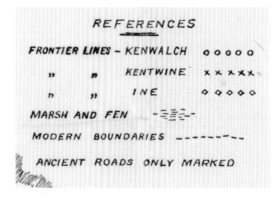

Below: St Cuthbert's Image found near Athelney' as depicted by the map maker Herman Moll (*c*.1654-1732) in his map of *Somerset Shire*, published in London in 1708. Moll's image is better known as the Alfred Jewel and was actually found in the parish of North Petherton (shown in the map left) in 1693. The jewel was bequeathed to Oxford University by Colonel Nathaniel Palmer (*c*.1661-1718) and today is in the Ashmolean Museum in Oxford. (Adrian Webb collection.)

Above: An extract from the *Mid-Somerset* map showing Athelney, King Alfred's Causeway and 'Borobridge' set within the 'Fens' of Somerset. The line of circles represents the frontier of 'Kenwalch' (Cenwealh 642-672) from the mid to late seventh century. The line of crosses shows the frontier line of Kentwine (Centwine *fl.*676-?685).

Right: The key to the symbology used by Whistler.

Source: *Mid-Somerset illustrating the Saxon conquest, probable Danish settlements and King Alfred's campaign from Athelney*, published in *The early wars of Wessex*.

A map showing a depiction of the county of Somerset during Saxon times. Based on information obtained from the Anglo Saxon chronicle. Note how the Kingdom of the West Saxons has been shaded green. The map was published with a Saxon alphabet. (Adrian Webb collection.)

Source: *Saxon England according to the Saxon Chronicle*, engraved by A.Bell and published in *The history of Great Britain* (London, 1790).

Part of Somerset county boundary
James Bridge Davidson
854 (1882)

James Bridge Davidson M.A. (1824-1885) was the son of James Davidson (1793–1864), a well-published antiquarian and bibliographer of Sektor House, Axminster. James Bridge Davidson was educated at Kingsbridge Grammar School and called to the Bar, working most of his adult life at Lincoln's Inn when not pursuing antiquarian interests. He wrote two papers for the Somerset Archaeological and Natural History Society on Anglo Saxon boundaries, a further ten for the Devonshire Association, the first being published in 1876.

Davidson's paper on part of the county boundary between Somerset and Devon was published in 1882. He combined field work, research into original sources and map work to write a detailed account of the county boundary skirting the parishes of West Buckland, Pitminster, Otterford and Buckland St Mary. He described his map (reproduced opposite):

> The pink line shows the course of the modern county boundary. The numbers in the circles mark the stations of the perambulation of the boundary of 854. The other numbers mark the stations of the perambulation of 1367, so far as they can now be identified. There is no reason to suppose that the modern boundary has departed from that of 1367, except at the point of Whitewall corner.

Source: J.B. Davidson, 'Notes on part of the county boundary between Somerset and Devon' in *Somerset Archaeological and Natural History Society Proceedings* 28:2 (1882). Original size: 320 x 230mm.

The county boundary, matching the area depicted opposite from West Buckland to Whitestaunton, as surveyed by Christopher Saxton and published in 1575 (see Chapter Two). Note the Yarty River mapped as 'Yart fluvius' and the shading for the different counties; green for Dorset.

Source: C. Saxton, *Somersetensem* (London, 1575) (Robin Bush collection).

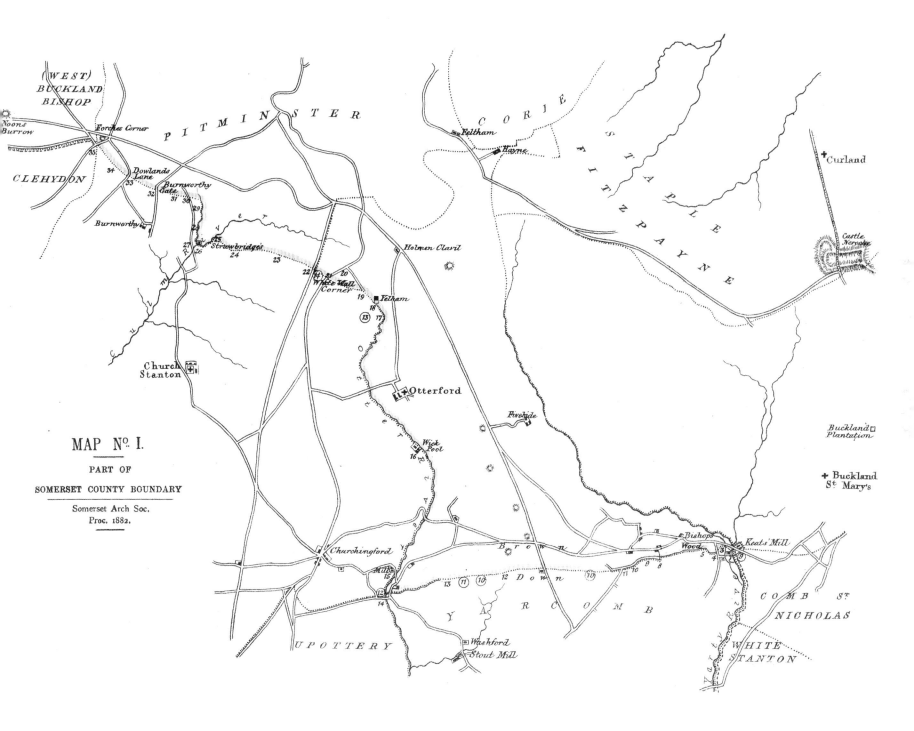

(WEST)
BUCKLAND
BISHOP

Noons Burrow

Forches Corner

CLEHYDON

35

34 *Dowlands Lane*

33

Burnworthy Gate

32

31 30 29

Burnworthy

P I T M I N S T E R

28

27 26 25 *Strawbridges*

24 23

22 21 20

White Wall Corner

19 18 *Yelham*

13 17

Church Stanton

Holmen Clavil

Otterford

Fivehde

Wick Pool

16

MAP Nº I.

PART OF

SOMERSET COUNTY BOUNDARY

Somerset Arch Soc.
Proc. 1882.

Churchingford

Mills
15

12

14

Brown

Bishops Wood

3
Keats' Mill

5 4

13 11 10 12 Down 10 11 10 9 8

Washford Stout Mill

U P O T T E R Y

Y A R C O M B

C O R I E

F I T Z P A Y N E

S T A P L E

Feltham

Hayne

Curland

Castle Neroche

Buckland Plantation

Buckland Sᵗ Mary's

C O M B Sᵗ
NICHOLAS

WHITE STANTON

Map of Somerset shewing the chief estates as recorded in Domesday Book, A.D. 1086
The Right Reverend Edmund Hobhouse
1086 (1889)

The Right Reverend Edmund Hobhouse (1817-1904), born in London on the 17th of April 1817, was second son of Henry, Permanent Under-secretary of State for the Home Department and Keeper of State Papers. He retired to Wells in 1881. He was an active member of both the Somerset Archaeological and Natural History Society, and the Somerset Record Society which he helped to found. For the Somerset Record Society he edited the register of Bishop John de Drokensford, churchwardens' accounts, the *rentalia et custumaria* of Michaelis de Ambresbury and contributed to the editing of the cartularies of Bruton and Montacute priories. He died at Wells on the 20th of April 1904.

His map of the Somerset Domesday estates was printed by W. Griggs, Photo-lithographers of Peckham. It was one of the earliest maps of Somerset published by the Society to contain such a range of colours. There appears to have been no rationale behind the choice of colours, but it can be clearly seen how the estates belonging to William the Conqueror (in yellow) and those belonging to Glastonbury Abbey (in blue) covered the largest geographical areas within the county. The Conqueror's manors were scattered across the county, as opposed to those belonging to Glastonbury which dominated central Somerset.

Opposite: A reduced reproduction of Hobhouse's map.

Source: Rt Reverend Bishop Hobhouse, *Map of Somerset shewing the chief estates as recorded in Domesday Book, A.D. 1086* published in *Somerset Archaeological and Natural History Society Proceedings* 35 (1889). Original size: 452 x 308mm.

The Right Reverend Edmund Hobhouse (SANHS).

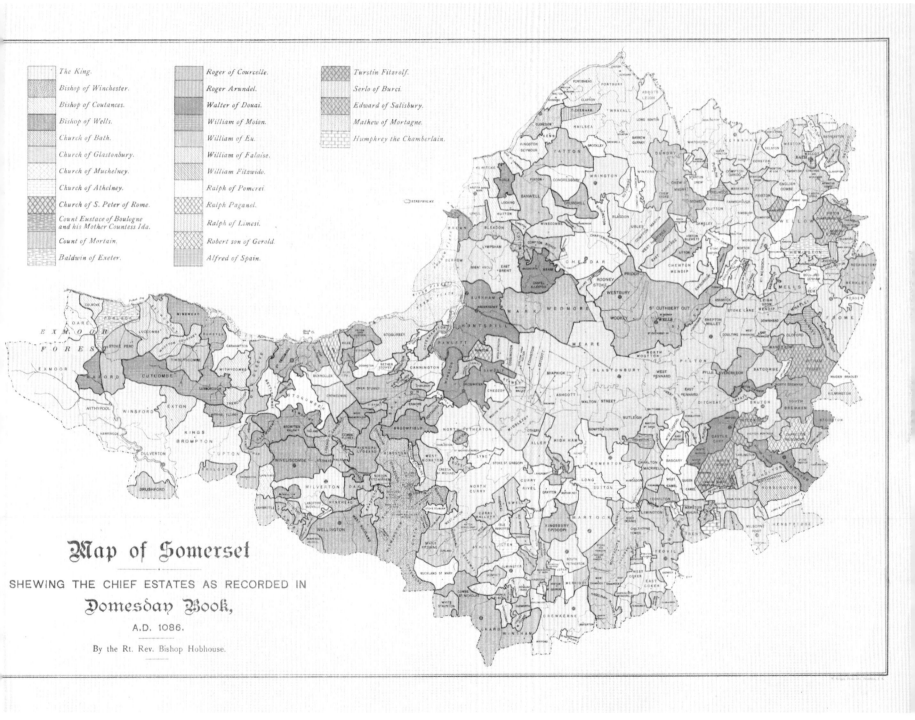

Legend:

- The King.
- Bishop of Winchester.
- Bishop of Coutances.
- Bishop of Wells.
- Church of Bath.
- Church of Glastonbury.
- Church of Muchelney.
- Church of Athelney.
- Church of S. Peter of Rome.
- Count Eustace of Boulogne and his Mother Countess Ida.
- Count of Mortain.
- Baldwin of Exeter.
- Roger of Courcelle.
- Roger Arundel.
- Walter of Douai.
- William of Moion.
- William of Eu.
- William of Falaise.
- William Fitzwido.
- Ralph of Pomerei.
- Ralph Paganel.
- Ralph of Limesi.
- Robert son of Gerold.
- Alfred of Spain.
- Turstin Fitzrolf.
- Serlo of Burci.
- Edward of Salisbury.
- Mathew of Mortagne.
- Humphrey the Chamberlain.

Map of Somerset

SHEWING THE CHIEF ESTATES AS RECORDED IN

Domesday Book,

A.D. 1086.

By the Rt. Rev. Bishop Hobhouse.

[Bounds of the Forest of Mendip]
J.W. Gough
1219 (1931)

John Weidhofft Gough (1900-1976), obtained firsts at Oxford in both Classics and Modern History and was awarded his D.Litt. in 1965. He wrote on many philosophical, biographical and historical subjects, including *John Locke's political philosophy* (1950), with his most important work being *The social contract: a critical study of its development* (1936). Gough was Emeritus Fellow of Oriel College.

Gough wrote two books on Mendip mining. In 1931, in his *Mendip mining laws and forest bounds*, he wrote how although the original extent of the Forest of Mendip could not be exactly determined, the heart of the estate was the royal estate at Cheddar, often referred to as the 'Forest of Cheddar'. At one stage the forest extended from as far as the coast, at the mouth of the River Axe where *le Blacstone*, or Black Rock can be found. To 'map' the extent of the forest, a perambulation, or walk along its boundary, was undertaken in 1219 and the observations that were made were written down. Further perambulations were needed and from the resulting records Gough produced his map, shown opposite.

Gough's map shows the limits of the forest and how, during the thirteenth century, it extended into the parishes of Shipham, Charterhouse, Axbridge and Priddy. He also produced another map, based upon the Ordnance Survey, showing the 'Boundaries and Liberties of the Lords Royal' which appeared in his classic work on *The mines of Mendip*.

J.W. Gough, *c*.1940. Source: Oriel College, Oxford, MPP/K 11/1.

Opposite: A reproduction of Gough's map showing the limits of the Forest of Mendip.

Source: J.W. Gough, *Mendip mining laws and forest bounds*, S.R.S. 45 (Taunton, 1931). Original size: 259 x 196mm.

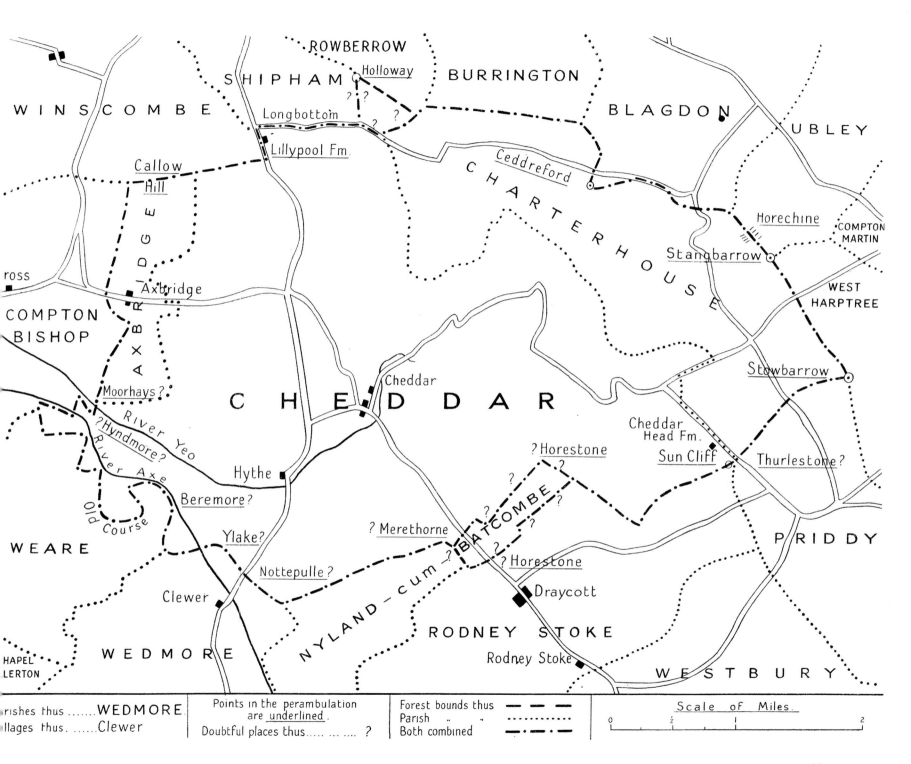

ROWBERROW

SHIPHAM   Holloway   BURRINGTON

WINSCOMBE   Longbottom   ? ?   BLAGDON   UBLEY

Lillypool Fm.   ?   Ceddreford

Callow   CHARTERHOUSE   Horechine   COMPTON MARTIN

Hill   Stangbarrow

ross   Axbridge   WEST HARPTREE

COMPTON
BISHOP   Stowbarrow

CHEDDAR   Cheddar

Moorhays?   Cheddar
Head Fm.

River Yeo   ?Hyndmore?   ?Horestone   Sun Cliff   Thurlestone?

River Axe   Hythe   ?

Beremore?   BATCOMBE   ?

Old Course   ?   ?

WEARE   Ylake?   ?Merethorne   ?   Horestone

Nottepulle?   NYLAND-cum-   ?   PRIDDY

Clewer   Draycott

HAPEL
LERTON   WEDMORE   RODNEY STOKE

Rodney Stoke   WESTBURY

rishes thus ...... WEDMORE   Points in the perambulation   Forest bounds thus — — —   Scale of Miles
llages thus. ...... Clewer   are underlined   Parish   " ....
    Doubtful places thus..... ... . ?   Both combined   0   ½   1   2

19

The Forest of Exmoor
E.T. MacDermot
1301 (1911)

Edward Terence MacDermot (1873-1950) was educated at Downside and Magdalen College, Oxford, before training as a barrister, but did not practice. He wrote *The history of the Forest of Exmoor* (published in 1911), which included several maps, including facsimiles of seventeeth century maps and historical interpretations of medieval documents. His map of the Forest of Exmoor in 1301 is reproduced opposite, in which he also included information from the first detailed perambulation undertaken in 1219.

Defining the ancient boundary of Exmoor Forest was the result of the Crown's need to carefully regulate its assets and at the same time to derive an income from them. Thus on the 6th of November 1217 regulations were issued on behalf of the infant King Henry the Third for all forests to be 'viewed by good and lawful men', and that any afforestations, apart from those lawfully undertaken by the Crown, be disafforested. Subsequently letters patent were issued to John Marshal, justice of the forest, to order four knights to choose 12 knights in several counties to oversee a perambulation on Exmoor.

Peter de Maulay, sheriff of Somerset and Dorset, was commissioned on the 22nd of April 1219 to instruct the knights to summon foresters and verderers (who dealt with the day-to-day forest administration and minor offences, such as the taking of venison and the illegal cutting of wood) to undertake a perambulation. They had to cause the 'metes and bounds' to be set and 'distinctly put in writing', but alas not on a map. The record of their perambulation was inrolled and, subsequently, the resulting record has been held within the public records system for nearly 800 years. The wording of the perambulation reads:

The Lord King's Forest of Essemore begins from Corsneshet and stretches to Whiteston, from Whiteston to Hauekescumeshead, from Hauekescumeshead by the top of the hill to Osmundesburgh, from Osmundesburgh to the little Eisse, from the little Eisse to the great Eisse by the course of the water, by the course of the great Eisse to la Rode, and from thence to Ernesburg by the great way, from Ernesburg by the great way to Wamburg, from Wamburg to Langeston, from Langeston to Mageldene …, and from thence by the great way between the two Eisseweis to the water of Bergel, and along the water of Bergel to [where] Donekesbroch falls into Bergel. And from these bounds towards the West as far as Devon is the ancient forest, and towards the East is outside the forest. All the other woods, which have been afforested, have been afforested since the coronation of the Lord King Henry son of the Lord King John.

Today some of those places can still be identified, such as Corneshet which is Cosgate, Hauekescumeshead which is Hawkcombe Head on Porlock Common, Osmundesburgh is Alderman's Barrow, or Owlaman's Barrow, where the four parishes of Porlock, Stoke Pero, Exford and Exmoor meet, and the Great Eisse is the River Exe. MacDermot referred to E.J. Rawle's *Annals of the ancient Royal Forest of Exmoor. Compiled chiefly from documents in the Record Office together with some account of the forest laws and charters and officers*, published in 1893, for the identification of these (and other) ancient placenames.

As for MacDermot he was equally well known for his *History of the Great Western Railway* published in two volumes as three between 1927 and 1931. His history of Exmoor was reprinted in 1973.

———⊗⊗⊗———

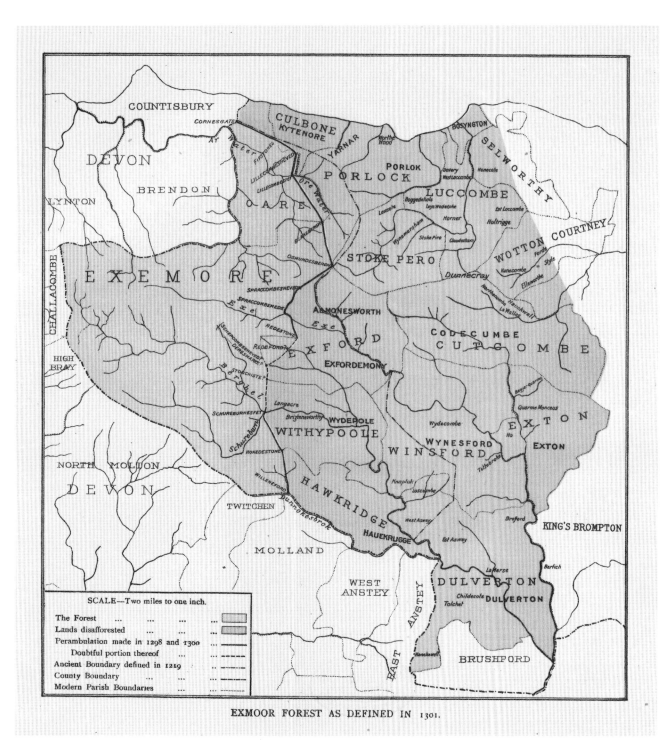

EXMOOR FOREST AS DEFINED IN 1301.

Called by MacDermot a 'Map of Exmoor Forest as defined in 1301', this also contains information gleaned from perambulations undertaken in 1219 and 1298. MacDermot added the limits of the modern county boundary and those of the parishes affected by perambulations undertaken some six centuries ago.

Source: E.T. MacDermot, *The history of the Forest of Exmoor* (London, 1911). Original size: 208 x 221mm.

Fourteenth and fifteenth century Somerset

Cartographic images of pre-Reformation Somerset are rare survivals from an age when map making was limited to a small number of mathematically educated men, both lay and clerical. Some imagery survives to show how people from this period portrayed cities such as Bath and Wells, as well as the abbey town of Glastonbury. But the earliest map to show any significant detail of Somerset can be found in the Bodleian Library and is famously known as the 'Gough map', named after its owner in the eighteenth century, Richard Gough F.S.A. (1735-1809), but its origins in the fourteenth century are obscure.

Its portrayal, or mapping, of Somerset reveals thirteen places, *i.e.* Axbridge, Bridgwater, Bruton, Chard, Cleeve Abbey, Crewkerne, Dunster, Frome, Glastonbury, Ilchester, Taunton, Uphill and Wells. Only two of these places stand out, both of which are shown without any colour: Dunster and Taunton. Dunster is shown as what could well be a square keep, with a smaller building to the left, which might be symbolic of the priory. Taunton is interesting when it is compared with Bristol. Does the bottom part of the drawing represent the town walls, or even Taunton Castle, with the building in the background being the priory? We may never know. There is one large river shown running through part of north Somerset, thought to represent the River Axe. By including it on a map with other much larger places in Somerset, puts the small parish of Uphill in a more significant light than has previously been thought. Perhaps its importance as a landmark for navigation brought it to the attention of the mapmaker over 650 years ago.

———⊶⊷———

Right: A reproduction of a depiction of the city of Wells, *c.*1460.

Source: New College, Oxford, MS C.288 f.4v.

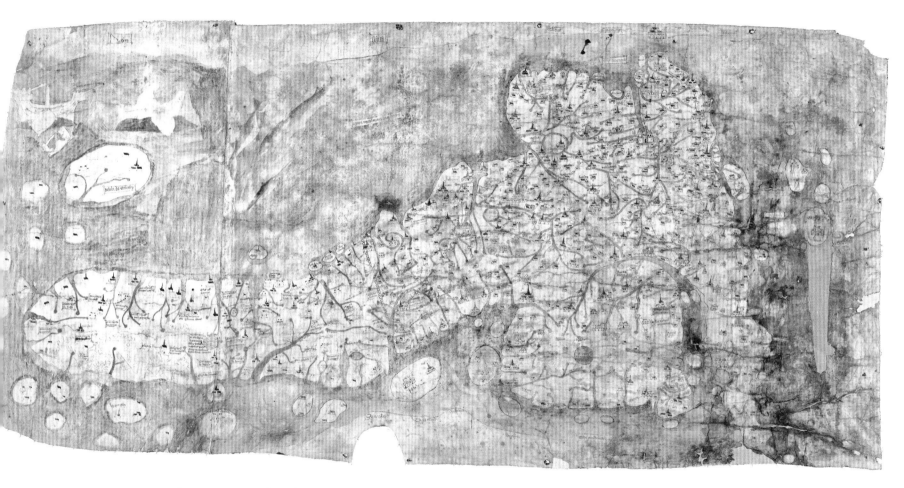

A reduced reproduction of the Gough map of *c.*1360.

Source: Bodleian Library, MS. Gough Gen.Top. 16. Original size: 1150 x 560 mm.

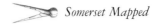

An extract from the Gough map showing the ancient county of Somerset, with Bristol shown in the top left and Exeter in the bottom right. To the right can be seen a red line joining several buildings. This represents the road from Exeter (in the bottom right hand corner) to Shaftesbury at the top of the extract. On the facing page is a key to the places shown on the extract.

Today Somerset is renowned for its perpendicular church towers. The Gough map only shows two such towers in Somerset. Churches with spires, or without any tower at all, dominate the map, suggesting the buildings without towers simply signify the location of a town.

Source: Bodleian Library, MS. Gough Gen. Top. 16.

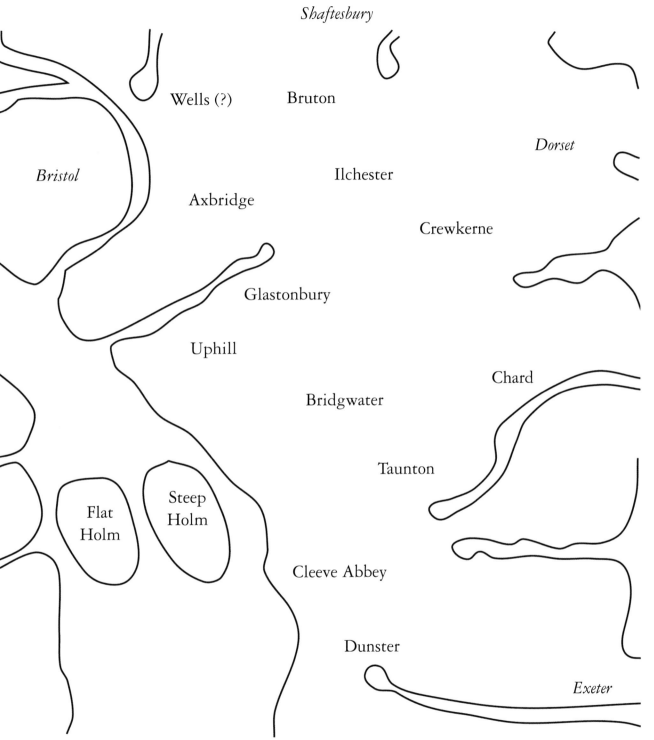

Shaftesbury

Bristol

Wells (?)   Bruton

Dorset

Ilchester

Axbridge

Crewkerne

Glastonbury

Uphill

Chard

Bridgwater

Flat Holm   Steep Holm

Taunton

Cleeve Abbey

Dunster

Exeter

Left: A key to the places shown on the extract on the opposite page. Places outside of Somerset are shown in italics. Shaftesbury lies just outside the map but has been included to help explain the geography of the region. The coastline and rivers are shown to help locate the place names.

Source: Adrian Webb.

Above: The remains of the old church of Uphill. The church depicted on the Gough map once had a spire, which today has one of the shortest towers in Somerset.

Source: Adrian Webb.

25

A sketch map of Somersetshire, shewing the places where crosses have been erected
Charles Pooley
1877

Charles Pooley F.S.A., F.R.C.S. (1817-1890) possessed interests in medicine, antiquities, natural history and science. He was a medical practitioner in Weston-super-Mare, taught at the University of Bonn, and was a member of the Royal Archaeological Institute of Great Britain and Ireland and of the Somersetshire Archaeological and Natural History Society. As a fellow of the Royal Chemical Society he produced calotype views for his publications in the 1850s and published *On Engraving Collodion Photographs, by Means of Fluoric Acid Gas*. Pooley discovered a cave on the south side of Weston-super-Mare, wrote *Ozone, not Iodine; the cause of the salubrity of Weston-Super-Mare* and *A word on mesmerism* both in 1862. He served as president of the Weston-super-Mare Natural History Society, and was a great supporter of the West of England Sanatorium. He was a Fellow of the Society of Antiquaries and in 1864 was admitted as a Fellow of the Royal College of Surgeons.

He was best known for his interests in ancient stone crosses, of which he wrote volumes for Gloucestershire and Somerset. He attended a Somersetshire Archaeological and Natural History Society meeting in 1869 and reported on a head of a thirteenth-century cross discovered in an old cottage in West Harptree, which represented the crucifixion. His volume on Somerset crosses, published in 1877, the majority dating from the fourteenth and fifteenth centuries, includes a map 'in order to give a comprehensive view of the different stations where Crosses were erected . . . with a red cross against the name of each place'.

WEST CAMEL.

Above: The stem of an 'ancient Saxon' cross from page 57 of Pooley's *Stone crosses of Somerset*. It had been discovered by the Reverend W.L. Metcalf, rector of West Camel, when the church was restored in 1866 where it had been built into a wall. A great deal of Victorian 'restoration' ruined many churches forever, but a by-product of the Gothic Revival was the discovery of ancient relics which had been hidden for centuries.

Opposite: A reduced reproduction of Charles Pooley's *A sketch map of Somersetshire, shewing the places where crosses have been erected*.
Source: C.Pooley, *Stone crosses of Somerset* (London, 1877).
Original size: 330 x 235mm.

A SKETCH MAP OF

SOMERSETSHIRE,

SHEWING THE PLACES
WHERE CROSSES HAVE BEEN ERECTED.

Pooley highlighted the 'heads of those [crosses] from Tellisford and Ditcheat, and the almost entire crosses of Wedmore, Stringston, Spaxton, and Chewton Mendip' as being 'amongst the finest instances' from the fourteenth century. That of Tellisford is reproduced above. It was discovered by the Reverend E.F. Baker when an old wall was taken down in the church during some repair work. It measures 43 cms in height and 40.5 cms in width.

Source: C.Pooley, *Stone crosses of Somerset* (London, 1877).
Original size: 330 x 235mm.

Pooley described the crosses for the fifteenth century as being 'conspicuous for the massiveness of their design, and the contrast their ornamentation presents to the graceful style of the previous age'. He mentioned those at Yatton, Wraxall, Dundry, Wick St Lawrence, Doulting and West Pennard as particularly notable. The latter is reproduced above and contains the arms of Richard Beere (d.1524), the last but one Abbot of Glastonbury.

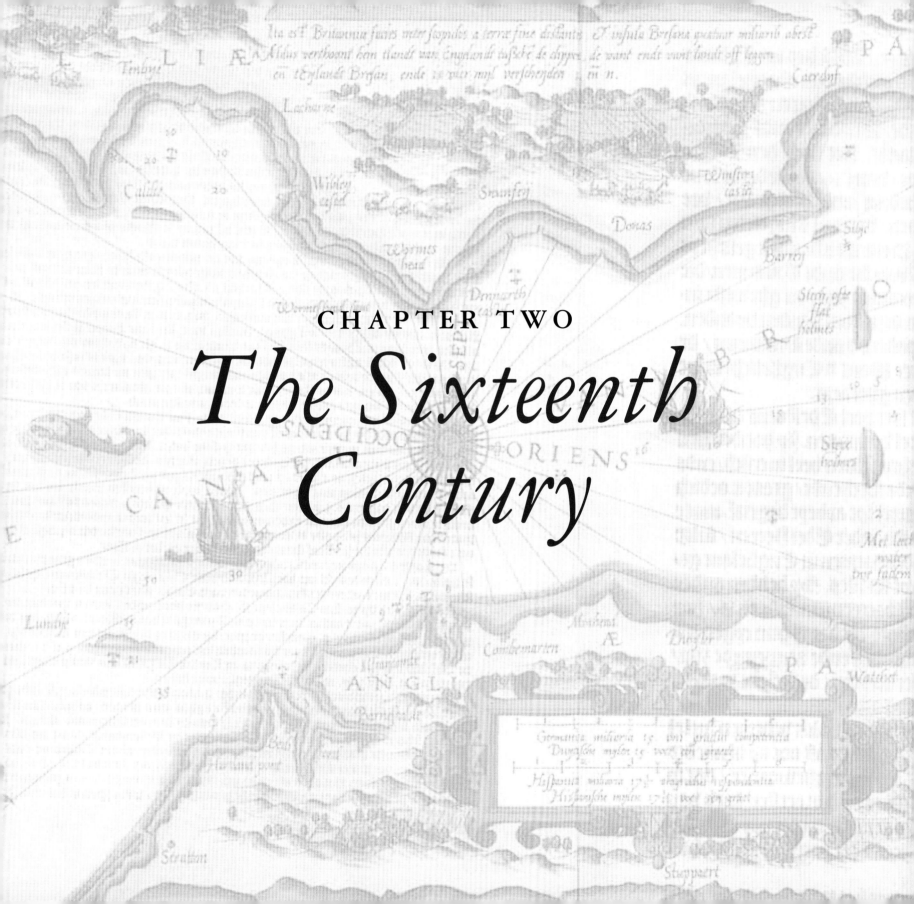

CHAPTER TWO
The Sixteenth Century

A map to illustrate the annals of Bath and Wells [Valor Ecclesiasticus]
Aaron Arrowsmith
1535 (published 1810-1825)

This map of Somerset is based on a fine series of maps drawn by Aaron Arrowsmith (1750–1823), cartographer, engraver, publisher and founding member of a family of geographers. Arrowsmith founded a mapmaking and publishing dynasty in London, which included his two sons, Aaron and Samuel. The business was thus carried on in company with John Arrowsmith (1790-1873), nephew of the elder Aaron.

The survey of church lands, on which this map is based, was undertaken by order from King Henry the Eighth and became known as the '*Valor Ecclesiasticus*'. This important historical reference was published in the 1810s by the Record Commissioners. One of the earliest 'historical' interpretations to be portrayed in map form, the publication of the *Valor* included important information on the ecclesiastical structure of Somerset prior to the Reformation.

The version reproduced opposite appeared in 1885 in the Diocesan Histories Series published by the Society for Promoting Christian Knowledge. The volume covering *The Somerset Diocese, Bath and Wells* was written by the Reverend William Hunt, late vicar of Congresbury with Wick St Lawrence. The map was produced by Stanfords Geographical Department, one of the leading map producers of their day. Abbeys, nunneries, monasteries, priories, churches and chapels appear as symbols, and the boundaries of the pre-Reformation diocese and deaneries are also shown.

Above: Aaron Arrowsmith, holding his draughtsman's dividers in his right hand (from a print based on a drawing by H.W. Pickersgill engraved by T.A. Dean).

Opposite: *A map to illustrate the annals of Bath & Wells*.

Source: W. Hunt, *The Somerset Diocese, Bath and Wells* (London, 1885). Original size: 206 x 133mm.

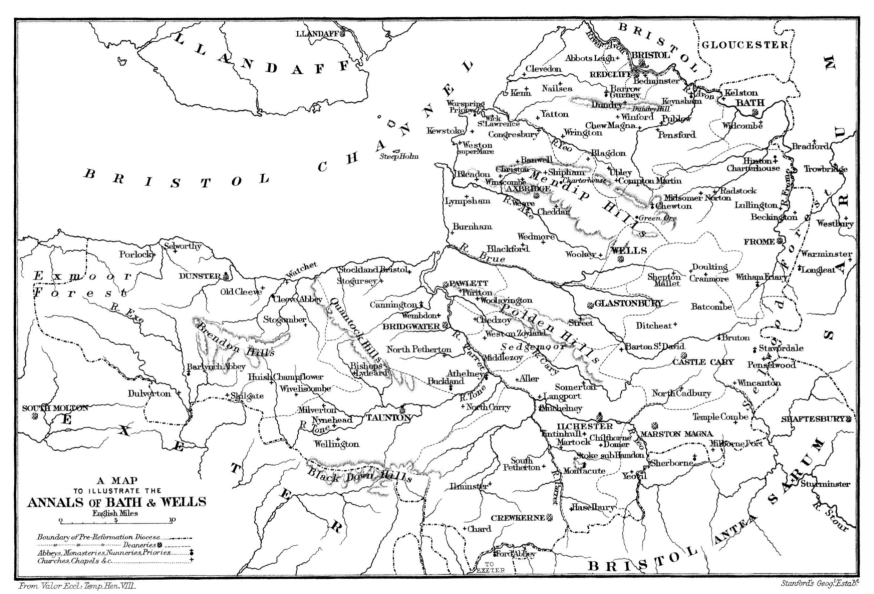

A MAP
TO ILLUSTRATE THE
ANNALS OF BATH & WELLS
English Miles

Boundary of Pre-Reformation Diocese
Deaneries
Abbeys, Monasteries, Nunneries, Priories
Churches, Chapels &c.

From Valor Eccl: Temp. Hen. VIII.

Stanford's Geogl. Estabt.

London: Published by the Society for Promoting Christian Knowledge

31

The coste of England uppon Severne
Anonymous
1539

Although not strictly a map, rather a view or panorama of the whole coast of Somerset survives from 1539. It contains proposals to fortify the coast at a time when there was a real threat of invasion by France and her Spanish allies. Following a peace treaty between King Francis the First of France and Charles the Fifth, Holy Roman Emperor King of Spain, Henry the Eighth's decision to divorce Catherine of Aragon put him at odds with two of the greatest powers in Christendom. Henry's kingdom needed defending. Although the defences were not put in place in Somerset, this magnificent drawing gives a unique view of the topography all along the coast. It has been described as defence mapping and was part of a massive fortification scheme along the coast stretching from Land's End to Berwick.

At the mouth of the River Avon a large group of ships can be seen at anchor in King Road, either loading or unloading, or transiting the port of Bristol. Moving down the coast to Portishead, with much smaller ships in the pill compared to those at King Road, another group of ships can be seen at anchor off Kettles Wood, an anchorage once used to handle an illicit consignment of leather being sent down from Newnham, Gloucestershire to be loaded aboard two Spanish ships.

A large proposed gun tower at Woodspring is overshadowed by a church with a spire on a hill. But what is this church? Is it the church of St Martin, at Worle, which still retains its spire to this day? Further down the coast in the un-named but easily identifiable Weston Bay, is another group of ships taking shelter. This bay is easily identifiable as it sits beneath Knightstone but further north than Black Rock at the mouth of the River Axe. And the Black Rock appears like a mountain jutting from the sea, and acted as a

mark for the ships running in and out of the River Axe.

Further offshore, between Flat Holm and Steep Holm, a ship can be seen flying the flag of St George, clearly not one of the Spanish ships involved in the trade in illicit goods, but one that was heading towards Bristol. This would have been one of those larger ships that followed the ancient shipping route between the Holms on their way to Bristol. In the early seventeenth century navigators were advised to

> goe nearest Flatholme side, for there is deepest water, with an open winde you may sayle as neare as you will, yea so neare as that you may cast a stone thereon.

Then to Bridgwater, with its bridge clearly drawn and there are ships waiting at the mouth of the River Parrett. The rest of the coast is dominated with fishing weirs off Watchet and Porlock and four distinct groynes stretching out from Minehead 'key'. Many ships can be seen taking refuge at Minehead and Porlock.

A copy of this panorama was published in 1888 as the frontispiece in Emanuel Green's book on *The preparations in Somerset against the Spanish Armada, A.D. 1558-1588* and is reproduced opposite and over.

Source: The original is in the British Library, Cotton Augustus I.i f.8. Original size: 1875 x 349mm.
Opposite and overleaf: A reduced reproduction of the whole panorama. Modern place names have been added outside of the edge adjacent to their location shown on the panorama.

Hollowbacks Portishead Fresemare Clevedon Sluts Pill Woodspring Pill

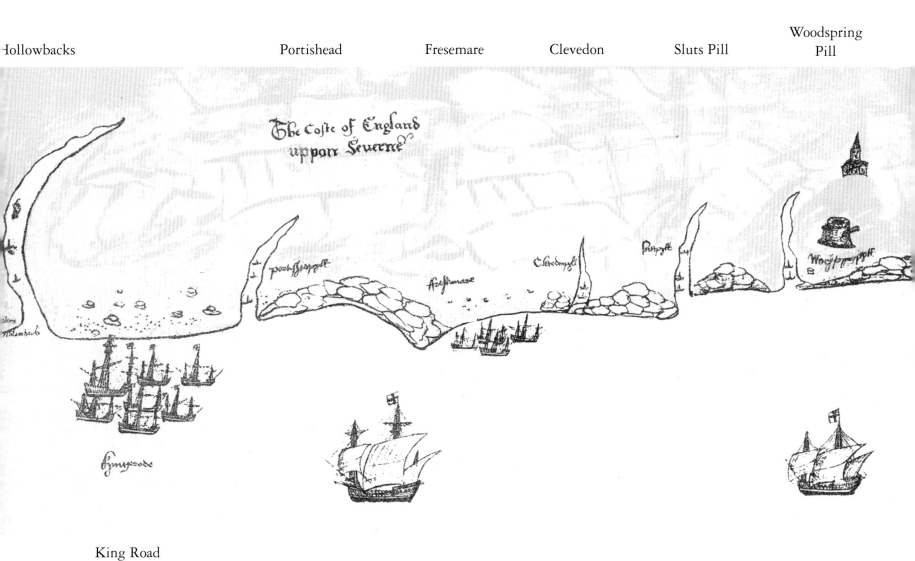

King Road

Continued from previous page

Bridgwater

Knightstone   Uphill   Steart   Combwich

Anchor Head   Flat Holm   Black Rock   Steep Holm

Porlock

Watchet Minehead Hurlestone Porlock Bay

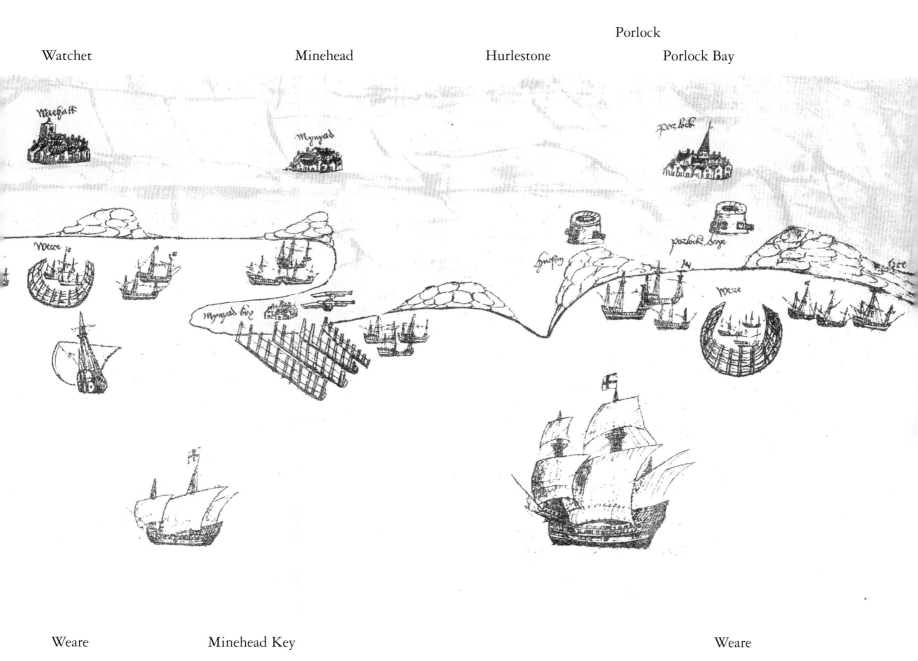

Weare Minehead Key Weare

[Map of Mendip]
*c.*1550
Anon

Arguably one of the earliest and most informative maps of any region within Somerset is one showing part of the Mendips, its roads, churches and mining operations. The map is complex and may have originally been drawn up as a result of a dispute concerning the rights of the commons in the ancient Forest of Mendip. That dispute occurred in 1550 but the date of this map is thought to be around 1590 because of its style. Therefore is this map, or at least part of it, a later copy of an earlier map which is now lost?

The map is thought possibly to have belonged to the May family of Charterhouse on Mendip who may have commissioned it. It is known to have definitely been in the ownership of Earl Fortescue who sold the manor of 'Ashweek' (Ashwick) to J.C. Hippisley towards the end of the eighteenth century. The text on the map, now much decayed, recites the ownership of Charterhouse Down and part of the Forest of Mendip passing from the Crown to the Fitzjames family, then to Sir Ralph Hopton, from whom it passed to Mr Robert May deceased and to his son, also named Robert. The text refers to the 'Queen's Forest' thus putting the date between the 17th of November 1558 and the 24th of March 1603. However, Robert May senior (d.1549) was granted the manor in September 1544 and by 1554 it had passed to Robert junior (following his father's decease). Robert junior's will was proved in 1582, so the text must have been referring to a dispute dated before that time.

Against each of the churches are two or three names of men with their ages. The burials of some of these men can be found in only half a dozen surviving ancient parish registers, such as John Addams the elder who was buried at Chewton Mendip on the 20th of March 1556/7. Another man mentioned on the map was John Bees who

was buried at Chewton Mendip on the 29th of September 1558 and a man of the same name of 'Watry Coome' (Watery Combe in Chewton Mendip) was also buried there on the 24th of October 1562. Others mentioned who also died in the 1550s include John Bisse, a clothier of Croscombe, John Sherborne of 'Whitecombe' (Witcombe in West Harptree), John Millard (or Milward) and William Plumer both of Compton Martin. The majority of the other men are mentioned in Elizabethan documents showing that they lived in the same parishes, albeit after the case.

Therefore there are three things of note. First is the statement about the dispute. Although thought to have been in Queen Elizabeth's reign, the deaths of John Addams the elder in March 1557 and John Bees in September 1558 must mean the dispute took place between 1549 and 1557. A Chancery dispute of 1550-1, concerning the boundaries of Black Down, narrows down the date even further. Secondly, the lettering on the map is not from such an early date and appears to be in a clear late Elizabethan or early seventeenth century hand. So is this a copy of an earlier map, drawn up to give a pictorial record of the dispute and the tenants' rights should they ever need to refer to them? Thirdly, how did it end up with the Ashwick court rolls when there is no depiction of Ashwick church on the map? Perhaps it was used as a wrapper.

(continued over)

Opposite: A reduced reproduction of a tracing of the map made by Harry Savory and published in 1911 in the *Proceedings of the Wells Natural History and Archaeological Society* (Wells, 1911).

Source: The original is in Wells Museum. Original size: 444 x 520mm.

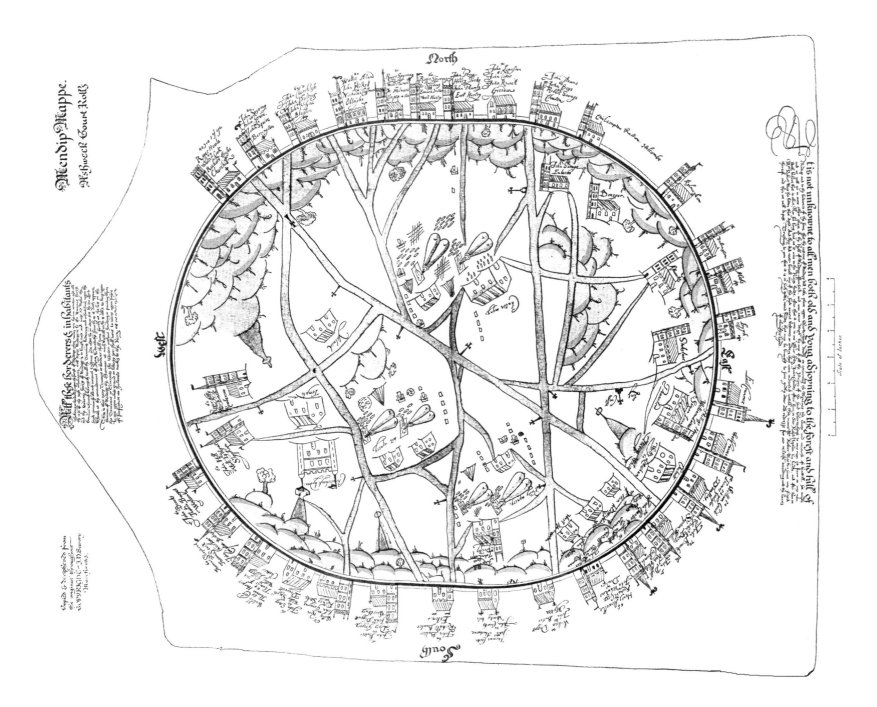

(*continued*)

Although the map predominantly concerns itself with details of the case and the rights of common on Black Down, it includes many other fascinating pieces of information. Arguably the most interesting are the parts of the map showing the different mineries and the processing of the ore dug up from the depths of the earth.

The map shows three of the four ancient mineries of Mendip, namely Chewton and Priddy, as well as the 'West Minery'. In the mid sixteenth century the Chewton Minery was owned by the Waldegrave family of Chewton Mendip, the Priddy Minery by the bishops of Bath and Wells and the West Minery by the May family of Charterhouse. The connection to Ashwick is slight.

The map was exhibited at the Society of Antiquaries in London by Sir J.C. Hippisley in 1809. It was donated to Wells Museum at the end of the nineteenth century by Bishop Hobhouse who thought the numbers by the names perhaps represented 'the head of cattle for which pasturage was claimed', but is undoubtedly the age of men. The map may have been purchased in a curiosity-shop in Bristol before being brought to Wells. I have termed this the "Hobhouse" map.

An extract, right, shows some details of the mining activities above ground. J.H. Savory identified the bellows and hearths, with piles of 'hard-earned ore' nearby. Recent research by Barry Lane, Curator of Wells Museum, has identified the criss-cross feature as a pile of whitecoal as shown in a woodcut of 1556. The triangular feature is thought to be a clamp of charcoal and the sausage shapes represent moulds for molten lead, which can be seen being filled from the hearths.

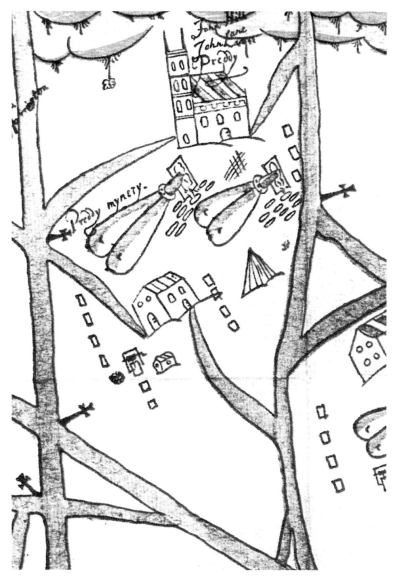

A section from a tracing of the map showing the 'Preddy mynery' situated to the north of the church; the extract is reproduced with north at the bottom. To the north of Priddy is the Chewton Minery.

Source: J.H. Savory, 'Mendip mappe Ashweek court rolls' in *Proceedings of the Wells Natural History and Archaeological Society* (Wells, 1911).

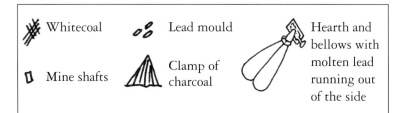

Whitecoal

Mine shafts

Lead mould

Clamp of charcoal

Hearth and bellows with molten lead running out of the side

Above: A close-up view (from the original map) of 'Shypham' church and the names of John Hill and William Lythyat. Note how clear and distinct the handwriting is, with their ages written above them; both men were 60 years of age. Families of this name continued to live in the area during the 1570s.

Whoever drew the map decided not to draw each church as it actually appeared, but they stylised them showing few, if any, differences between them. Ironically the neighbouring church of Rowberrow (drawn on the other side of the road) resembles the drawing of Shipham, suggesting that perhaps some of the churches may have been more familiar to the map maker than others. Or if this is a copy, perhaps the copyist did not pay close attention to what he was copying.

The grey line to the right of the church is a road with a cross towards the top. There are several such crosses shown on the map, none of which survived into the twentieth century.

Top right: The illustration is orientated with north at the bottom and south at the top. To the east of Shipham and Rowberrow is Charterhouse on Mendip, or as it is depicted on the map, 'Charterhouse hydon'. No church is shown at Charterhouse, so a drawing of what appears to be a castle or an impressive looking domestic manor house is inserted. Was this therefore the manor house of the May family at Charterhouse, drawn with its towers and fortifications? Could this be the site known today as Haydon Grange?

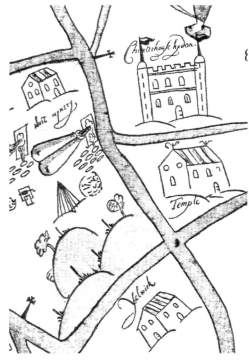

Left: Further north east is 'Yelwick', which survives today as Ellick in the parish of Blagdon, and in the 1780s was mapped as 'Elick'.

Between Charterhouse and Ellick is another small domestic building, similar to that at Ellick, which is given the name Temple. But where is this today? Temple Down (in West Harptree) was owned by the May family and it is shown on a map (below) from the 1780s. Today the area is marked by Templedown Farm in West Harptree.

Below: 'Temple down' as mapped in the 1780s. Charterhouse is to the left, Compton Martin is top right.

Sources: Day and Masters, *Somerset* (1782) (SANHS). An extract from a tracing of the map made by Harry Savory and published in 1911 in the *Proceedings of the Wells Natural History and Archaeological Society.* The 'Hobhouse Map' in Wells Museum.

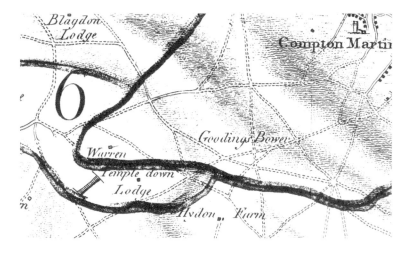

Angliae, Scotiae & Hiberniae nova descriptio
1564
Gerardus Mercator

Gerardus Mercator (1512-1594) was born in Flanders (modern day Belgium). His career started when he engraved maps but in 1537 he produced his own map and in 1538 produced his first map of the world. He went on to write the first book on the italic script published in the Western world. He moved to Duisburg, in Germany where he worked as a surveyor, taught mathematics and was appointed court cosmographer to Wilhelm, Duke of Jülich-Cleves-Berg. He later became a leading globe maker in Europe.

His map, containing a detailed depiction of Somerset's hills, rivers, towns and cities, was orientated to read with west at the top and north to the right. This orientation has left us with a very unusual depiction of the county particularly the way in which he showed the Mendip Hills, *Mendepius mons*, stretching from Sherborne, in Dorset to Warminster, in Wiltshire. Another range of hills runs in a westerly direction from Taunton to Molton, in Devon, which must surely be the Quantock Hills. Equally inaccurate is the way he showed the River Tone, *Thone flu*, running straight to Ilchester, with no spur running from Taunton, and an island named *Athelnea insula*.

Today Mercator is best known by navigators as the originator of the map projection used on navigational charts across the globe.

Opposite: A reproduction of a section of the map showing the county of Somerset.

Source: Bibliothèque Nationale de France, GED-17776.
Original size of each plate: 323 x 443mm.

A portrait of Gerardus Mercator. (Private collection.)

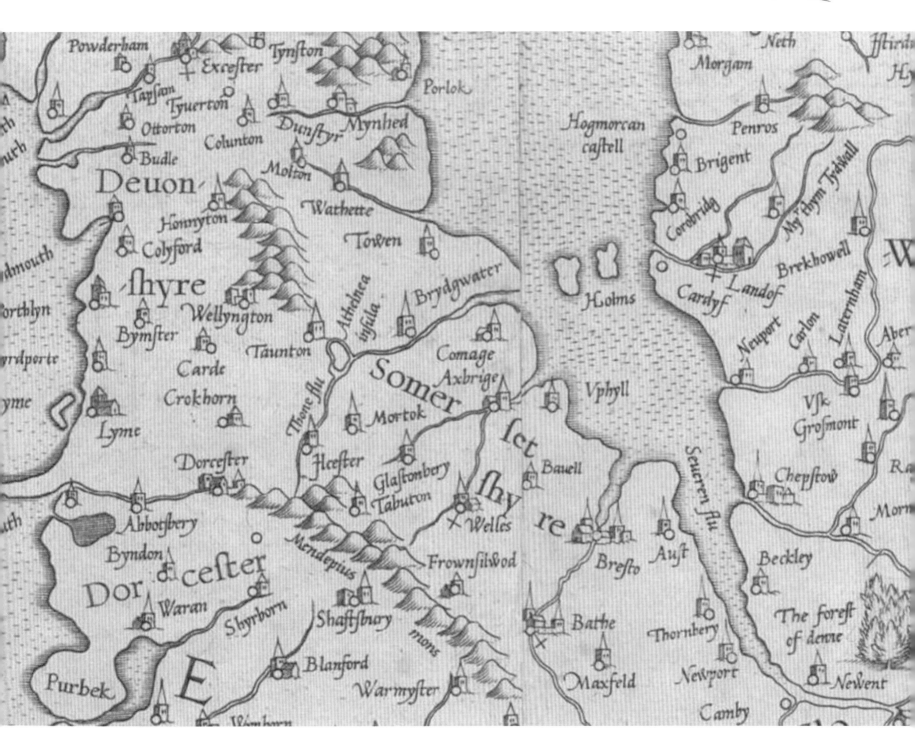

Bath and *Brightstowe*
William Smith
1568

Today Bristol has grown into a major conurbation but before 1373 Redcliffe was part of the ancient and large parish of Bedminster in Somerset. Because of its size Bedminster had chapels of ease including Abbots Leigh, St Mary Redcliffe and St Thomas. In 1373, Redcliffe became part of Bristol for administrative purposes but remained in the Diocese of Bath and Wells ecclesiastical jurisdiction, whereas the rest of Bristol (north of the River Avon) was within the diocese of Worcester. Redcliffe was originally part of the manor of Bedminster and was held by the earls of Gloucester, although divided from Bristol by the River Avon.

This situation continued throughout the Middle Ages and was only changed in 1542 when the diocese of Bristol was created with its own bishop and its cathedral in the former Augustinian abbey. Bedminster and its chapelries then became part of the new diocese. In the sixteenth century when the view opposite was executed by William Smith, he included the church at 'Ratliffe', or Redcliffe, which had changed little since it was in the county of Somerset. The area around the church appears to be almost rural compared to the housing crammed in behind the city walls. The sheep in the foreground are symbolic of the woollen industry in the west of England and the fortunes that were being made by Elizabethan clothiers.

Right: An enlargement of Redcliffe. (Robin Bush collection.)

Source: Braun & Hogenburg, *Civitates Orbis Terrarum* 3 (Cologne, 1581). Original size: 490 x 330mm.

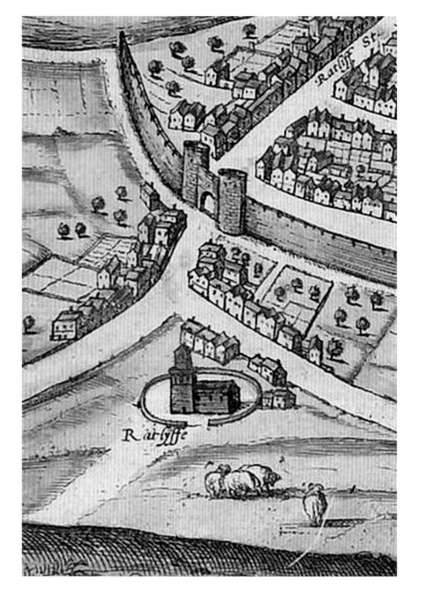

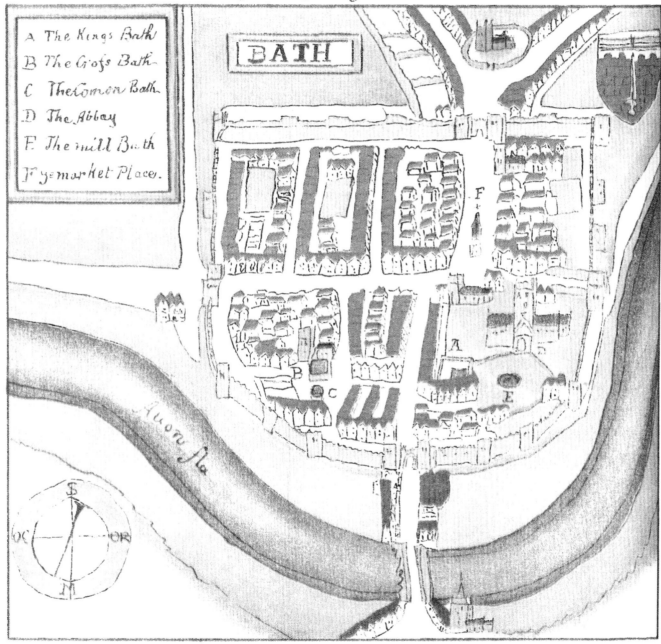

A The Kings Bath
B The Cross Bath
C The Common Bath
D The Abbey
E The mill Bath
F ye market Place.

William Smith also drew a map of Bath that remained unpublished, unlike his map of Bristol. Drawn before 1588, Smith described Bath as a 'little Cittie, yet one of ye most auncientest in England'. When Emmanuel Green published a copy of the map in a paper, in 1889, he proposed that this was not so much a 'map' but more of a view of the city. He described it as 'a bird's eye-view - "a portrature" as if taken from Beechen cliff'. Widcombe church can be seen at the bottom of the map by a bridge across the River Avon.

Source: E. Green, 'The earliest map of Bath' in *Proceedings of the Bath Natural History and Antiquarian Field Club*, 6 (1889), 58-74. Size: 120 x 114mm.

Somersetensem
Christopher Saxton
1575

Christopher Saxton was originally from Dunningley in Yorkshire and was probably educated at Dewsbury. It was here that he most likely came in contact with the vicar John Rudd, who was a keen cartographer, and who is thought to have fostered Saxton's passion for the subject.

Saxton began his survey of the English and Welsh counties in 1574 and completed the work five years later in 1579. The same year it was published in atlas form, and became the first national atlas of England and Wales. Saxton systematically surveyed the country, beginning his task in eastern England, perhaps in Norfolk or Suffolk. He then proceeded westwards from Kent across southern England, before heading northwards through the midlands. The last counties to be mapped were probably the Welsh ones around 1577. The maps were compiled from field observations and very likely from existing cartographic material, especially local surveys, suggested by the speed with which Saxton completed his work. However, the work of cartographers such as Lawrence Nowell and Gerard Mercator were probably of little use to Saxton as their work was too generalised and at too small a scale.

The map of Somerset was completed in 1575 and engraved by Lenaert Terwoort, a Flemish engraver who also engraved the maps of Hampshire and Suffolk. Similar to the other county maps, it features the arms and motto of Thomas Seckford of Woodbridge in Suffolk, Saxton's patron. However, it differs slightly in that it does not show the Royal Arms of Queen Elizabeth. Saxton's proof map of Somerset, which entered Lord Burghley's collection, does not have a title panel, or the Seckford motto but the word 'Summersetshre' added in manuscript, suggesting it was incomplete when sent to

The arms of Thomas Seckford (1515-1587), member of Queen Elizabeth's Privy Council, lawyer, politician and knight of the shire for Suffolk (as they appear on Saxton's map). His role in Saxton's mapping project ensured that his arms were engraved for posterity, although the motto underneath was subsequently changed in a later edition.

Lord Burghley. But why either Saxton or Terwoort rushed to get it finished may never be known.

The maps were all completed by the end of 1577 and Saxton was granted a license to publish them exclusively for ten years. Despite producing the first systematic survey of the country, Saxton's work was not always favourably received. The main criticism was that Saxton had, on occasion, grouped counties together meaning less detail could be portrayed on the maps. The maps also often lacked consistency, with hill signs varying greatly across the different counties. This prompted cartographers such as John Norden and William Smith to focus their efforts in the late sixteenth and early seventeenth century on producing something more accurate. Pieter van der Keere also printed the maps, including the county of Somerset, in the Netherlands in miniature form. Most notably, the maps were updated by John Speed who turned them into works of art, as well as more accurate maps.

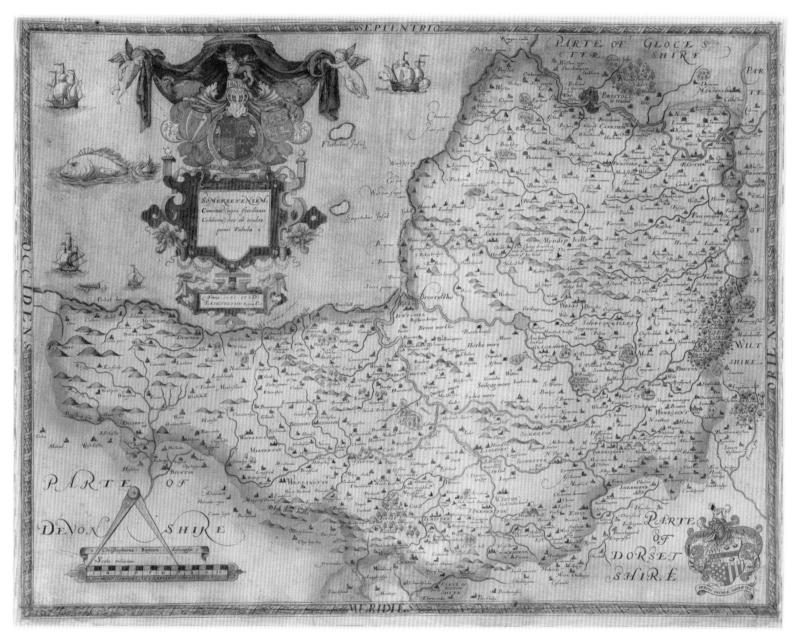

A reduced reproduction of Saxton's map of Somerset, 1575. Original size: 512 x 390mm.

Source: Robin Bush collection.

An enlarged image depicting Cadbury Castle, or 'Camellek' at South Cadbury. A Bronze- and Iron-age hillfort, it has been speculated that it may have been King Arthur's legendary court of Camelot. Saxton interestingly adopted the 'Camelot' name from John Leland.

An enlarged image of the Mendip hills, including Cheddar, Charterhouse and Priddy. The hills have been a place of settlement from the Neolithic period. The caves at Cheddar were places of early human habitation and Britain's oldest complete human skeleton was found in the Cheddar gorge in 1903. The village was important in the Roman and Saxon periods and was home to a royal palace. Later, as industry developed, watermills appeared along the river grinding corn and making paper. Saxton noted how 12 mills were found within 'one quarter of a myle'.

An enlarged image of Downend Castle, or 'Cheif chattle of ye mount at Downe ende'. Also known as Chisley Mount or Chidley Mount, it was the site of a motte and bailey castle thought to have been built around the turn of the twelfth century. It is thought the castle was built by the Columber family who also built Stowey Castle. The castle was built on a good defensive position within easy reach of the River Parrett for trade.

An enlarged version of Peter Keere's map of Somerset that was based upon that of Saxton. Published from 1599 to 1676 under different titles, this map was further reproduced by John Speed. (SANHS.)

Source: P. Koerius, *A collection of maps in the counties of England and Wales* (1599). Original size: 121 x 86mm.

[Compton Martin and adjacent lands]
c.1574
Anon

This wonderful Elizabethan map gives a unique view of the topography of Compton Martin and its setting within Mendip, the roads leading to the adjacent parishes and small pictures of over a dozen churches and domestic buildings. The map maker is not known, neither is the author of the writing in the four panels. There is no date written on the map, which raises the questions exactly when was this document drawn up, and why?

The first question is easily answered. A dispute in 1574, brought before the Court of Chancery, includes exactly the same details which are on the map but does not explicitly mention one being made. But why was a map needed? This is a question which causes much debate. A statement on the map reads:

> From West harptrie to Bickfelde tenne furlonges thyrtie fyve perches. Memorandum that the hole comon of pasture in question conteyneth one thowsand too hunderythe and threescore Acers.

The problem with this statement in relation to what is drawn on the map is that there it contains no scale, Also the important section showing the common in question is drawn disproportionately compared to the roads and the churches shown around the edge. This suggests that before 1574 there was no detailed map of the area. Equally that there was, possibly, a lack of records, such as one showing the extent of the lands in question, therefore a map was needed to determine the area in question in the court case.

The family at the centre of the case lived in their manor house at Bickfield, now called Moat Farm. Their name was Roynon and they had come into the lands through marriage into the Raymond family.

The Devil's Punchbowl (left) and Knight Barrow (right) as depicted in 1574. The Devil's Punchbowl is a swallet hole 80 feet deep.

The Raymonds were descended from the Bickfold family who purchased Smethan (in West Harptree) in the mid thirteenth century.

As a document this map represents three things. First, of course, is the map itself, portraying in glorious colour the meaning of the texts written on it and in the court papers. Secondly, it is a perambulation of the parish of Compton Martin, describing its extent, boundary markers and the distance from one to another. Thirdly, it is a description of the distances between five places, for example 'From Compton to Blagdon too Myles tenne perches'. An analysis of these distances by David Hart shows that the surveyor who measured the distances with a rood pole, using a compass to plot the angle from place to place, did a very accurate job under the circumstances. For its age the map is in incredibly good condition and its content makes it a rare survival for Somerset. As for its wider place in the history of surveying, it is equally rare for the way its maker portrayed such a large geographical area alongside a great deal of accurate detail, including the crosses on top of churches.

Source: SHC, DD/SPY 110 . Original size: 860 x 860mm.

A reduced reproduction of the whole map. The area in yellow signifies hillside pastures and the common land on Mendip claimed by Compton Martin. The area in brown shows the land under cultivation that had been ploughed. The dark green colour has been used to show land on neighbouring estates. The colours are thought to have possibly been made using ochre (hydrated iron oxide) which can be found at sites in the Mendip Hills area.

A reproduction showing the churches of East Harptree on the left and West Harptree with its spire on the right. In the middle, dominating the scene, is 'Richmond Castle', or Richmont Castle in the parish of East Harptree. The castle is thought to have been constructed in the late eleventh century and by the 1650s it was in ruins, a state of affairs which continued until the end of the nineteenth century. Green noted how the 'castle's field of influence is reflected by the early 19th century map of the Honor of Richmond where it's bounds extended south as far as Priddy and the ecclesiastical parishes on the plateau of East Harptree, West Harptree, Compton Martin and Ubley'.

Top (left to right) Shepton Mallet, Wells ('Wellys') and Priddy ('Preddye').

Middle (left to right): Stoke St Michael, Cheddar ('Chedder') and Axbridge.

Bottom left: the 'chaunselers howse at thend of d[re]ey wey' which is Chancellor's Farm in the parish of Priddy.

Bottom middle: A substantial house at Bickfield with a blue flag flying over one end. Whoever drew the map made unique observations of the architecture of the area in enough detail to show a flag pole, different stages of church towers, brick or blockwork and even buttresses on the sides of churches.

Canael Van Brostu
Lucas Jansz Waghenaer
1589

Lucas Jansz Waghenaer's (1533/4-1606) chart of the Bristol Channel, was published by Cornelis Claesz in the *Spieghel der zeevaerdt* in 1589. As the title of the volume suggests this chart was not of English origin but was published in Amsterdam. The chart was also accompanied by the first detailed printed sailing directions that were included on the verso of his chart of the Bristol Channel. Those directions for navigators were potentially more useful than the chart as, from time out of mind, navigators had been using written (or oral) directions to navigate from one port to another.

Waghenaer, described as a pilot, as well as issuing his *Spieghel* in different editions and languages, such as French, German and Latin, produced a smaller revised version in 1592, the *Thresoor der zeevaert*. He issued a French version as the *Thresorie ou cabinet de la route marinesque* in 1601, which was more like the old style pilot guide in size, containing many coastal profiles in the text. Waghenaer's work was copied by many others, including Willem Janszoon Blaeu (1571-1638) whose work was copied by John Seller senior (1625-1697), Hydrographer in Ordinary to Charles the First, when he produced his great cartographic fraud *The coasting pilot* in 1671. Nevertheless Waghenaer produced a landmark volume in the history of both cartography and navigation. His charts became so well known that English chart users referred to them as 'waggoners'.

Right: A reduced reproduction of Waghenaer's chart of the Bristol Channel, or '*De Canael van Brostv*'. (Robin Bush collection.)

Source: L.J. Waghenaer, *Spieghel der Zeevaerdt* (Amsterdam, 1589). Original size: 520 x 360mm.

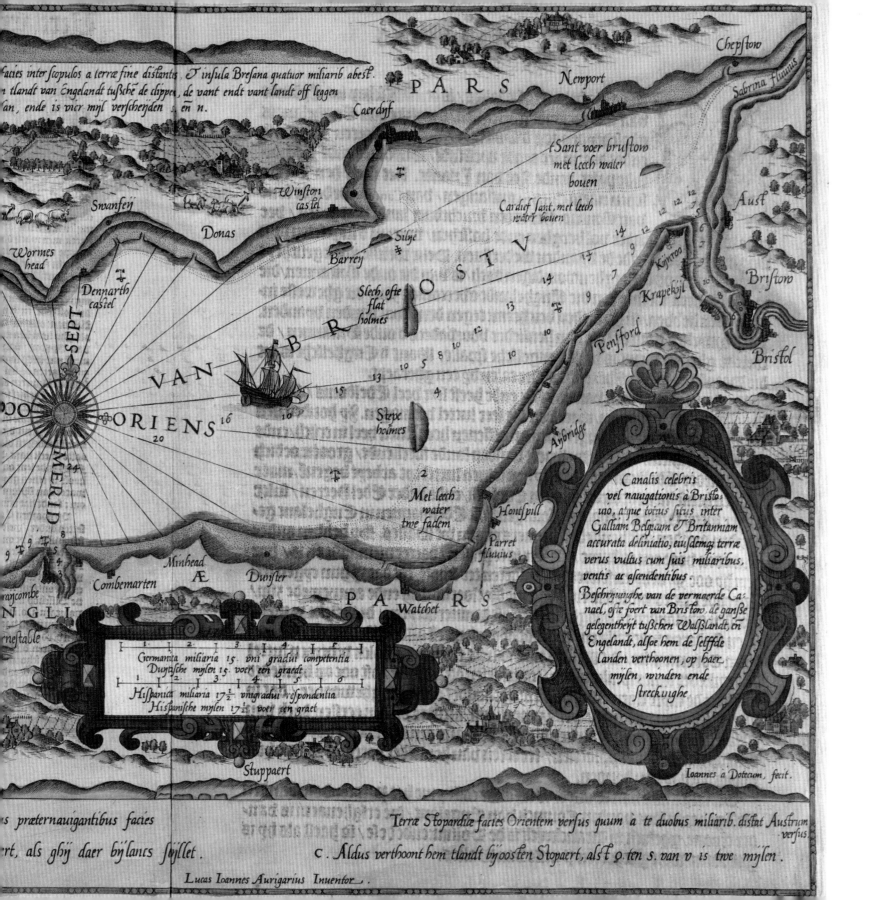

facies inter scopulos a terræ fine distantis, T insula Bresana quatuor miliarib abest.
tlandt van Engelandt tusschē de clippen, de vant endt vant landt off leggen
an, ende is vier mijl verscheyden, en n.

PARS

Chepstow

Newport

Sabrina fluuius

Caerdyf

Sant voer brustow
met leech water
bouen

Cardief sant, met leech
water bouen

Aust

Swanfey

Winston castel

12 12 12
12 12

Donas

Bristow

14 14 12

Wormes head

SEPT

Barrey

Silye

Krenroo

14 7

Denparth castel

BROSTV

Krapekyl

Pensford

13

Slech, ofte flat holmes

14

9

12

7

Bristol

VAN

10

10 5 8 10

10

ORIENS 16

13

4

20

Stepe holmes

Anbridge

24

2

9 9 8
5 4
4 3

Met leech
water
twe fadem

Houtspill

Canalis celebris
vel nauigationis à Bristo-
uo, atque totius situs inter
Galliam Belgicam T Britanniam
accurata deliniatio, eiusdemqs terræ
verus vultus cum suis miliaribus,
ventis ac ascendentibus
Beschryuinghe, van de vermaerde Canael, ofte foert van Bristow, de gansse
gelegentheyt tusschen Walsslandt, en
Engelandt, alsoe hem de selffde
landen verthoonen, op haer
mijlen, winden ende
streckuighe.

Parret fluuius

Minhead

Æ

Dunster

Combemarten

PA R S

Watchet

Germania miliaria 15. vni gradui competentia
Duytsche mylen 15. voer een graedt
Hispanica miliaria 17½ vnigradui respondentia
Hispanische mylen 17½ voer een graet

Stuppaert

Ioannes à Dotecum, fecit.

Lucas Ioannes Aurigarius Inuentor.

s præternauigantibus facies

als ghy daer by lancs seyllet.

Terræ Stopardiæ facies Orientem versus quum à te duobus miliarib. distat Austrum
versus
C. Aldus verthoont hem tlandt by oosten Stopaert, alst 9 ten s. van v is twe mylen.

Above: An illustration taken from the title page of Waghenaer's *Thresorie ou cabinet de la route marinesque* published in 1601. The man on the left is handing what is probably an atlas to the man at the table. On the table a pair of dividers is being used on a map, or chart, to plot a maritime voyage by the look of the ships in the background. On the table is a globe, a cross staff and possibly a nocturnal and hanging up, in the top right corner, is a mariner's astrolabe. All instruments used for navigation. Exactly what the person sat looking at the map or chart is doing is unclear. Perhaps the man with the hat is teaching the other person the art of navigation. (Admiralty Library.)

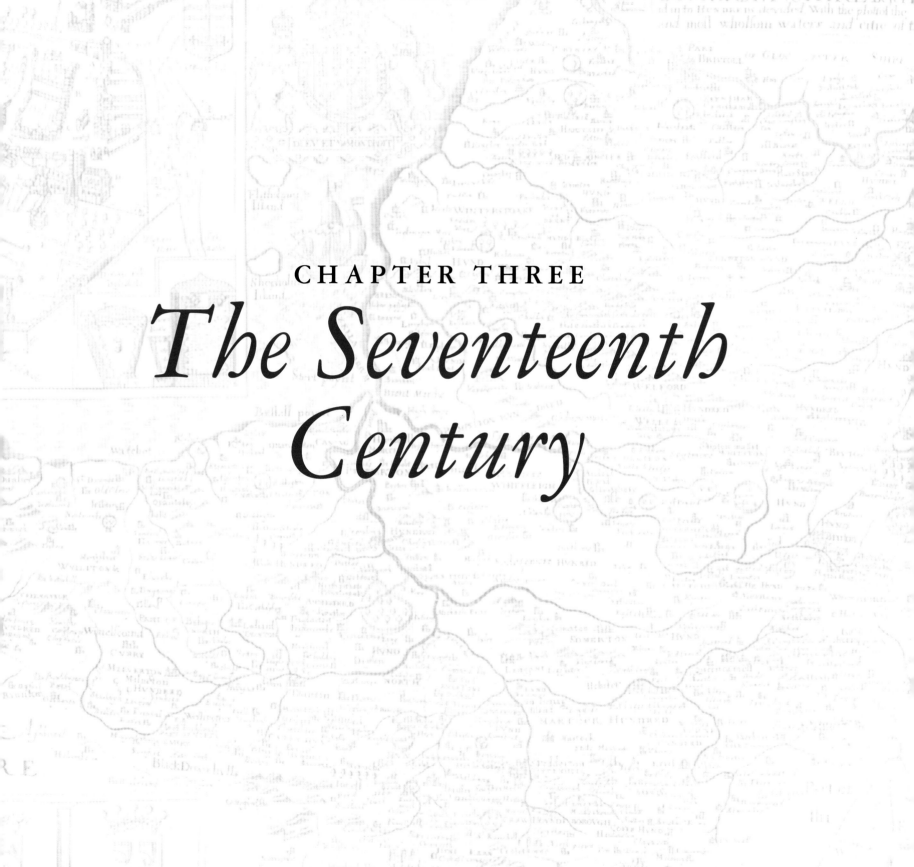

CHAPTER THREE
The Seventeenth Century

Somerset shire
John Speed
1610

John Speed's (1552-1629) map of Somerset is possibly the most easily recognised and reprinted of all the county maps. How could this mapmaker ever have imagined his maps would be printed on tablemats, tea trays and as vellum facsimiles. Even during his lifetime his maps were reprinted half a dozen times, then over a dozen times after his death, appearing in atlases with titles such as *The theatre of the Empire of Great Britaine* and *A collection of maps of England* (both from 1610), *England fully described* (from 1713) and the *English atlas* (in 1770).

Speed was both a mapmaker and an historian who was admitted to the Merchant Taylors' Company of London in 1580. He based his maps on the surveys of John Norden and Christopher Saxton. Speed also published other great works, such as *The genealogies recorded in the sacred scriptures according to euery family and tribe with the line of our sauior Jesus Christ obserued from Adam to the Blessed Virgin Mary* (printed in 1611), and his *Prospect of the most famous parts of the World* (printed in 1627), which was the first world atlas produced by an Englishman to be brought into print.

The inset plan of the city of Bath contains what is claimed to be the earliest depiction of a tennis court shown on a map. It is situated between the 'Kings Bathe' and St Peters.

Opposite: A reduced reproduction of the version 'Performed by JOHN SPEEDE and are to be sold in popes head Alley by John Sudbury et George Humble' from the first Latin edition of 1616 published in his *Theatrum imperii Magnae Britanniae*. (Robin Bush collection.)

Source: *The theatre of the Empire of Great Britaine* and *A collection of maps of England* (London, 1610). Original size: 508 x 375mm.

A portrait of John Speed, holding a pair of dividers over a map, signifying his map making expertise, from a contemporary engraving. (Robin Bush collection.)

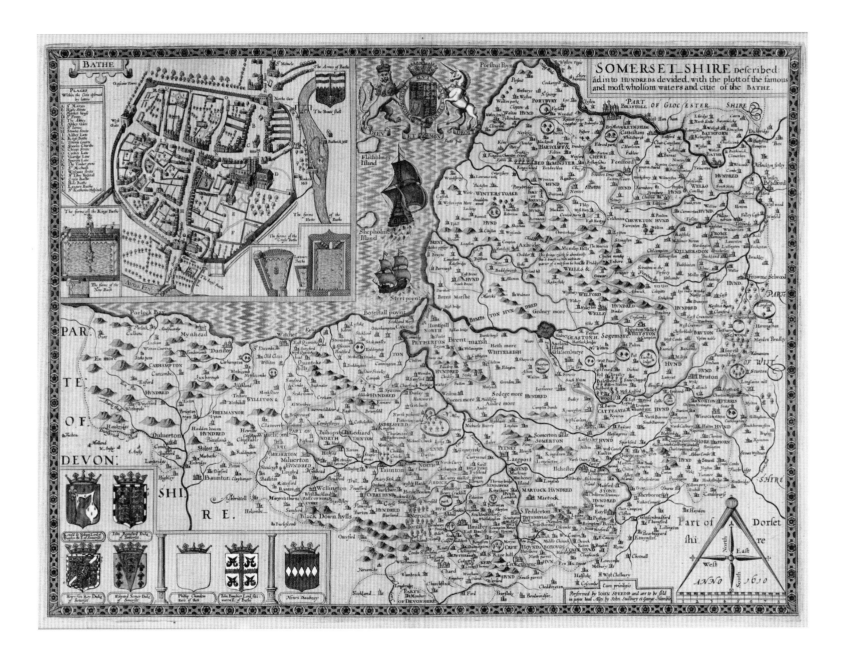

Poly-Olbion
William Hole
1612

Michael Drayton (1563-1631) wrote *Poly-Olbion* which was first published in 1612. It included work by John Selden (1584-1654) and the maps were drawn by William Hole (d.1624). The book is described as an 'expansive poetic journey through the landscape, history, traditions and customs of early modern England and Wales'. In this unusual work Drayton included a 15,000-line poem, which includes much about the county of Somerset and how it was viewed in Jacobean times.

In his third song he describes the rivers and adjacent countryside after leaving the River Avon at Bath:

> The views the Sommersetian soil;
> Through Marshes, Mines, and Moors doth toil,
> To Avalon to Arthur's Grave,
> Sadly bemoan'd of Ochy Cave.
> Then with delight she bravely brings
> The princely Parret from her springs
> Preparing for the learned plea
> in the Severne Sea.

Drayton went on to tell of the nymphs in 'Selwood's shades' and

> The Sommersetian maids, by swelling Sabryn's bank
> Shall strew the way with flowers (where thou art coming on)
> Brought from the marshy grounds by aged Avalon'.

A very romantic view of the county and one that is continued, more verbosely, part of which is reproduced below:

This said, she many a sigh from her full stomach cast,
Which issued through her breast in many a boist'rous blast;
And with such floods of tears her sorrows doth condole,
As into rivers turn within that darksome hole:
Like sorrow for herself, this goodly Isle doth try;
Imbrac'd by Selwood's son, her flood the lovely Bry,
On whom the Fates bestow'd (when he conceivéd was)
He should be much belov'd of many a dainty lass;
Who gives all leave to like, yet of them liketh none:
But his affection sets on beauteous Avalon;
Through many a plump-thigh'd moor, and full-flank'd marsh
    do prove
To force his chaste desires, so dainty of his love.
First Sedgemore shews this flood her bosom all unbrac'd,
And casts her wanton arms about his slender waist:
Her lover to obtain, so amorous Audry seeks:
And Gedney softly steals sweet kisses from his cheeks.
One takes him by the hand, intreating him to stay:
Another plucks him back, when he would fain away:
But, having caught at length, whom long he did persue,
Is so intranc'd with love, her godly parts to view,
That alt'ring quite his shape, to her he doth appear,
And casts his crystal self into an ample mere:
But for his greater growth when needs he must depart,
And forc'd to leave his love (though with a heavy heart)
As he his back doth turn, and is departing out,
The natning marshy Brent environs him about:

Opposite: A reduced reproduction of the map covering Somerset.
(Robin Bush collection.)
Source: M. Drayton, *Poly-Olbion* (London, 1612). Original size: 335 x 253mm.

BRISTOW

SOMERSET

Brent marsh

Cheder Rokes

Chute

BATH

SHERE

Mendip hils

Ax Gedny more

Ochy hoole

Scage more

The Ile of avalon

Audrey more

Qwantock hils

Parret

Bry

Car

Tone

Blackdowne hils

Neroch fo:

The Ile of Muchney

Wil

Selwood fo:

Nader

Dyver

Willy

Salsbury Plane

Wansdike

Blakmore fo:

froume

Auon

Bradon fo:

Colne

Isis

Rhe

Barbury hill

Martingsall hill

Oldbury hill

Pewsham fo:

St Ans hill

Bagden hill

Badbury hill

Alburne chase

Kennet

Sauernake fo:

WILT SHERE

Stoneindg

Harrodon hill

Auon

Bourne

SALSBVRY

Above: An enlargement of a female sitting in Wookey Hole. Is this the witch of Wookey Hole?

Below: Exmoor on the edge of the 'Sabrinian Sea', as shown in the top right corner of the map covering Devon and Cornwall. It is included with Devon and Cornwall because its waters run into the River Exe and a figure can be seen pouring water into the River Barle.

Above: In a map covering the Bristol Channel from Lundy ('Londy') as far up the channel as Bristol, mythical figures dominate the scene. King Neptune with his trident and crown rides on the back of a monstrous fish. His queen stands on the belly of a beast which looks like a dog whilst another naked lady stands on top of Lundy with a bird on her head.

This view of the River 'Severne' includes part of the Bristol Channel with the coast of Somerset poorly depicted. Despite the lack of names on the English side of the Bristol Channel, this is the Somerset coast as opposite lie the Welsh rivers (from left to right) of 'Elwy' (Ely), 'Taf' (Taff), 'Remny' (Rhymney), 'Srowy' (Sirhowey), 'Ebwith' (Ebbw), Usk and Wye. Along the north Somerset coast can be seen a group of ladies playing musical instruments and flying the flag of St George for England. On the opposite coast is another group of women also playing musical instruments, the majority of which are harps, with a flag inscribed 'Wales & St David'.

[Map of Mendip]
Early seventeenth century
Anon

The most colourful and decorative version of the Mendip mining maps from this period is one that was in the ownership of the Reverend J.D.C. Wickham B.A., formerly lord of the manor of Holcombe and rector of Horsington from 1875 to 1897. We have termed this map the "Wickham" map.

Although the central pictorial information is very similar in its arrangement to the "Hobhouse" map of Mendip, its purpose was to show both the ancient grazing rights and the mining laws. At the side of the map, in what appears to be an early seventeenth-century hand, is a record of the enrolment of the the rights and laws in the Court of Exchequer during the reign of King Edward the Fourth. The dispute was between the tenants of Lord Bonville, of Chewton, and the Prior of Green Ore; the king ordered Lord Chokke, Chief Justice, to go 'into the Country of Meyndeepe and set a concord and peace in the Countrey upon Meyndeepe'. Chokke assembled the Lords Royal and some ten thousand men in order to settle the dispute. A description of the mining laws includes ten clauses.

A copy of this map was made in the nineteenth century and was sent to the Museum of Practical Geology at Jermyn Street. The original was donated to the Somerset Archaeological and Natural History Society. A much reduced version appeared in Wickham's *Records by spade and terrier* published in 1918.

Above: An enlarged image of the area described as the 'West Mynery', situated to the north east of Cheddar Gorge.

Opposite: A reduced reproduction of the map.

Source: SHC, DD/SAS S.32. Original size: 669 x 908mm; the green coloured area measures 340 x 791mm.

The circumference of the forrest of Exmoore
John More
1637

This map, possibly one of the earliest of Exmoor, depicts the bounds of the forest. Dated 12 February 1637, it shows a perambulation of the forest. The perambulation began at the Hooked Stone and, as was traditional, worked clockwise around the forest. It not only detailed the boundary of the forest, but also the limits of the adjoining commons, suggesting the map was produced for some legal purpose possibly relating to rights of common.

During 1637 two court cases were brought in the Court of the Exchequer concerning the rights within the forest. The first concerned royal tithes, and decreed that the plaintiff, George Cottington, had the right to the tithes. The second was brought by Cottington (at Michaelmas) against Christopher Crang and Joseph Hounndle of Exford, and argued that many of the marking stones of the bordering commons, which were part of the forest, had been removed. Significantly the bill stated 'The commons are only encroachments on the forest, and are all of them bounded and compassed into the forest by the last perambulation recorded'. Could this compassing refer to the map opposite? It seems logical that a case such as this would need evidence of the boundaries of the forest, and the easiest way to show this would be on a map. This map could then be presented to the parties to agree upon. The map ended up among the records of the Office of Land Revenues, perhaps because the dispute with which it was associated involved royal tithes.

There has been debate about the authorship of the map. Previously some historians had attributed it to Jeramie Baines, who later surveyed the forest in 1651. While it is not unreasonable that Baines may have taken part in the perambulation in 1637, an annotation at the bottom of the map reads 'donne by me John

Moore of ...... in Devon'. Unfortunately the place from which Moore is likely to have originated or resided is too faded to read with any clarity. Little is known about John More in Somerset, but a man of this name produced surveys from 1599 to 1637 in Dorset, Hampshire, Kent, Sussex and Surrey. If this is the same man, then such a longevity in surveying activity was unusual.

Black Barrow, near Porlock, is 22 metres in diameter and 1.5 metres high. It is a Bronze Age round barrow that is mentioned in a perambulation of 1279 and named on the map opposite. (Phillip Ashford.)

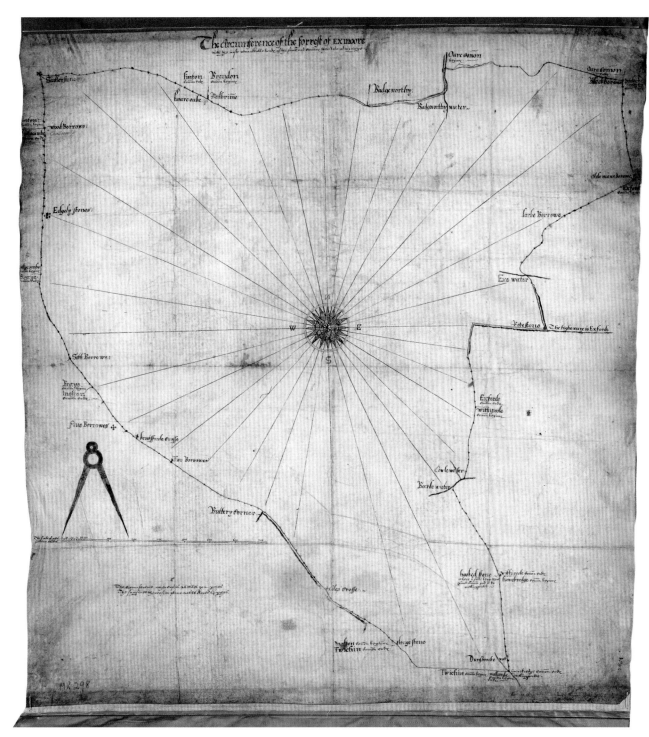

A reduced reproduction of John More's map showing the ancient boundary of the Forest of Exmoor. The full title reads 'The circumference of the forrest of Exmoore with the moste remarkeable bonds of the same and Commons thereunto adioyninge' drawn on vellum and used in a court case.

Source: TNA, MR 1/298. Original size: 800 x 725mm.

Hopton's itinerary from July 1642 to March 1644
July 1642 to March 1644 (1902)
Charles E.H. Chadwick Healey

In 1902 Charles E.H. Chadwick Healey (1845-1919) edited a key primary source detailing the activities of the royalist forces in Somerset from 1642 to 1644. The source was Sir Ralph Hopton's (1598-1652) narrative of his campaign in the west of England, to which Chadwick Healey added other relevant papers. Hopton had been a Parliamentarian, but in the spring of 1642 changed his allegiance and, shortly afterwards was sent to the Tower of London for his strong language in the House of Commons.

In the summer of 1642 he was sent by King Charles the First, with the Marquess of Hertford, upon an 'expedition' to the West. As a professional soldier Hopton fought with great conviction and was created a peer in 1643. Following defeats at Torrington, in Devon and Truro, in Cornwall he fled England for Jersey. He died at Bruges and his body was brought back to Somerset after the Restoration and interred at Witham. Henry Hyde, 1st Earl of Clarendon (1609-1674), wrote that Hopton was 'as faultless a person as I ever knew man'.

Chadwick Healey included three maps in his book published by the Somerset Record Society, of very different styles and purposes. In the front he included a modern map of the Battle of Lansdown (near Bath) in July 1643. He copied this map (with permission) from one that had already been published in volume 41 of the *Proceedings of the Somerset Archaeological and Natural History Society*. The author of the paper was the Very Reverend T. Jex-Blake, D.D., (1832-1915) Dean of Wells who had written about the battle to coincide with a field visit. Jex-Blake obtained the map from William Bidgood, Curator

Ralph, 1st Lord Hopton (SANHS).

of the Somerset Archaeological and Natural History Society, who had prepared it from the Ordnance Survey. Bidgood's cartographic style provides a clear picture of the landscape and the key sites referred to in the text.

The Chadwyck-Healey Baronetcy, of Wyphurst in the county of Surrey, was created on the 6th of May 1919 for Charles Chadwyck-Healey.

(continued over)

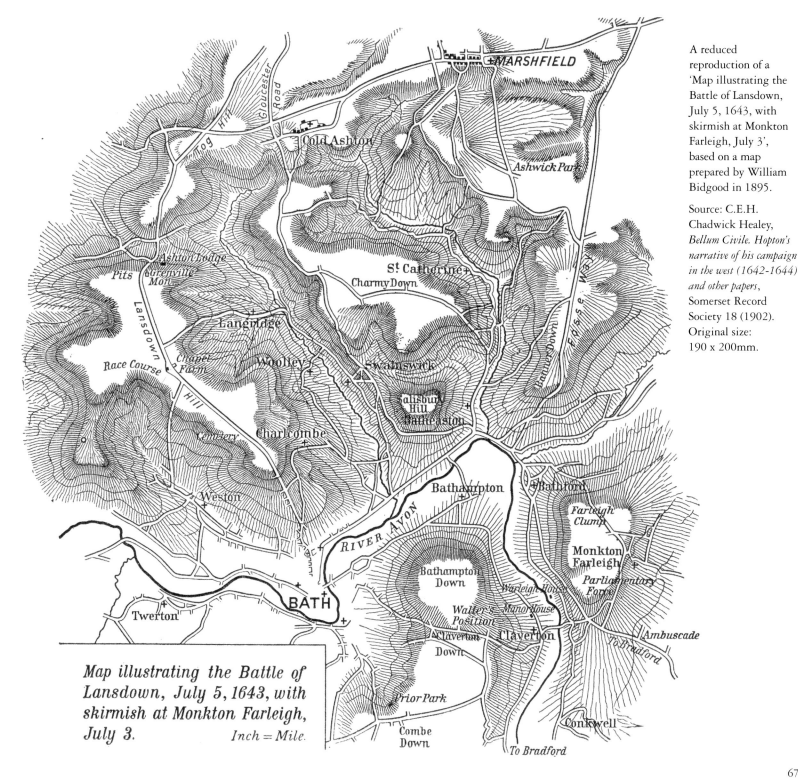

Map illustrating the Battle of Lansdown, July 5, 1643, with skirmish at Monkton Farleigh, July 3. *Inch = Mile.*

A reduced reproduction of a 'Map illustrating the Battle of Lansdown, July 5, 1643, with skirmish at Monkton Farleigh, July 3', based on a map prepared by William Bidgood in 1895.

Source: C.E.H. Chadwick Healey, *Bellum Civile. Hopton's narrative of his campaign in the west (1642-1644) and other papers*, Somerset Record Society 18 (1902). Original size: 190 x 200mm.

(continued)

The second map Chadwick Healey included (located at the back of the volume) shows Hopton's itinerary from July 1642 to March 1644. He described this map as

> an endeavour has been made to trace upon a map Hopton's movements during the period covered by this narrative. The line of march so laid down is intended merely to show the movements of the headquarters of the army. The operations of bodies of troops detached from the main force could not be added except at the expense of clearness. As it is, the marchings and counter-marchings, around Launceston for example, are sufficiently complicated.

From this map it is possible to see at a glance the tremendous distances the Royalist army travelled in their attemps to overcome the Parliamentary forces.

In Somerset Hopton was up against Parliamentarians like Robert Blake (1598-1657) of Bridgwater. But it is not just for his efforts at the sieges of Taunton and Dunster in 1645 that Blake is well-known, it is for his achievements at sea. Appointed 'General at Sea' from 1649 and described as the 'Father of the Royal Navy', he earned such a title after overhauling the navy, revising its tactics and discipline, and increasing the number of ships in commission to unprecedented numbers. Shortly before his death he was appointed Warden of Cinque Ports.

⸺ ◆◆◆ ⸺

A reproduction of Chadwick Healey's map of Hopton's itinerary from July 1642 to March 1644.

Source: C.E.H. Chadwick Healey, *Bellum Civile. Hopton's narrative of his campaign in the west (1642-1644) and other papers*, Somerset Record Society 18 (1902). Original size: 371 x 195mm.

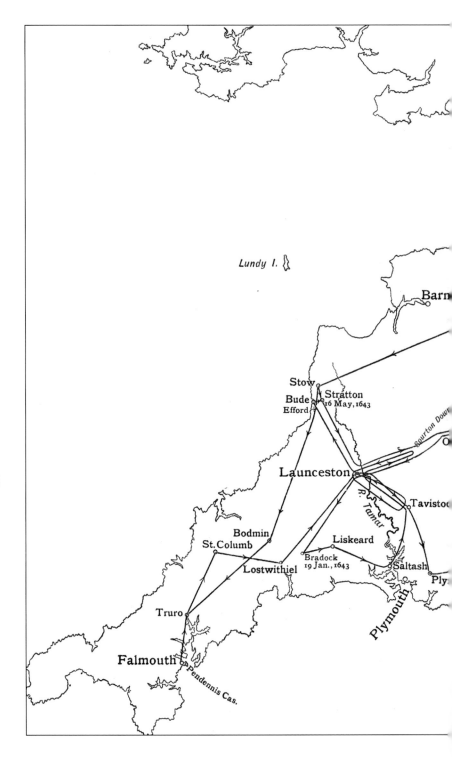

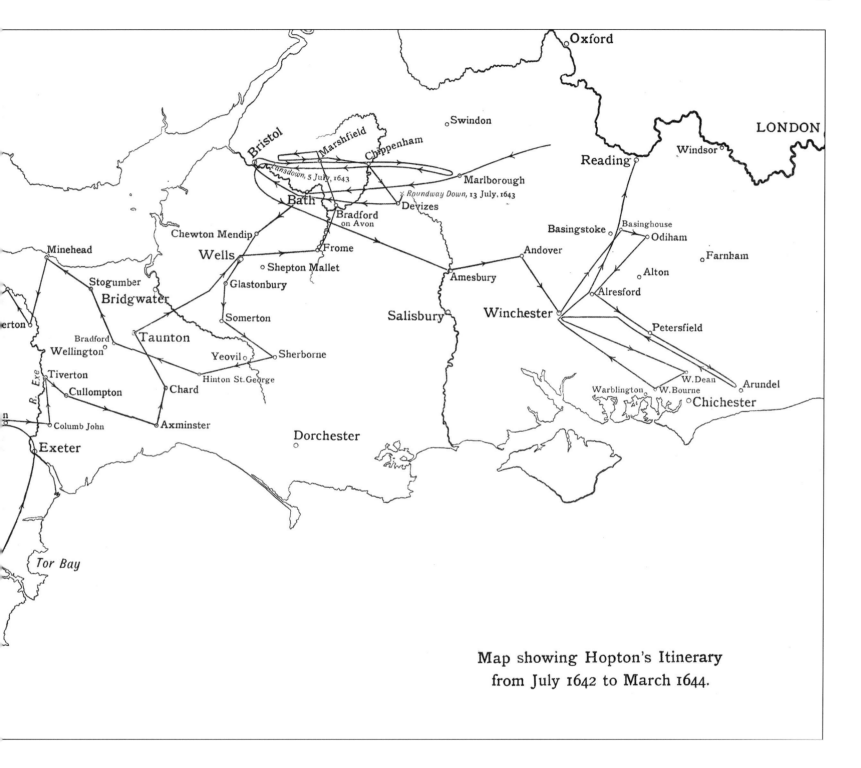

Map showing Hopton's Itinerary
from July 1642 to March 1644.

Somerset
Jacob van Langeren
1643

The famous surveyor and map maker John Norden (*c*.1547-1625) was the author of a series of distance tables published in 1625 in *England, an intended guyde for English travailers*. In that 1625 edition he included instructions to the reader about how to use the table. Norden claimed that he had invented the idea and his instructions read:

The use of this Table.

THe Townes or places betweene which you desire to know, the distance you may finde in the names of the Townes in the vpper part and in the side, and bring them in a square as the lines will guide you : and in the square you shall finde the figures which declare the distance of miles.

And if you finde any place in the side which will not extend to make asquare with that aboue, then seeking that aboue which will not extend to make a square, and see that in the vpper, and the other side, and it will showe you the distance, it is familiar and easie.

Beare with defectes, the vse is necessarie.

Inuented by IOHN NORDEN.

Although Norden travelled extensively the distances he showed are most unlikely to all have been measured road distances. In the introduction He described how he measured distances from maps by Saxton, Speed and himself.

When this work was reprinted in 1635, a small map with a capital letter, first published by William Bowes in 1590, each representing a place on the distance table, the names of the adjacent counties and a scale bar replaced the instructions. In 1643 the map was replaced with the map reproduced opposite. That map is much larger than the 1635 version but in doing so it is very cluttered.

The 1643 edition was sold by Thomas Jenner at the South entrance of the Exchange and the maps were engraved by Jacob van Langeren. Jacob Floris van Langeren (fl.1525-1610) was a member of a Dutch family of globe makers who were established in Amsterdam in 1580.

The full title reads:

A DIRECTION FOR the English TRAVILLER By which he Shal be inabled to Coast about all England and Wales. And also to know how farre any Market or noteable Towne in any Shire lyeth one from an other and Whether the same be East, West, North, or South from ye Shire Towne. As also the distance betweene London and any other Shire or great towne with the scituation thereof East, West, North, or South from London. By the help also of this worke one may know (in What Parish, Village or Mansion house soever he be in) What Shires he is to passe through & which way he is to travell till he comes to his journies End.

The map and distance table appeared in Jenner's *A book of the names of all the hundreds contained in the shires of the Kingdom of England* from 1644 and in his *A book of the names of all parishes, market towns, villages, hamlets, and smallest places, in England and Wales* from 1657.

Somerset

	Bristoll	Bathe	Welles	Shepton	Bruton	Somerton	Ilchester	Glastonbury	Bridgewater	Taunton	Charde	Euell	Wellington	Willcombe	Dunster	Crooke-horne	Froome	Wincaunto	Hunspill	Lamporte	Miluerto	Duluerton	Mynehead	Whatchet	Pensforde	Ilmister
Ax-bridge. S	12	16	8	11	16	14	17	9	13	18	21	21	24	23	26	23	18	20	10	15	23	32	30	22	11	21
Ilmister. S	32	32	19	20	21	10	12	15	11	7	4	12	12	15	23	5	28	21	11	5	6	13	23	25	20	29 109
Pensforde. S	5	7	11	11	18	20	22	15	22	20	23	27	15	34	36	30	12	19	19	31	42	39	32		129	
Watchet	34	36	25	27	31	22	25	22	20	13	20	27	12	7	5	24	36	33	14	19	11	7	129			
Mynehead W	36	43	31	34	36	26	30	10	17	26	34	15	11	3	27	42	38	20	24	10	135					
Duluerton SW	43	46	34	36	40	30	31	23	20	16	22	33	11	8	18	45	41	22	24	140						
Miluerton SW	34	36	25	27	30	19	21	22	11	6	14	24	3	3	13	18	35	31	14	15	115					
Lamporte S	27	26	14	15	15	5		6	8	12	11	16	17	22	6	22	16	116								
Hunspill SW	20	24	13	16	20	13	16	11	6	13	20	17	16	8	19	24	23	117								
Wincaunto SE	24	22	12	9	3	12	10	13	23	25	23	12	30	33	37	19	10	98								
Froome SE	10	8	11	6	18	18	15	30	31	20	36	37	40	27	66											
Crooke-horne S	33	22	20	20	10	8	16	15	6	10	20	27	112													
Dunster W	33	42	30	31	35	26	27	26	10	6	23	13	8	132												
Willcombe SW	36	40	30	31	35	22	23	23	13	5	23	129														
Wellingto SW	37	39	26	28	30	19	21	22	13	5	22	129														
Euell S	29	27	15	14	12	7	4	12	17	18	110															
Charde SW	35	36	22	23	27	13	13	18	14	9	121															
Taunton W	31	33	20	22	24	15	16	7	129																	
Bridgewater SW	24	27	16	20	11	13	116																			
Glastonbury S	19	18	4	6	10	6	3	108																		
Ilchester S	26	24	12	12	11	4	102																			
Somerton S	24	23	10	10	11	102																				
Bruton S	20	16	8	5	108																					
Shepton S	16	13	4	101																						
Welles S	15	14	102																							
Bathe E	11	92																								

An enlarged reproduction of the 1643 map engraved by Jacob van Langeren, one of a Dutch family of globe makers. Although issued after Norden's death it is known from Needell's study of Somerset maps that editions published after 1644 included folded maps. Also that the plates were becoming very worn so the lettering and linework on the maps was strengthened. (Adrian Webb collection.)

Source: J. Norden, *A direction for the English traviller by which he shal be inabled to coast about all England and Wales* (London, 1643). Original size: 102 x 100mm.

Somersettensis comitatus
Joan Blaeu
1648

The mapmaking house of Blaeu had its roots in the golden age of cartography for the Netherlands. Rather than follow his father as a herring salesman Willem Janszoon Blaeu (1571-1638) followed his own interests in astronomy and mathematics. He made maps and globes, and in 1633 was appointed map-maker of the Dutch East India Company. The business passed to his son Joan Blaeu (1596-1673) and his brother Cornelius (1610-1648) who produced some of the most attractive and detailed maps of their time.

In 1620, Joan became a doctor of law, and in 1651 he was voted into the Amsterdam council. Blaeu's map of Somerset was published in 1648 but is based on the work of Saxton and Speed, although it lacks the inset plan of the city of Bath. However, when Speed's map was re-engraved, and subsequently re-issued by John Overton 'at y[e] White horse wi'out Newgate neere the fountaine tavern' in 1668, there were differences due to copying mistakes, including the hundredal boundary between the hundreds of Whitley and Glastonbury Twelve Hides, as well as 'Balsboro Wood'; Blaeu included both of these but Overton did not. Blaeu's copyist was more proficient than Overton's. Sadly for the Blaeu family a disastrous fire completely destroyed their business in 1672.

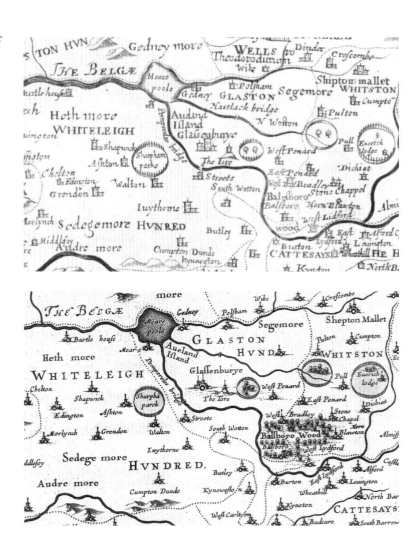

Right: Extracts from Speed by Overton (top) showing the missing hundredal boundary and name in 1668 (SANHS) and (below) Blaeu's 1648 edition. (Robin Bush collection.)

Opposite: A reduced reproduction of Blaeu's *Somersettensis comitatus*.
Source: J. Blaeu, *Atlas novus* (Amsterdam, 1648). Original size: 501 x 385mm.
(Robin Bush collection.)

SOMERSET-TENSIS COMITATVS.
Somerset shire.

The mapp of Sedgmoore with adjacent places
Richard Newcourt
1662

Richard Newcourt (d.1679) was from Devon but his father's half-brother was Sir Edward Hext (*c*.1550-1624), of the Middle Temple and Low Ham, Somerset. Hext's daughter Elizabeth married Sir John Stawell (1600-1662) of Cothelstone, Somerset and Newcourt obtained an estate in Somerton.

Newcourt became associated with Sir William Dugdale (1605-1686), an English antiquary, historian and herald. He was a capable artist and his two drawings of the west front and south prospect of Wells cathedral were published by Dugdale in *Monasticon Anglicanum*. Newcourt dedicated the south prospect to Sir John Strangways (1585-1666). He also drew views of Glastonbury and its famous abbey that were engraved by Wenceslaus Hollar (1607-1677).

In the map reproduced opposite Dugdale used Newcourt's work in *The history of imbanking and drayning of divers fenns and marshes both in foreign parts and in this kingdom and of the improvements thereby* published in London in 1662. Newcourt's talent for mapmaking came to the fore in 1658 when his map of London, entitled 'An Exact Delineation of the Cities of London and Westminster and the Suburbs thereof, Together wth ye Burrough of Southwark And all ye Thorough-fares Highwaies Streetes Lanes and Common Allies wthin ye same Composed by a Scale, and Ichnographically described' was published. It is described as the most important map of London executed before the great fire.

—⸺∞⸺—

Source: W. Dugdale, *The history of imbanking and drayning of divers fenns and marshes both in foreign parts and in this kingdom and of the improvements thereby* (London, 1662). Original size: 411 x 304mm.

Above: William Dugdale, author of *The history of imbanking and drayning* published in 1662 which contained a map of Sedgemoor drawn and most likely surveyed by Richard Newcourt of Somerton.
Opposite: A reduced reproduction of Newcourt's map. (Robin Bush collection.)

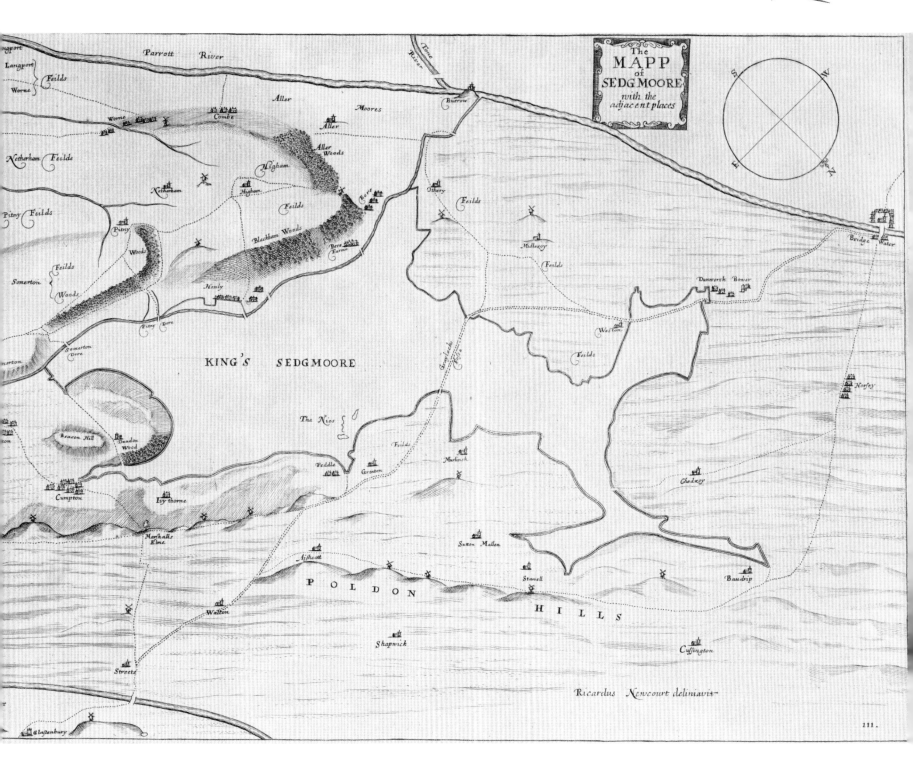

The
MAPP
of
SEDG MOORE
with the
adjacent places

Parrott River

Langport

Langport
Fields
Worne

Netherham Feilds

Pitny Feilds

Somerton
Feilds
Woods

Worne
Combe

Aller

Aller

Moores

Aller

Aller Woods

Higham

Netherham

Higham

Higham
Feilds

Bere

Pitny

Woods

Blackham Woods

Bere
Earme

Henly

Pitny Dore

Somerton Dore

KING'S SEDGMOORE

Burrow

Othery

Feilds

Midlezoy

Feilds

Gogliake Roo

Dunworch Bower

Weston

Feilds

Bridge
Water

Horsey

The Nios

Beacon Hill

Dundon
Wood

Peddle

Feilds

Grinton

Murloich

Chedzoy

Cumpton

Ivy thorne

Sutton Mallen

Marshalls
Elme

Aisheott

Stawell

Baudrip

P O L D O N

Walton

H I L L S

Streete

Shapwick

Cuffington

Ricardus Newcourt deliniavit

Glastenbury

The Map of Exmore
Anonymous
1676

This circular map of Exmoor was originally annexed to a bill in a case brought in the court of the Exchequer. The suit was that of Attorney General v George Arundell. As with the 1637 map of Exmoor, the easiest way to illustrate the forest boundaries was by way of a map. This seems to be a common proceeding used throughout the latter half of the seventeenth century, as six similar maps are known to exist within Exchequer records, attached to similar lawsuits.

The purpose of the map was to illustrate James Boevey's claim that the commons were part of the forest. Boevey purchased the freehold to the forest in 1653 from the Parliamentary commission responsible for distributing the property of King Charles the First, and a year later built a house on the moor, at what is now known as Simonsbath. The house can still be visited today. Boevey later moved to Surrey, but kept the freehold of the forest. He would often seek ways of increasing rents, and was consequently not always popular with the tenants. In the answers to the bill of complaint, there is mention of perambulations being undertaken of the commons to demarcate the land boundaries in order to pass on the information to younger generations.

One of the most significant features of this map are the churches around the edge which illustrate the parishes adjoining the forest. Four of the other maps of Exmoor also depict the same churches. In the map opposite these churches are drawn to a similar design, but those depicted on a map attached to another case show more individual characteristics, for example the churches of Hawkridge, Porlock and Oare are shown with spires. Today the churches at Hawkridge and Oare do not have spires, suggesting the mapmaker may have employed some artistic license or perhaps have not been familiar with the local area.

In all the maps the forest boundary markers are the same, including the Hooked Stone and the Hoare Oak; and the same rivers, including the Exe and Barle, are depicted. This begs the question as to why so many copies of this map were made, when the boundary information is almost identical. Two of the maps have evidence of pin pricks, showing some form of copying process was being undertaken, suggesting that maps of Exmoor at least were becoming important pieces of evidence during the second half of the seventeenth century.

Above: A drawing of Withypool church from 1849 by W.W. Wheatley, which has changed little since 1673.

Source: SANHS, Braikenridge Collection.

Opposite: A reduced reproduction of 'The Map of Exmore'. This is one of many examples and was used as evidence in court cases during the second half of the seventeenth century.

Source: TNA, MPB 1/54. Original size: 430 x 410mm.

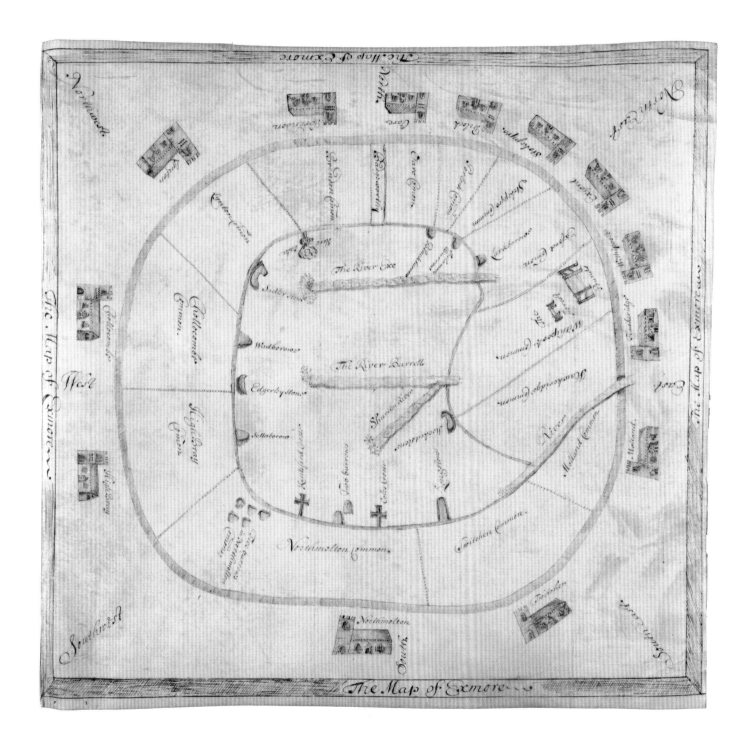

Britannia
John Ogilby
1675

John Ogilby (1600-1676) was a Scotsman who at one time or another during his lifetime was a translator, cartographer, dancing master, tutor, Deputy-Master of the Revels, publisher, composer, as well as Cosmographer and Geographic Printer to King Charles the Second. He was best known for publishing the first British road atlas in 1675, based upon his survey of some 26,700 miles of roads of which only 'the most considerable of them' (7,500) appeared in his atlas.

The design of the atlas was thought to be innovative with its strips of maps arranged side by side and its elaborate scrolls, but fundamentally the idea can be traced back to medieval times and itineraries recording journeys from one town to another. It was produced as an 'aid to commerce'. The maps were re-worked and engraved by Thomas Gardner in a smaller but more convenient size. Gardner stated the reason for doing so was:

> As the original plates are in large Sheets, the general Use of them has been hitherto lost, and the Book rather an Entertainment for a Traveller within Doors, than a guide to him upon the Road. . . . But this, besides its being the original work in Miniature . . . tis presum'd will be thought much more useful to the Ends those books were intended, and deserve the Title of A Pocket-Guide to the English Traveller.

Above: A portrait of John Ogilby (from Homer's *Iliad* (London, 1660)).

Source: T. Gardner, *A pocket guide to the English traveller* (London, 1719). Original size: 275 x 179mm.

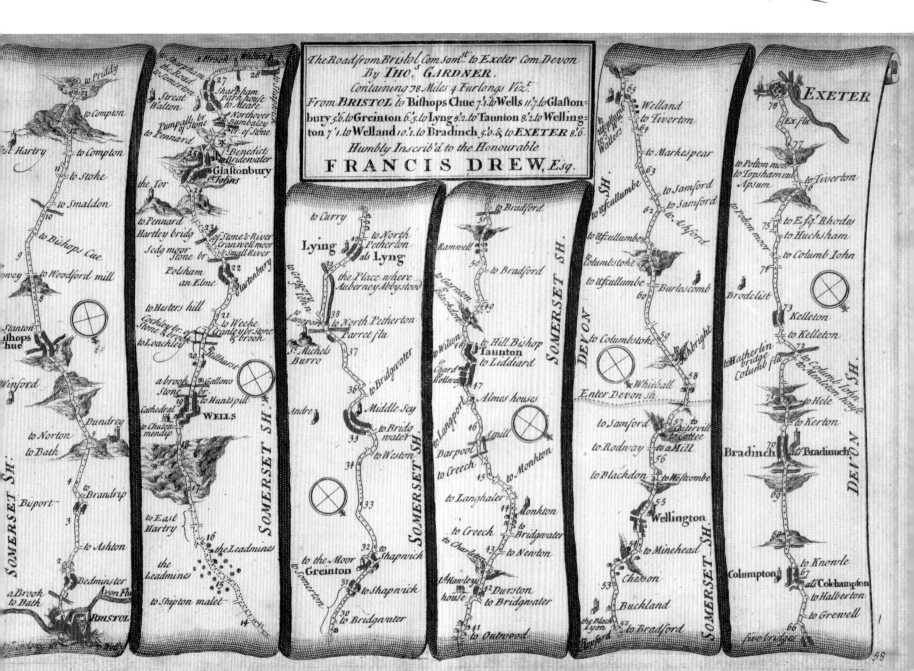

A version of the reduced and more practical edition of Ogilby by Thomas Gardner showing the road through the county from Bedminster to Wellington. Gardner dedicated this map to Francis Drew esquire, who served as a Member of Parliament for Exeter and later as High Sheriff of Devon. (Robin Bush collection.)

Angliae totius tabula cum distantiis notioribus in itinerantium usum accomodata
John Adams
1680

John Adams was a native of Shropshire who attended Shrewsbury School and later became a barrister at the Inner Temple.

Adam's *Index Villaris*, from which the map opposite was extracted, aimed to show the distances between the cities and market towns of England and Wales without the need for a compass or scale. The way in which Adams presented his information was relatively new, but it is thought that he borrowed many of the measured distances from Ogilby. However, it is probable that William, John Adams' brother, who was a professional surveyor, may have assisted with some of the field work. It was intended as an improvement of a similar map of England and Wales which Adams had produced in 1677, but which had been criticised for being roughly done. The Index was reprinted with additions in 1690 and again in 1700.

City names were depicted in squares such as Bath and Wells, whereas market towns were shown in circles. Hills and rivers were also shown, and for Somerset these included Exmoor, although it is not named. The rivers 'Ax' and 'Brent' are also shown, not on the 1677 version, and interestingly Brent Marsh is named. The map was dedicated to King Charles the Second and depicts his coat of arms.

Although Adams produced two surveys of England and Wales by 1680, he still knew his map could be improved, so he undertook a survey of the whole country, supported by several members of the Royal Society. He completed his travels prior to 1685 and in the same year published his revised map. Reduced and coloured copies of his revised map were sold with the later editions of the *Index Villaris*.

Above: Royal patronage was essential for the success of any national mapping scheme. Adams knew this and included an elaborate display to acknowledge his patron, signifying an official sanction for his map.

Source: J Adams, *Index villaris* (London, 1680) at TNA, MPI 1/463. Original size: 600 x 600mm.

Opposite: A close up from Adams' map showing the county of Somerset and the mapping he undertook. In 1681 Adams measured a baseline on the Somerset Levels as part of a national survey undertaken trigonometrically, to accurately map the whole country.

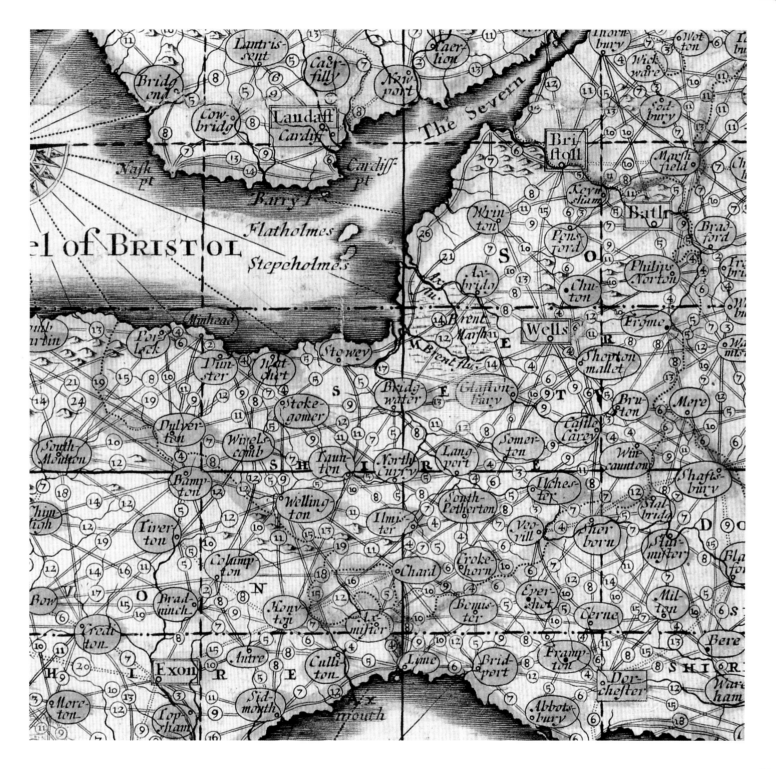

[A plan of the Battle of Sedgemore]
The Reverend Andrew Paschall
1685

The death of King Charles the Second signalled an opportunity for one of his illegitimate sons, James, Duke of Monmouth, to lay claim to the throne. After landing at Lyme Regis, Monmouth's route through Dorset, into the north of Somerset and his retreat to Bridgwater (shown opposite) is legendary. Defeat at the Battle of Sedgemoor and the 'Bloody Assize' that followed ensured that his name would go down in history. But who recorded the events on that fateful day on the battlefield in the map overleaf?

Different maps record events on that day. This map is a very simple and hurried depiction of the battlefield, based upon a sketch by the Reverend Andrew Paschall, rector of Chedzoy from 1662 to 1696. Paschall wrote to the Secretary of State:

> In ye want I am at present of a skilful hand that might enable me to serve your lordship with a exact draught of this place (to which God be praised we are returned in safety) I have impled some of my neighbours to measure the distances according to the enclosed paper, and I make no doubt but they have done it with care.

Paschall also prepared at least two versions of events, which as a noncombatant clergyman, although staunchly royalist, provides a fascinating account of the battle. One of the versions was deposited at Hoare's Bank in 1706 and did not materialise until 1940.

Today the rebellion by Monmouth is often referred to locally as the 'Pitchfork Rebellion'. However, back in 1685 Monmouth gave orders from Taunton to the local tithingmen to 'searche for, seize, and take all such scythes as can be found in your tything'. In return their owners were to be paid 'a reasonable price', and the scythes were to be delivered to the commissioned officers who were assembled in Taunton. So perhaps it was not just pitchforks that played a part in the battle, but an agricultural tool which used effectively could have been far more deadly and capable of inflicting more horrific injuries than the pitchfork, although futile compared to the muskets belonging to King James the Second.

James Scott, Duke of Monmouth (from a print of 1820). (Adrian Webb collection.)

Above: A collection of scythes.

Right: A reduced reproduction of 'The scene of the Duke of Monmouth's progress, 1680 and Rebellion, 1685'.

Source: G. Roberts, *The life, progresses, and rebellion of James, Duke of Monmouth, &c.* (London, 1844). Original size: 218 x 218mm.

The Scene of the
DUKE OF MONMOUTH'S PROGRESS, 1680
and
REBELLION, 1685.

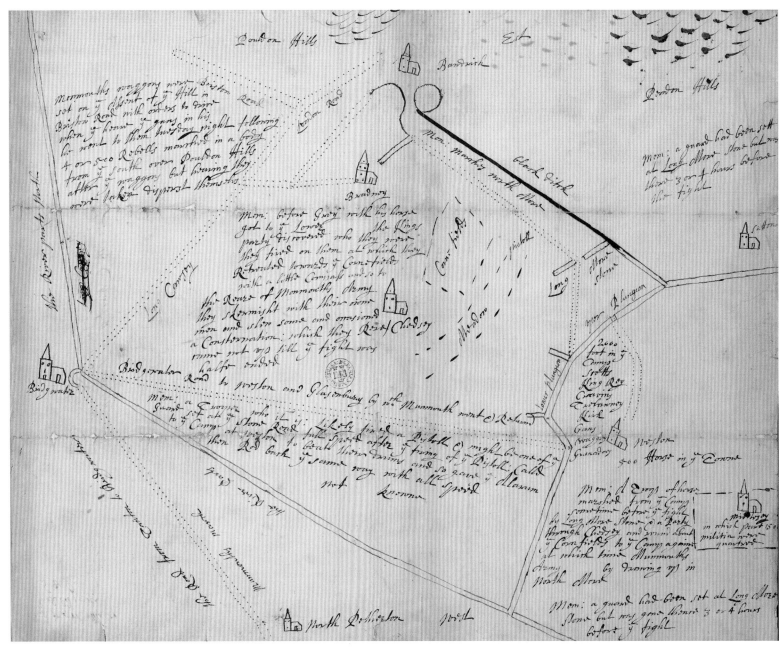

Above: His map stretches from Bridgwater in the west to Long Sutton in the east, and from North Petherton in the south to Bawdrip in the north. He included descriptions of events in the parishes of Middlezoy, Westonzoyland, Chedzoy, and the hamlet of Bradney.

Opposite: A transcription of the writing on Paschall's plan. (Adrian Webb.)

Source: Bodleian Library, MS. Ballard 48, fol. 74. Original size: 400 x 328mm.

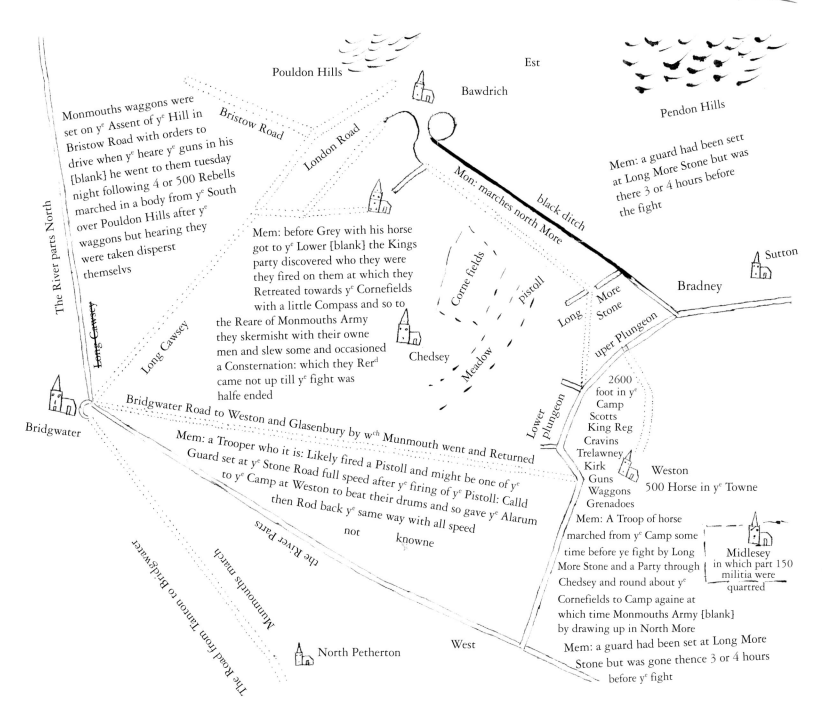

Pouldon Hills

Est

Bawdrich

Pendon Hills

Monmouths waggons were set on yᵉ Assent of yᵉ Hill in Bristow Road with orders to drive when yᵉ heare yᵉ guns in his [blank] he went to them tuesday night following 4 or 500 Rebells marched in a body from yᵉ South over Pouldon Hills after yᵉ waggons but hearing they were taken disperst themselvs

Bristow Road

Bristow Road

London Road

Mon: marches north More

black ditch

Mem: a guard had been sett at Long More Stone but was there 3 or 4 hours before the fight

The River parts North

Long Cawsey

Long Cawsey

Mem: before Grey with his horse got to yᵉ Lower [blank] the Kings party discovered who they were they fired on them at which they Retreated towards yᵉ Cornefields with a little Compass and so to the Reare of Monmouths Army they skermisht with their owne men and slew some and occasioned a Consternation: which they Rerᵈ came not up till yᵉ fight was halfe ended

Corne fields

pistoll

Long   More   Stone

Sutton

Bradney

uper Plungeon

Chedsey

Meadow

Lower plungeon

2600 foot in yᵉ Camp Scotts King Reg Cravins Trelawney Kirk Guns Waggons Grenadoes

Bridgwater

Bridgwater Road to Weston and Glasenbury by wᶜʰ Munmouth went and Returned

Weston 500 Horse in yᵉ Towne

Mem: a Trooper who it is: Likely fired a Pistoll and might be one of yᵉ Guard set at yᵉ Stone Road full speed after yᵉ firing of yᵉ Pistoll: Calld to yᵉ Camp at Weston to beat their drums and so gave yᵉ Alarum then Rod back yᵉ same way with all speed

not   knowne

the River Parts

Munmouths march

The Road from Tanton to Bridgwater

North Petherton

West

Mem: A Troop of horse marched from yᵉ Camp some time before ye fight by Long More Stone and a Party through Chedsey and round about yᵉ Cornefields to Camp againe at which time Monmouths Army [blank] by drawing up in North More

Midlesey in which part 150 militia were quartred

Mem: a guard had been set at Long More Stone but was gone thence 3 or 4 hours before yᵉ fight

The city of Bath
Joseph Gilmore
1694

This map was the first major survey of the city to be completed since the time of Henry Savile's map-making exercise of *c.*1600. Joseph Gilmore (d.1723?) of Nettleton, Wiltshire, is described as a teacher of mathematics in Bristol. He may have been influenced by James Millerd's map of the city of Bristol as both are in a similar style. The map was sold by Thomas Taylor at 'ye Golden Lyon in Fleet Street'.

Gilmore possibly, also taught at Marlborough, Wiltshire, in the 1680s and later worked as a surveyor to the 2nd Duke of Beaufort from 1708 until at least 1717. He was employed by Thomas Taylor as a draughtsman and also authored a work on how to transport live fish in purpose-built ships with Sir Richard Steele in 1718 called *An account of the Fish-Pool*. He was also involved in a Chancery Court case in 1718 with Steele against John Sansom esquire of London concerning this scheme. Gilmore undertook a mathematical study to consider the nature of the dams needed following the breach of the sea wall in 1707 at Dagenham, Essex, which created an area of flooded marsh land. His recommendations were published in *A letter to a member of parliament, concerning Dagenham-Breach: occasion'd by the late ruin of the works there* in London in 1718. Three dams were built, the last one standing firm against the tide. It was completed on 18th June 1719, about twelve years after the accident first occurred.

The later versions of his Bath map include a large panel of text, views of public buildings, including 29 lodging houses and a list of 23 principal inns. It was so popular it was reissued six times with few alterations. The first version measured 310 x 240mm but the later version was much larger measuring 945 x 744mm.

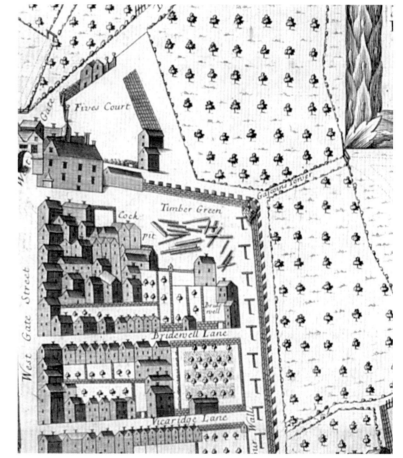

Above: A section from Gilmore's map of Bath of 1694 showing the Fives Court, Timber Green and the Cock pit in the West Gate area of the city.
Opposite: A reduced reproduction of Gilmore's map of Bath of 1694 (reprinted with additional images of buildings in 1731 or later).

Source: Private collection. Original size: 954 x 744mm.

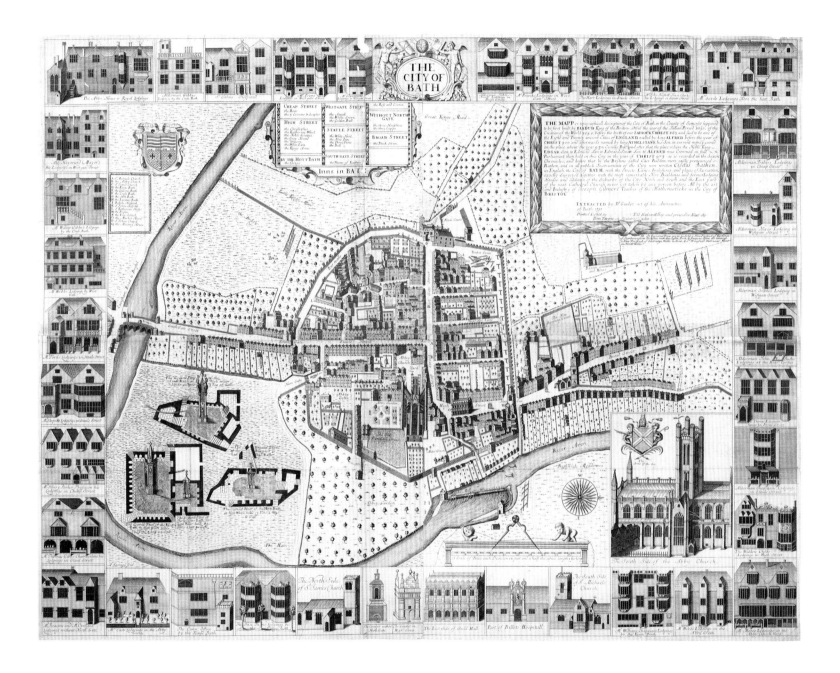

[The Bristol Channel]
Captain Greenvile Collins R.N.
1694

For nearly a century the published charting of British waters was dominated by charts originating in the Netherlands. Following three Anglo-Dutch wars, King Charles the Second appointed Captain Greenvile Collins (1644-1694) to undertake a new hydrographic survey of Britain's waters. Collins used a royal yacht and a small crew of around 20 or so men, combined with some rudimentary equipment, including a land surveyor's chain and a waywiser for measuring the coast.

Collins surveyed the Somerset coast in the early 1680s, also taking the opportunity to visit Sir Robert Southwell at Kings Weston and explore Pen Park Hole. Collins returned to the Somerset coast in 1690 after he was involved with King William the Third's expedition to Ireland. They sailed from Duncannon Fort to King Road in 27 hours.

Collins' chart, or draught, of the 'Severn' was 'not so well finished as intended' due to the engraver having lost the original. He also produced a chart of the River Avon from King Road to Bristol. Nevertheless Collins' surveys were printed by his cousin, Freeman Collins, and published by William Fisher in *Great Britain's Coasting Pilot* in London in 1693. Many of the charts remained in print for over a century.

(continued over)

Opposite: A reduced reproduction of 'The Severn or the Channell of Bristoll' from *Great Britain's coasting pilot*. (Robin Bush collection.)

Source: G. Collins, *Great Britain's coasting pilot* (London, 1693).
Original size: 550 x 435mm.

Top: An extract from 'A Prospect of Carreck-fergus. Being the Place where King William landed in Ireland' showing Collins and King William the Third in the *Mary* yacht (from plate 32 of *Great Britain's coasting pilot* (London, 1693)).

Above: The man on the right is using a waywiser (UKHO, A584).

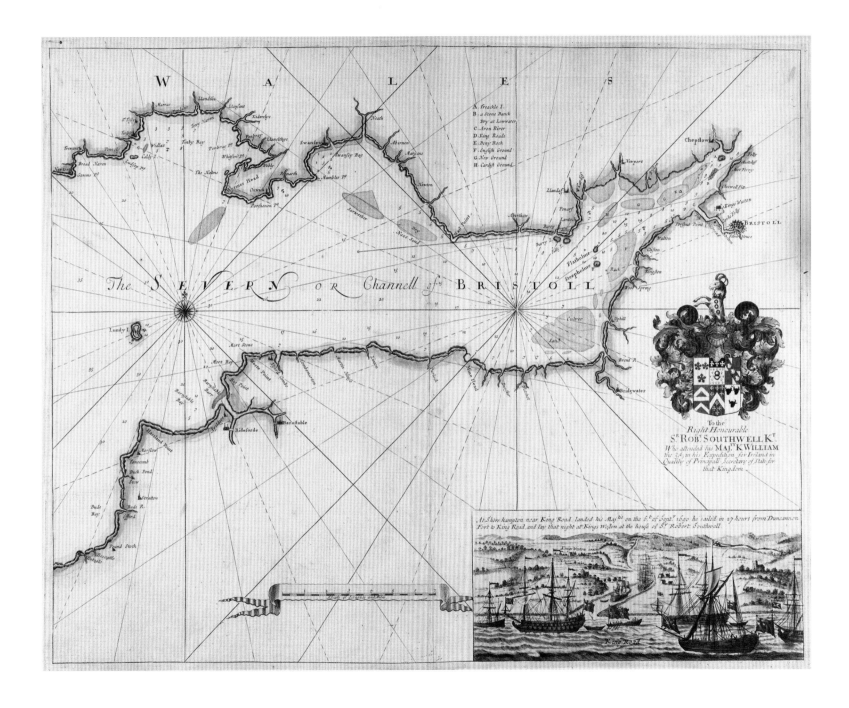

(continued)

Robert Yate (1643-1737) was a late inclusion by Collins into his *Pilot*. Described as one of the wealthiest merchants in the city of Bristol it is not surprising that Collins dedicated his chart of King Road and the River Avon to this wealthy man. Shortly after starting his survey of Great Britain's waters, Collins offered people the chance to subscribe to the project. Compared to other ares of the country, such as Cornwall and London, support from the region was small. Only Sir Samuel Astry of Gloucestershire, Sir Robert Southwell of Kings Weston, Robert Yate and two other Bristol merchants, Mr Thomas Alcock and Mr Robert Henley subscribed to the *Pilot*.

Yate's background is an interesting one as his father was staunchly royalist but changed his allegiance and fell out of favour in 1661. Collins was from a staunchly royalist family but could not have held a grudge against the Yate family. During the reigns of William and Anne, Robert Yate was a key figure in Bristol and he was supported through his family connexions to a number of the most prominent members of the city's civic and mercantile elite. He supported king and country whenever possible, so his subscription to a project sponsored by a former king, albeit over a decade before, is not surprising.

He held property interests in Wine Street, owned The Red Lodge, Bristol, as well as Charlton House, Wraxall, Somerset. He served as a common councilman, sheriff, mayor, alderman, a member and master of the Society of Merchant Venturers, honorary guardian of the Bristol corporation of the poor, as well as deputy-master of the Bristol mint. He died at his country seat at Wraxall in 1737, and his burial at Christ Church in the city was a 'grand civic affair'.

Opposite: A reduced reproduction of Collins' chart of the River Avon. (Robin Bush collection.)

Source: *Great Britain's coasting pilot* (London, 1693).
Original size: 915 x 397mm.

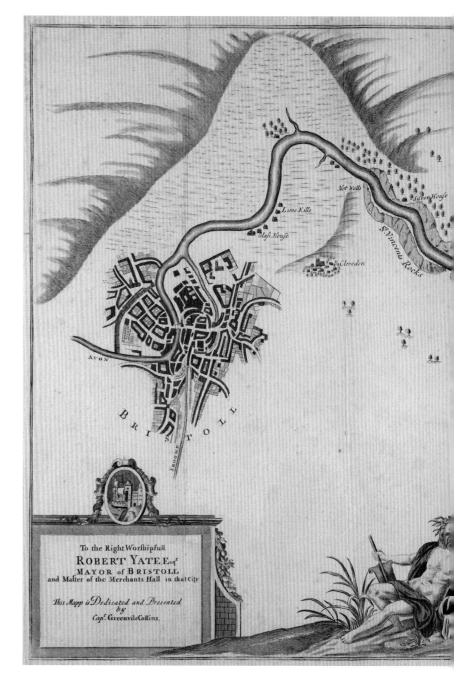

90

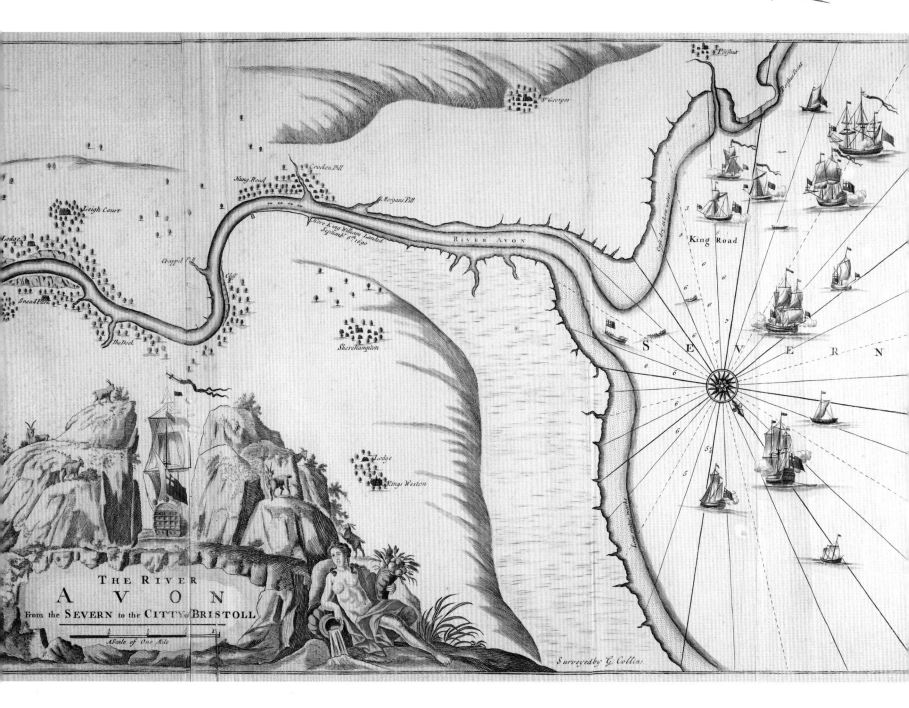

St: Georges

Crocken Pill

King Road

Leigh Court

M: Morgans Pill

RIVER AVON

Here King William Landed
Septemb: 6th 1690

Lodge

Chappel Pill

Snead Park

Cliff

The Dock

Shere Hampton

SEVERN

King Road

Poyshut

Poyshut Point

Lodge

Kings Weston

THE RIVER
AVON
From the SEVERN to the CITTY of BRISTOLL

A Scale of One Mile

Surveyed by G: Collins

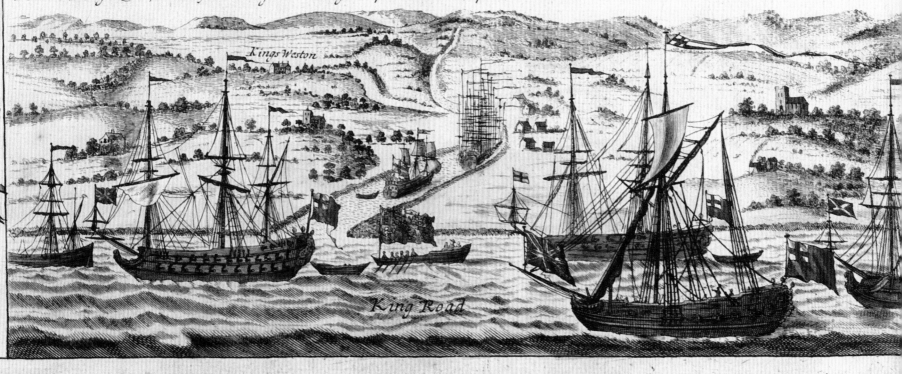

At Shore hampton near King Road, landed his Maj.tie on the 6.t of Sept.r 1690 he sailed in 27 hours from Duncannon Fort to King Road, and lay that night at Kings Weston at the house of Sr Robert Southwell.

Kings Weston

King Road

A reproduction of the scene at the mouth of the River Avon in 1690 which Collins included in his chart of the Bristol Channel.
(Robin Bush collection.)

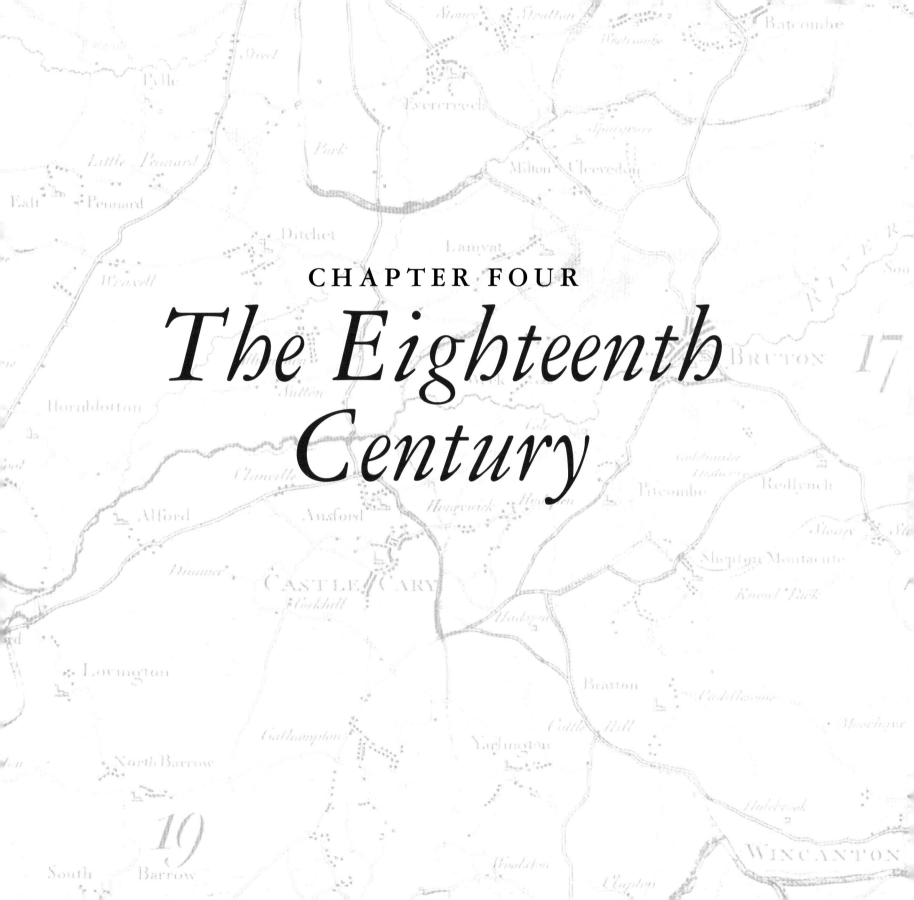

CHAPTER FOUR

The Eighteenth Century

Somerset Shire
Robert Morden
1701

This map was first published in 1701 in *The new description & state of England* by Robert Morden (*c.*1650-1703). Morden was an English bookseller, publisher, and maker of maps and globes based in London. He was among the first successful commercial map makers and was inventive in his approach. He also published a larger version of a map of Somerset in 1695 that appeared in William Camden's *Britannia*. A smaller version was published in Thomas Cox's *Magna Britannia antiqua & nova: or, a new, exact, and comprehensive survey of the ancient and present state of Great-Britain*, first published in 1727.

The table of distances published by Cox (pictured to the right) was a throwback to 1625 and the publication of John Norden's *England, an intended guyde, for English travailers*. A 1635 version by Jacob Florensz van Langeren contained a small thumb-nail size map of the county, compared to Morden's version which was adorned with statistics and coats of arms belonging to the county's corporations.

The distances contained in the table make for interesting reading. Today Google Maps can instantly give you any distance and when compared to those published in the 1720s there are some surprises. Milverton to Bristol was 34 miles but Google gives 50, Chard to Bristol was 35 miles which today is 55, and Yeovil (spelled 'Euell') to Bath 27 miles but now it is 52. Cox's 'mile' in the 1720s was longer than that of today's, not helped by Morden using three different scales of mileage!

Above: Cox's table of distances.

Opposite: A reduced reproduction of Morden's smaller map of Somerset. (Adrian Webb collection.)

Source: T. Cox, *Magna Britannia* (London, 1727). Size: 208 x 175mm.

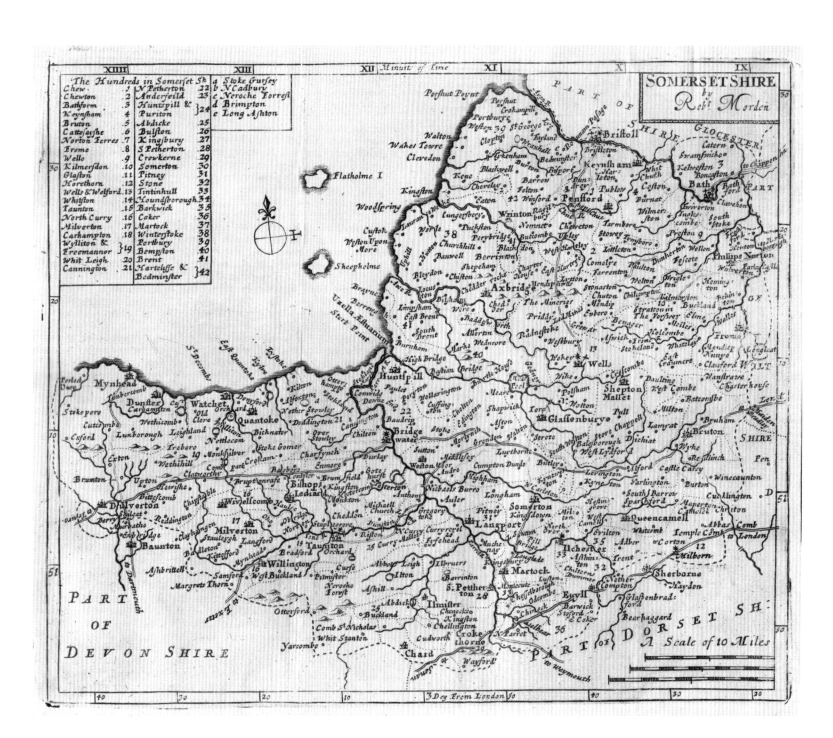

SOMERSETSHIRE
by
Robt Morden

The Hundreds in Somersetsh

Chew	1	N Petherton	22
Chewton	2	Anderfeild	23
Bathform	3	Huntfpill & Puriton }	24
Keynsham	4		
Bruton	5	Abdicke	25
Cattezafshe	6	Bulston	26
Norton Ferres	7	Kingsbury	27
Frome	8	S Petherton	28
Wells	9	Crewkerne	29
Kilmerfdon	10	Somerton	30
Glafton	11	Pitney	31
Horethorn	12	Stone	32
Wells & Welford	13	Cloundfborough	34
Whitston	14	Barkwick	35
Taunton	15	Coker	36
North Curry	16	Martock	37
Milverton	17	Winterftoke	38
Carhampton	18	Portbury	39
Wylliton & Freemannor }	19	Bempston	40
Whit Leigh	20	Brent	41
Cannington	21	Hartclitte & Bedminfter }	42

a Stoke Gurfey
b N Cadbury
c Neroche Forreft
d Brimpton
e Long Afhton

PART OF DEVONSHIRE

PART OF DORSETSH.

A Scale of 10 Miles

Somerset Shire
Herman Moll
1708

Herman Moll, who is thought to have come from Amsterdam to London, was a cartographer, engraver, and publisher. His maps were finely executed and clearly engraved, with his depiction of Somerset and its antiquities being no exception. He embellished his map with depictions of the recently discovered Alfred Jewel, the Glastonbury cross, a Roman pavement at Wellow and Roman remains at Bath.

Moll's connections to the Royal Society, publishing and the arts in London gave him links with Jonathan Swift, Robert Boyle, Daniel Defoe, Robert Hooke and to the most famous privateer and explorer of his age, Somerset's William Dampier. Dampier is thought to have been the first Englishman to set foot in Australia. As well as engraving the illustrations for Dampier's celebrated voyages he used Dampier's surveys and observations to show more accurate depictions of his discoveries. The Moll-Dampier-Swift connection resulted in the passage in Swift's famous book, *Gulliver's travels*, in chapter four, part eleven:

I arrived in seven hours to the south-east point of New Holland. This confirmed me in the opinion I have long entertained, that the maps and charts place this country at least three degrees more to the east than it really is; which I thought I communicated many years ago to my worthy friend, Mr. Herman Moll, and gave him my reasons for it, . . .

A Caſſawaris

Above: Cassowary, that are native to Borneo, originally drawn by Dampier and engraved by Moll (W. Dampier, *et al*, *A collection of voyages* (London, 1729).

Opposite: A reduced reproduction of Moll's map of 'Somerset Shire'. (Adrian Webb collection.)

Source: H. Moll, *Fifty six maps new and accurate maps of Great Britain* (London, 1708). Original size: 318 x 197mm.

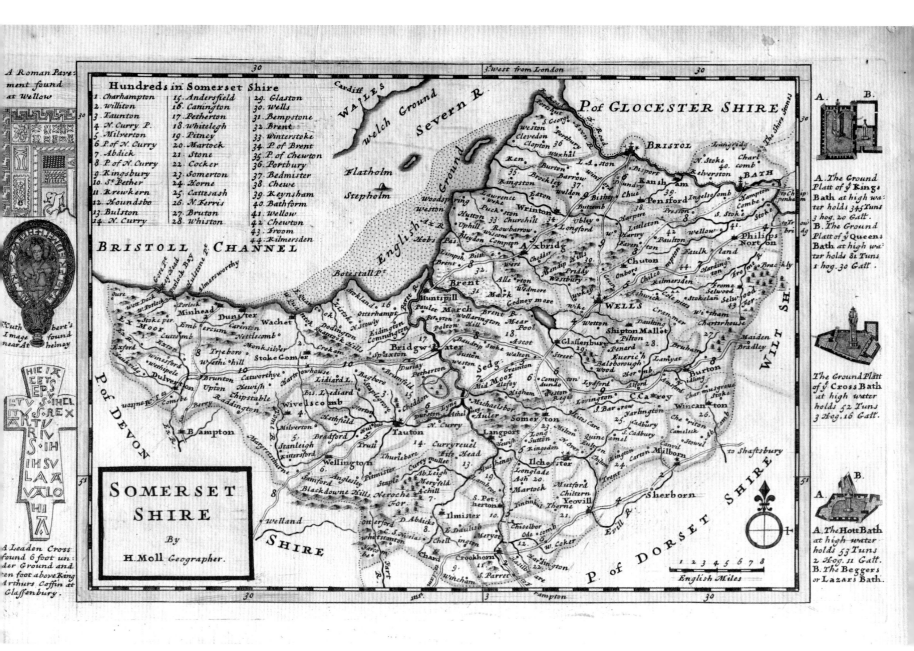

A Roman Pavement found at Wellow

Kuth bert's Image found near At helney

HIC IA CET EPS ETV S HEL ITY S REX AR TVI S IH IH SV LA A VALO HI A

A Leaden Cross found 6 foot under Ground and ten foot above King Arthurs Coffin at Glassenbury.

Hundreds in Somerset Shire

1. Charhampton	15. Andersfield	29. Glaston
2. Williton	16. Canington	30. Wells
3. Taunton	17. Petherton	31. Bempstone
4. N. Curry P.	18. Whitelegh	32. Brent
5. Milverton	19. Pitney	33. Winterstoke
6. P. of N. Curry	20. Martock	34. P. of Brent
7. Abdick	21. Stone	35. P. of Chewton
8. P. of N. Curry	22. Cocker	36. Portbury
9. Kingsbury	23. Somerton	37. Bedmister
10. St Pether	24. Horne	38. Chewe
11. Krewkern	25. Cattesash	39. Keynsham
12. Houndsbo	26. N. Ferris	40. Bathform
13. Bulston	27. Bruton	41. Wellow
14. N. Curry	28. Whiston	42. Chewton
		43. Froom
		44. Kilmersden

SOMERSET SHIRE

By

H. Moll *Geographer.*

A. *The Ground Platt of y Kings Bath at high water holds 345 Tuns 3 hog. 20 Gall.*
B. *The Ground Platt of y Queens Bath at high water holds 81 Tuns 1 hog. 30 Gall.*

The Ground Platt of y Cross Bath at high water holds 52 Tuns 3 Hog. 16 Gall.

A. *The Hott Bath at high water holds 53 Tuns 2 Hog. 11 Gall.*
B. *The Beggers or Lazars Bath.*

English Miles

The roads of England according to Mr Ogilby's survey
Charles Western
1713

An attempt to condense the information on Ogilby's road maps appeared in the form of a circular map with the title *The roads of England according to Mr Ogilby's survey* (a reduced version of which is reproduced opposite). This was published in 1713 some time after the act of union of 1707 depicted in the heraldry. It was made and sold by Charles Western at the Nags Head in Bishopsgate and sold by Nathaniel Crouch at the Bell in Poultry. A copy of this rare map hangs on a wall at Forde Abbey. The version printed here is a later reprint sold by George Willdey from his toy and print shop at the corner of Ludgate Street. Willdey went bankrupt in 1741.

From Chichester to Carlisle the map is dominated by the double line post roads and all roads emanate from London like a spider's web in a mis-shaped rare map of England and Wales.

The distances from London to cities in rectangular boxes coloured green. Intermediate distances to larger towns are shown in circles coloured red. Distances in between the circles and rectangles are shown without a circle or square around them.

Above: A close-up of the south west section of the map showing the main routes through the county of Somerset. Bath is shown as being 108 miles and Wells 127 miles from London.

Opposite: A reduced reproduction of *The roads of England according to Mr Ogilby's survey* (London, 1713).

Source: Bonhams Auctioneers. Original size: 569 x 576mm.

A Map of Somerset Shire
Emanuel Bowen
1720

The inevitable copying of earlier works, coupled with the demand for 'new' maps, led to the production of an improved version of Ogilby's road maps. John Owen, gentleman, of the Middle Temple was behind this scheme which saw county maps, distances and descriptions crammed into small pages and published as *Britannia depicta or Ogilby improv'd*. This was printed and sold by Thomas Bowles, print and map seller next to the Chapter House in St Paul's Church-yard and Emanuel Bowen, engraver and print seller near the Stairs in St Katherine's.

Chubb described this map of Somerset (reproduced opposite) as 'small, overcrowded' and 'sketchy' and it is almost unusable because of the vast amount of information crammed into such a small area. The map contains the coat of arms of the Duke of Somerset, a list of the hundreds in the county, as well as a scale bar. Because so much information has been included many of the place names have been split and many are arranged in a haphazard way. Some are badly mis-spelt, such as 'West Hartley' instead of West Harptree, 'Comwidge' for Combwich, 'Nerodie Forrest' for Neroche Forest

The description of the county, at the bottom of the sheet, includes facts such as that the county contained 44,606 houses and 'The Air is generally very good, unless it be in ye Marsh Country, where it inclines to Agues & other Distempers'.

———— ✦ ————

Right: A reduced reproduction of *A map of Somerset Shire*.
(Robin Bush collection.)

Source: J. Owen, *Britannia depicta* (London, 1720).
Original size: 115 x 180mm.

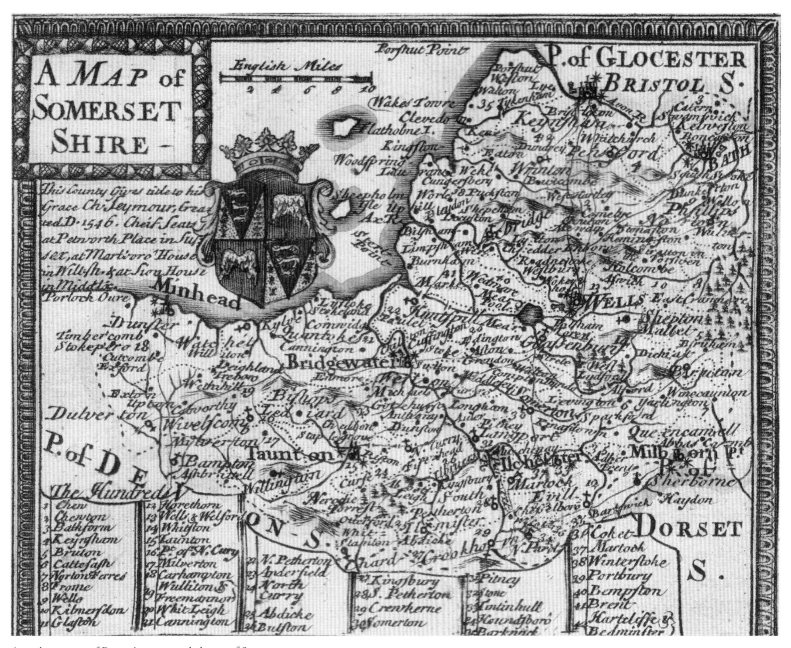

An enlargement of Bowen's overcrowded map of Somerset.

Somersetshire survey'd and protracted
Mr Strachy
1736

One of the rarest of all the maps showing just the county of Somerset was the brainchild of a Somerset squire, John Strachey F.R.S. (1671-1743) of Sutton Court. Strachey, born at Chew Magna, matriculated at Trinity College, Oxford, and was admitted at the Middle Temple, London, in 1688. He was elected a Fellow of the Royal Society in 1719. He collected a vast amount of antiquarian and topographical information and proposed publishing a county history.

Strachey very cleverly measured the thicknesses of seams of coal and projected their course underground, in order to try and work out the value of the coal. This led to a major breakthrough in the history of geology. After drawing a cross-section of the layers of rocks under his estate in north Somerset, Strachey was the first man to come up with the concept of layers of rocks being known as strata. Many years later this breakthrough was developed by William Smith (1769-1839).

In addition to his antiquarian and scientific interests, Strachey was an accomplished surveyor and map maker. Fortunately the detailed records of how he accumulated enough information to produce a new map of the county survive in abundance. His field books, in which he recorded his basic observations, show how he used suitable vantage points, such as Glastonbury Tor and Dundry Beacon, to make his compass readings. He could not have covered the whole county all on his own. Examples from these books can be found on the opposite page.

Later in the mapmaking process when he checked his observations he found some errors. He used small pieces of paper to cover up these incorrect observations in his field books. He obtained information from a number of contacts including Colonel Jepp Clarke of Chipley, the Reverend William Dodd, Richard Codrington bookseller of Bridgwater, to name but a few contributors.

After the basic information had been drawn up and proof states of the map returned to Strachey, he took the opportunity to add missing information and make any amendments. Some of those amendments were extensive, especially along the north Somerset coast, which are reproduced overleaf.

Not only did Strachey undertake his own surveys, compiled his own map, but he also marketed it as well. He offered the map at a special subscription rate of 7s 6d, but this was too steep for some. For 15s he offered people the chance to have their coats of arms included on the map. Others were happy to wait until it was published then pirated by rival publishers and sold at a lower price. The entrepreneurial Strachey was not to be thwarted by a small minority who did not want to support his publication. A copy of his proposal is reproduced overleaf.

The map he finally produced was head and shoulders above all those of the county that came before it, not only because of the scale he published his map but because of its unique content. He included inset plans of Wells, Bath and Ilchester that clearly showed their urban development. He also included many coats of arms which the wealthy families of the county paid to have included.

Opposite and over leaf: Reduced reproduction from Strachey's pocket-size field book and proposals. Source: SHC, DD/SH 1/91 and 2/110.

Original observations recorded in Strachey's field book . . .

A sketch of places observed.

A list of observations.

The map making process continued . . .

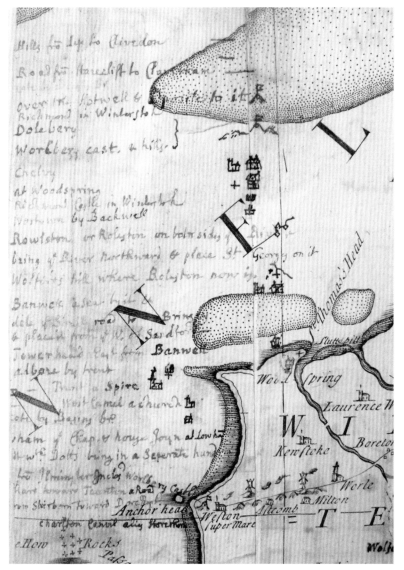

Correcting the observations.

S I R,   22ᵈ May 1736.

THE Copper-Plates of a NEW MAP OF
SOMERSETSHIRE (*actually survey'd*)
being now finished by Mr. SENEX, *and will be
ready to be published as soon as the Coats of Arms
of the Subscribers can be engraved: If you
please to subscribe, and send the Blazon of your
Coat of Arms to either of the following Persons,
before the* 12ᵗʰ *of June next, it shall be inserted
in the Margin of the Map; and will oblige,*

Sir,

Your Humble Servant,

JOHN STRACHEY.

No more will be printed with the
Coat of Arms than what shall
be subscribed for.

7 s. 6 d. *to be paid at Subscribing, and* 7 s. 6 d. *more
on Delivery of the Map.*

SUBSCRIPTIONS are taken in by
Mr. SENEX, over against St. *Dunstan's Church*, in *Fleet-
Street*; Mr. STAGG, in *Westminster-Hall*; Mr. COSE-
LEY, in *Bristol*; Mr. LEAKE, in *Bath*; Mr.
BROWN, in *Wells*; Mr. CODRINGTON, in *Bridg-
water*; Mr. NORRIS, in *Taunton*, Booksellers: The
Reverend Mr. DODD, at *Charleton Mackerel*; Mr.
WICKHAM, Attorney, at *Frome*; and Mr. JOHN
THOMAS, Post-Master, at *Crewkhern*.

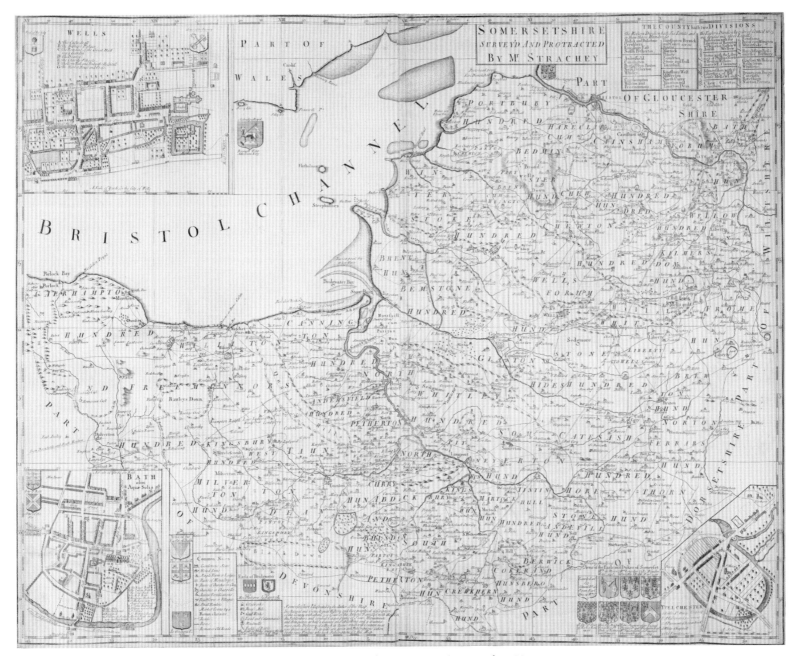

A much reduced reproduction of Strachey's final map, including the coats of arms. Original size: 996 x 755mm.

Source: SANHS.

An actual survey of the city of Bath . . . and of five miles round
Thomas Thorpe
1742

This is the first detailed map of the area around Bath, based on a survey by Thomas Thorpe in 1742. It was published according to Act of Parliament on the 5th of March 1743/4 for the proprietor, Thomas Thorpe, land surveyor. It was sold by him and Mr Leake and Mr Frederick, booksellers in Bath, Mr Hitch, bookseller in Paternoster Row London and various other print sellers. It was engraved by James Cole in Hatton Garden. Thorpe is thought to have been trained by John Dougharty (1677-1755) and had surveyed a farm belonging to Mr Jeremiah Peirce in Cold Ashton, Gloucestershire in 1741.

This detailed map of the Bath area is merged from nine individual sheets and it includes a key explaining the main features to be found in the city centre. An alphabetical list of subscribers includes Ralph Allen, the Right Honourable the Earl of Bath, Sir Abraham Elton Bart, and John Wood esquire (who made his own map of Bath that was published in 1735) amongst others. This map was so popular that it was reissued in different formats in 1771, 1773, 1787 and 1800.

A much smaller version was produced by Bath booksellers Leak and Taylor in 1759; Messrs Frederick, Leak and Taylor in 1770; Frederick and Taylor in 1776; Taylor and Meyler, or vice versa, in eight editions from 1783 to 1796 and by Savage and Meyler in 1805. The manuscript of the 1770 edition has survived and it was re-used for the 1776 edition, when the publisher's details were amended (reproduced to the right).

Thorpe undertook a survey for Sir Robert Throckmorton in Bampton, Oxfordshire, and constructed a plan of the lands belonging to the Right Honourable the Earl of Powis in the manor of Liswerry and Libennith in the parishes of Christchurch, Caerleon, Llanvrechea, etc. in 1752.

(continued over)

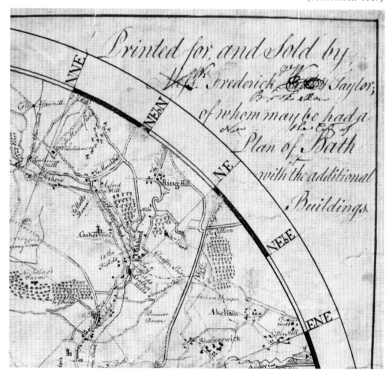

Above: An extract from a reduced manuscript version of Thorpe's survey of 'A Map of 5 Miles round the City of Bath, on a Scale of one Inch and half to a Mile, reduced from an Actual Survey by T. Thorpe'. Note the names which have been crossed out, which formerly read 'Messrs Frederick, Leak & Taylor', suggesting this correction was undertaken in or shortly before being printed in 1776.

Source: SHC, DD/PL C/1822/11. Original size: 415 x 417mm.

A reduced reproduction of 'An Actual Survey of the City of Bath, in the County of Somerset, and of Five Miles Round. Wherein are laid down all the Villages, Gentlemen's Seats, Farm Houses, Roads, High Ways, Rivers, Water Courses & all things Worthy of Observation. Surveyed by Tho. Thorpe in the Year 1742'.

Source: Bath in Time - Bath Central Library. Original size: 1020 x 1020mm.

(continued)

Patronage and subscription were important elements in any private map-making venture. One of those men who subscribed to the map was Ralph Allen. Many of his circle of friends also subscribed to the project and it is likely that Allen's influence was part of the reason for so many people subscribing to Thorpe's map. The extract to the right includes Allen's house at Prior Park, depicted as 'Mr Allen's House' showing the overall shape of the building, the avenues of trees and further to the south his 'Free Stone Quarry' one of the sources of his fortune.

Above: Prior Park, Bath and Ralph Allen's railway in 1750, from an engraving by Anthony Walker (SANHS).

Right: An extract from Thorpe's map of the Prior Park area (Bath in Time.)

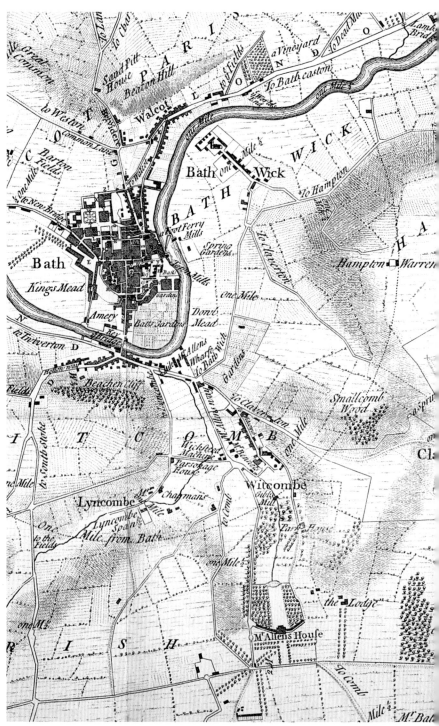

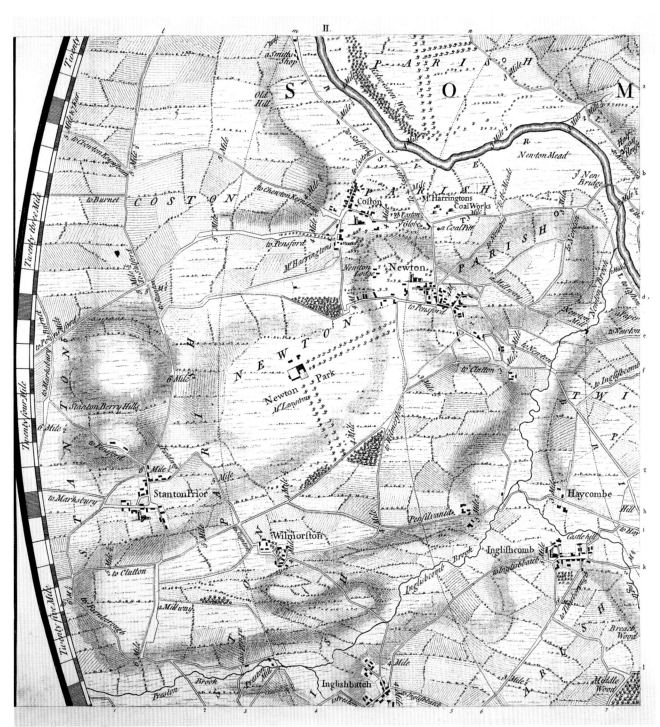

A reduced reproduction of a complete plate of Thorpe's survey. The dotted circular lines show the distance from Bath, with the distance between each line equalling one mile. In the border can be seen another unusual feature and that is the mileage from a 'zero' point at the bottom of the map.

This map is unusual for its time in that the field boundaries are shown in some detail along with hachuring to show hills and higher land. Wooded areas can clearly be seen and in some cases individual lines of trees have been included. In some cases the roads show directions to the next settlement and the distance from Bath. Individual buildings, woods and streams are named. Thorpe also went to great lengths to include more detailed drawings of the houses belonging to those who subscribed to his map.

Note the plate number at the top and the letters at the edge of the map showing the ends of roads so they could be matched up with the correct adjacent sheet.

Source: Bath in Time.

An accurate map of Somerset Shire
Emanuel Bowen
1762

Emanuel Bowen (*c*.1694-1767) was an English map engraver based in London, who at the height of his career worked for King George the Second of England and King Louis the Fifteenth of France as a geographer. Bowen's map of Somerset is arguably one of the most informative and attractive of its time, first published in *The Royal English atlas* in 1762.

Although similar to his map of the county published in *The large English atlas* in 1750, it is embellished with copious amounts of text relating to Somerset during the mid-eighteenth century. Bowen included information on distances, agriculture, antiquities, religion, the nobility, commerce, ancient and natural history, market days, and much more.

The illustration to the right of the cartouche (reproduced on the right) shows Somerset as a truly agricultural county. A man can be seen climbing a tree about to pick an apple or a pear, another man is feeding hay to a some oxen, behind which are a small number of sheep in a field. Cider, wool and livestock were commonplace across the county.

Sadly Bowen and his son, Thomas, who also went into the map trade, both died in poverty. Two of Emanuel's apprentices also became succesful mapmakers, one of whom, Thomas Kitchin, was involved in the publication of *The Royal English atlas*.

Opposite: A reduced reproduction of 'An accurate map of Somerset Shire divided into its Hundreds'.

Source: *The Royal English Atlas* (London, 1762). Original size: 500 x 404mm.

110

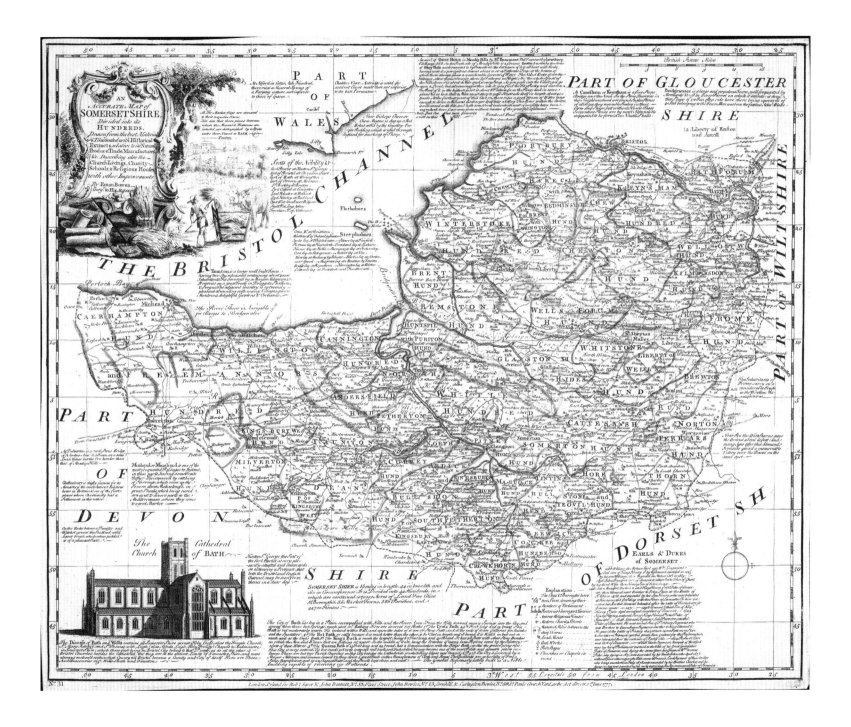

[The Rivers Avon and Parrett]
Lieutenant Colonel Paule St de Beville
1768

A French spy cum map-maker visited Somerset in 1768. Due to the difficulties between France and Great Britain during the eighteenth century, like those between most nations at war, a need arose for detailed geographical intelligence. Not only did countries need good quality surveys of their own lands for defensive purposes, but they also needed information on their enemy's lands if they were to invade them. Surveys were ordered by the Duc de Choiseul, French Minister of War and of the Marine, who was preparing for an invasion of Great Britain in the 1760s.

Lieutenant Colonel Paule St de Beville was instructed to determine the best places for an invasion. In addition to the main focus on London, action was considered against some of the ports along the coast. To achieve this Beville was required to

> reconnoitre carefully the roads leading to these different ports; to observe the best places to attack and to hold, on these routes; the rivers to be crossed and the camps that could be used; in short, the means of keeping up communication between the different corps which would have to be detached for these expeditions.

With this in mind he sailed for England on the 7th of September 1768, arriving at Dover he made his way to London then on to Oxford. From there he travelled through Woodstock, Gloucester, and Bristol when he undertook his survey of the Avon. He visited Bath and Wells before heading for Bridgwater for his next survey, after which he visited Taunton before going into Devon.

In the vicinity of the Avon on the 18th of September he recorded an inlet below Portishead (which dominated the Bristol Channel) as a pecked line of little significance. At the strategically important anchorage of King Road at the mouth of the River Avon, he described 'the place where vessels remain waiting for the tide so as to enter Bristol or which make ready to leave'. As he worked his way up the Avon towards Bristol he noted the place where the ferry crossed the river at Shirehampton, something that was well known to mariners since time out of mind. Having passed St George's and 'Kingsweston' he noted how 'parts [were] made of very high, sheer rock which form the bed of the river, which is very narrow'. He also noted on the Somerset side a 'favourable camp on the Nailsey rise which is very high' in front of which there was a 'large valley where it appears a brook runs, the meadow there being flooded'. All of this area was overlooked by a 'small turret where one keeps a look-out during the war' on the hill above 'Kingsweston' which he named the 'Mountain of the Spy'. Possibly indicating one of the places he used to observe the detail he recorded on his map.

In the Bridgwater area he noted, over two days on the 19th and 20th of September, the course of the River Parrett from Bridgwater, selectively recording the coast between Stogursey and Brent Knoll. His map shows the well cultivated land below Brent Knoll but to the south he mistakenly recorded a 'Gros' village to the south of the River Brue before reaching Huntspill; this is undoubtedly Burnham-on-Sea, which because his map was made in a hurry he placed it on the wrong side of the River Brue.

(continued over)

Opposite: A reduced reproduction of the River Avon and adjacent lands.

Source: TNA, MF 1/54/6. Original size: 310 x 355mm.

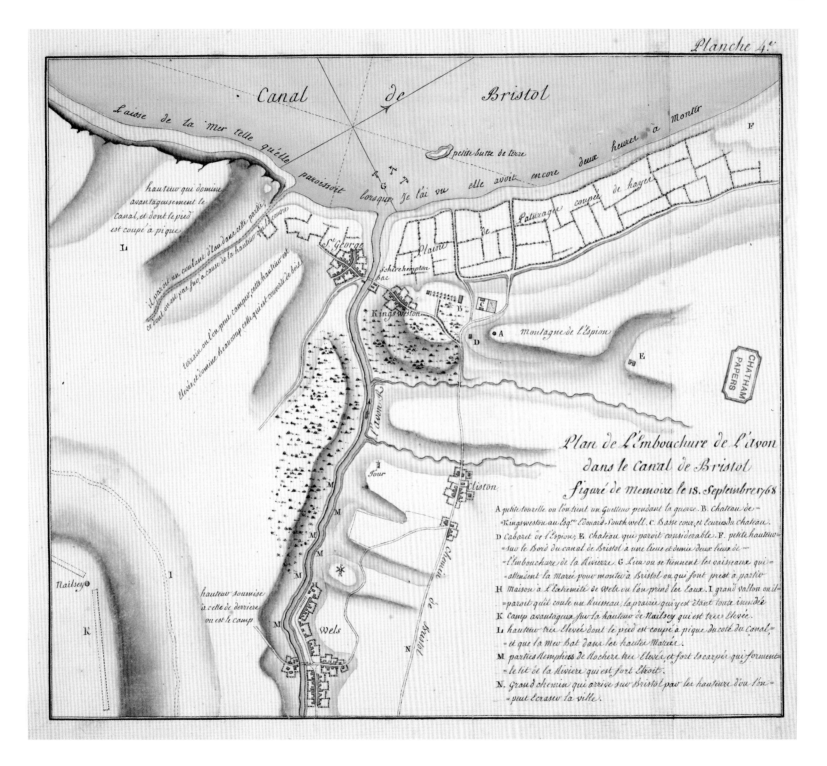

(*continued*)

Along the south side of the Brue he noted how the land was also broken up by hedges, but their depiction is highly generalised. Continuing towards the Parrett he noted the hamlets of Stretcholt and Pawlett Hill before reaching 'Paulett' itself, recording the low-lying terrain which would have been easy for troops to march over.

To the south of the Parrett, starting at its mouth, he did not record any of the islands lying off Huntspill but two further offshore as 'small islands which do not appear inhabited, the largest is high and cut perpendicular all around'. At Steart Point he noted a 'small castle belonging to George Parc and called Stratzum' which he had seen on a map marked as Warmhouse. Again his recording was not particularly accurate as the building was the Warren House, which was recorded on Strachey's map of Somerset in the 1730s. At Wall Common he found the coast to be 'low land where one can unload between these two headlands' and the 'high hills' at Stogursey were 'much further away to continue unloading'. He also recorded a windmill on the Poldens.

Beville's surveys were clearly made in haste. What Beville mapped was most likely undertaken at the end of the day from memory, as opposed to sailing up and down Somerset's main rivers with a sounding line that would have attracted far too much attention to his activities which were supposed to be clandestine. Subsequently his survey of the River Avon does not include an island adjacent to King Road at the mouth of the river. This may not appear too much of a problem unless you consider how important an anchorage area was to all shipping using the River Avon transiting to and from Bristol, as well as other vessels who used it in emergencies.

To survey the topography surrounding over twenty miles of river in only three days, including travelling from the Avon to the Parrett, explains why his surveys are far from accurate when compared to British mapping from the same period. However, such inaccuracies would have been of minor significance when his surveys were used for invasion planning, which fortunately did not materialise. If they had then the two rivers could have been of some importance had Somerset been chosen as a place for invasion.

For all of Beville's faults he has left behind a unique depiction of two important maritime areas of the county, maps that were once in the possession of William Pitt, 1st Earl of Chatham (1708-1778). His use of colour and a compass, but no scale, suggests he had time to record the bearings of important features but not enough time to measure their correct distances from each other, although it should be noted that he took some care of the maps' appearance. When compared to the map of the county produced by Strachey, which he might have seen, Beville's maps give us a little more detail of the topography of two areas of Somerset in the 1760s.

Opposite: A reduced reproduction of the River Parrett and adjacent lands.

Source: TNA, MF 1/54/7. Original size: 315 x 375mm.

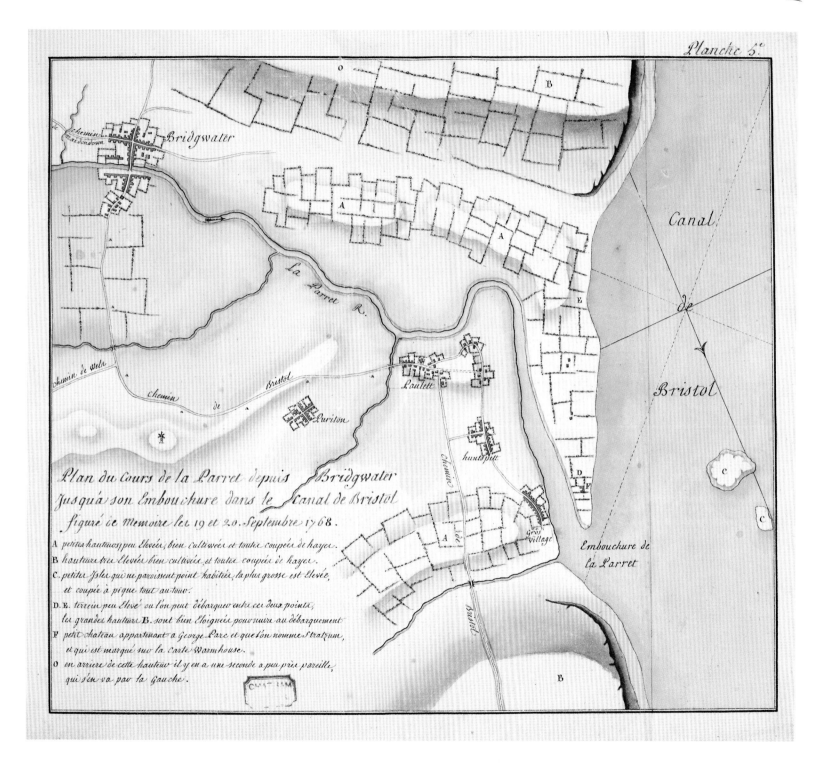

Planche 5.

Bridgwater

Canal

de

Bristol

La Parret R.

Paulett

Puriton

hunts pitt

Gros village

Embouchure de
la Parret

Plan du Cours de la Parret depuis Bridgwater
Jusqu'à son Embouchure dans le Canal de Bristol
figuré de Memoire les 19 et 20 Septembre 1768.

A. petites hauteurs peu Elevées, bien cultivées et toutes coupées de hayes.

B. hauteurs très Elevées bien cultivées et toutes coupées de hayes.

C. petites Isles qui ne paroissent point habitées, la plus grosse est Elevée,
et coupée à pique tout au tour.

D.E. terrein peu Elevé ou l'on peut débarquer entre ces deux points,
les grandes hauteurs B. sont bien Eloignées pour nuire au débarquement

F. petit chateau appartenant à George Parc et que l'on nomme Stratzum,
et qui est marqué sur la carte Warmhouse.

O. en arriere de cette hauteur il y en a une seconde à peu près pareille,
qui s'en va par la Gauche.

CHATHAM

115

Map of the country 11 miles round the city of Bristol delineated from an actual survey
Benjamin Donn
1769

The most northerly parts of the county were surveyed by Benjamin Donn (1729-1798) and published in 1769. Donn came from Devon where, in 1765, he had produced a celebrated map of that county. Following on from this success he produced a map centred on Bristol covering an area 11 miles around the city showing hundredal boundaries, roads, buildings of note, hachuring, land use and the inter-tidal area, the names of prominent landowners, and places of historical interest. Like Thorpe's map of 1742 (see pages 116-119) he used radiating circles to show the distance from a central point, which in this case was Bristol.

The map carries the title 'This Map of the Country 11 Miles round the City of Bristol Delineated from an Actual Survey Is Inscribed to the Rt. Worshipful T. Harris Esqr. Mayor: To the Worshipful the Recorder & Aldermen: The Sheriffs & Common Council: Also To the worshipful S. Munckley Esqr. Master, the Wardens, Assistants, & Commonalty of the Society of Merchants-Venturers of the said City: And To the other Subscribers by their hble. Servant B. Donn'. It was engraved by Richard Coffin of Exeter and printed for and sold by the author at his Mathematical Academy in King St., Bristol. Copies were also sold in London by Thomas Jefferys at the corner of St Martins Lane, Charing Cross.

After 1773 Donne ran an academy at Kingston St Mary near Taunton where he would have taught the mathematics which underpinned surveying.

Overleaf: A reduced reproduction of the lower section of Donn's map showing the north of the county of Somerset. Note how much more detailed Thorpe's map is compared to Donn's map for the Bath area.

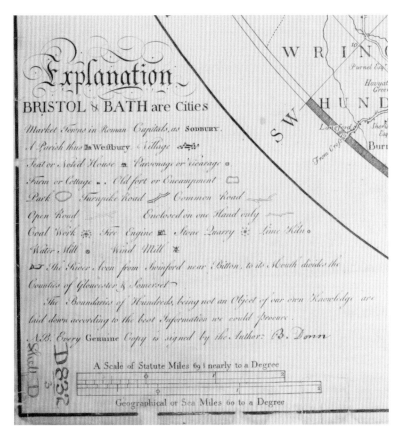

Above: The symbols used by Donn on his map. Note how every genuine copy of his map was signed, personally, by 'B. Donne'.

Left: A much reduced reproduction of Donn's complete map, centred on Bristol. He adorned the map with an illustration of a ship being towed towards the city, up the River Avon, by a boat full of hobblers. In the bottom corner he included a detailed plan of the 'Druidical Stones' at Stanton Drew. The cartouche includes illustrations relating to surveying and cartography.

Source: B. Donn, *Map of the Country 11 Miles round the City of Bristol* (Bristol, 1769) (UKHO, D832 shelf D). Original size: 950 x 920mm.

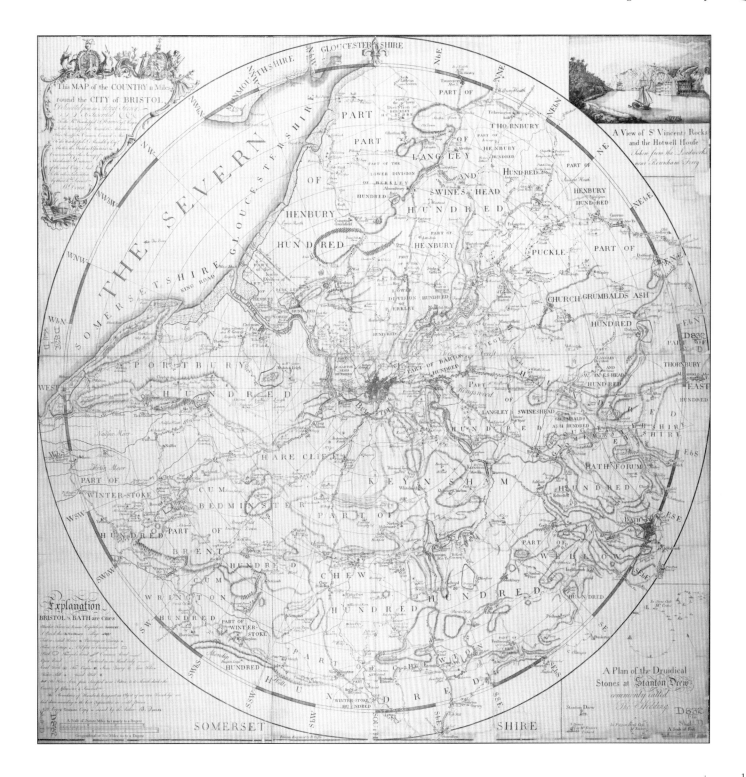

P O R T B U R Y

Weston in Gordine
Walton
Clapton
Naish Mr King
Mote House
The Ledge
Charlton Mugglesworth Esq
Abbots Leigh

PART Down OF BARTON REGIS HUNDRED

Mr House

H U N D R E D

Leigh

Cutberry Camp
Mr Stoake
Barnfield
A Warren
Fayland Farm
Fayland's Inn
A Warren
Leigh Down

Brickdale Esq
Sr Ab. Elton
Lower Tickenham
Tickenham
Mr Hollister
Wraxall
Mr Martindale
Barrett
Tynte's Place
Belmont
Mr Turner

Redcliff Mr Warren
Ashton Court J. Smith
Horseman's Green
Long Ashton
Mr Smith
Mr Weston
Mr Bayly

Nailsea Heath
Mr Bulloch
Mr Wells Combe
Backwell Common
Snuff Mills
Mr Twrne
Mr Sparrow
Bedminster Down
Mr Vigor

Nailsea Moor
Nailsea
Mr Sperron
Mr Burgum
Mr Burgum
Flax Bourton
H A R E   C L I F F
Mr Eastle
Mr Whippy
Bishop's worth vulgo Bishford
Mr Sage

Kenn
A Decoy Pond
Farley
Backwell
Barrow Court, Gore Esq
Hills
Barrow Mynchin
Barrow Gurney
Barrow Common
Mr Farrell
Highridge Baker Esq

Kenn Moor
Chelvy
West Town
Mr Filer
Mr Frampton
C U M
Downside
Freeman's Farm
Dundery
Free Stone
Mr Bagg

PART OF WINTER-STOKE
Mr Grimstead
Nailsea Court Sr R. Bampfield
Court Sr Ch. Tynte
Midghill Farm
Chelvey Batch
B E D M I N S T E R
P A R T

Mr Wilmot
Lower Claverham
Mr Came
Claram Green
vulgo Claram
Brockly
PART Court OF Brockcomb
CHELDON
Felton
North Willou

Yatton
Courtwich Earl Pawlet
Mr Markham
Quakers Meeting
Cleve
Mr Badcocks
HUNDRED
A Warren
Broad field Down
Lead Mine
Winford
Snuff Mill
Littleton G. Powder Mill

H U N D R E D
Cadbury Hill
Clove Pool
P A R T
O F
Troughs to wash the Ore
Lead Mine
King's
Mr Webb
Mr Walton Esq
Redding Pitts
G Powder Mill
Mr Colly
Ch Ma

King's Wood
B R E N T
Down
Mr Tommory
Poper

Congerbury
Yenwood Mr Richardson
Wrington Common
Mr Plaiften
Red Hill
H U N D R E D
Regilsbury Farm Sr Ch. Tynte
Regil
Mrs Willou
Mr Colly
Mr Carte

SWbW
WRINGTON Mar.Tu Court Pulteney Esq
CUM
Butcomb
Chew Stoke
Mr Griffin
Walley Court Mr Adams

tion
THE are Cities
W R I N G T O N   H U N D R E D
Purnel Esq
Havyat's Green
Butcomb Farm Baker Esq
Nempnet
Breach Hill Farm
Woodford
H U N
C H E W
Chew Park

PART OF

Part of Bristol Channel from Lundy Isle and Worms Head, to Watchet and Barry Isle
Lieutenant Murdoch Mackenzie Junior
1771

The records created during the late eighteenth century by officers in one of the greatest navies in the world, has left us with a unique view of how the Somerset coast and the murky waters of the Bristol Channel were mapped. One of those surveys was undertaken in the early 1770s by Lieutenant Murdoch Mackenzie, junior, R.N. (1743-1829).

In 1759 midshipman Mackenzie joined his uncle, Murdoch Mackenzie, senior, whilst surveying the west coast of Great Britain. After a brief spell under Captain Mouat he returned to serve with his uncle in the *Bird* on the 8th of May 1767 as an assistant surveyor. On the 24th of May 1771 Mackenzie, junior, took over command of the survey from his uncle, which by this time had reached the Bristol Channel.

Mackenzie used Minehead as his main centre of operations, from where he criss-crossed the Bristol Channel to South Wales over half a dozen times, as well as sailing to Bristol and King Road. He arrived at Minehead on the 25th of July 1771 and, with a break from surveying in the following February, it was not until the 3rd of July 1772 that he finally left the Somerset coast with all the information he needed to complete his charts. On the 8th of February 1773 he once again returned to Minehead to draw up his charts and then made his way to King Road on the 13th of March. From King Road he took a cutter to Bristol where he transferred to a coach for the journey to London to report to the Admiralty.

Mackenzie junior's survey of the Bristol Channel was so large it had to be divided into two parts. The part covering the area to the west of Watchet has survived but the adjacent part from Watchet to Bristol has not. In 1775, two years after Mackenzie junior's charts were drawn up in Minehead, Mackenzie senior's 'General Chart of the St. George and Bristol Channels' was published.

Mackenzie junior's cousin, Graeme Spence, was appointed to the post of Admiralty Surveyor in 1788 on his cousin's retirement from active surveying. He corrected many of Mackenzie junior's surveys for use by the Hydrographic Office, including 'A Mercator's Chart. Projected, and Drawn, from M: Mackenzie Junr's Surveys of England and Wales; and from G: Spence's Survey of the Scilly Isles' compiled in 1808, which included all of the Bristol Channel.

Although Spence's reworking was not published in its own right, it was used by Captain Thomas Hurd (1747-1823), Hydrographer to the Admiralty Board, as part of his three-sheet coverage of the English Channel. This was not published until 40 years after Mackenzie junior had completed his survey, and because of its scale it is a highly selective portrayal of the work Mackenzie junior undertook in the early 1770s.

Sadly, Mackenzie's survey for the coast of Somerset from Watchet to the mouth of the River Avon is probably now lost forever. Fortunately there are at least four different charts which contain extracts from it. Three of these have their origins within the Hydrographic Office and the fourth was a chart published by the commercial chart trade.

Opposite: A reduced extract of Mackenzie's survey of the Somerset coast from Watchet to Oare; the title is reproduced overleaf.

Source: UKHO, 640 shelf 13k. Original size: 1800 x 1000mm.

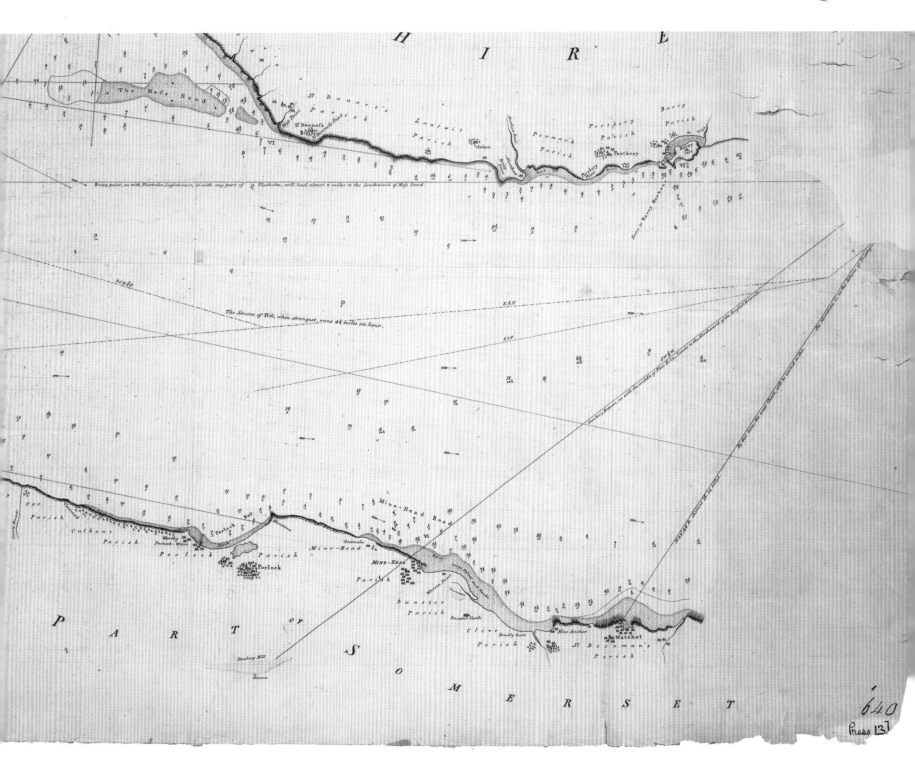

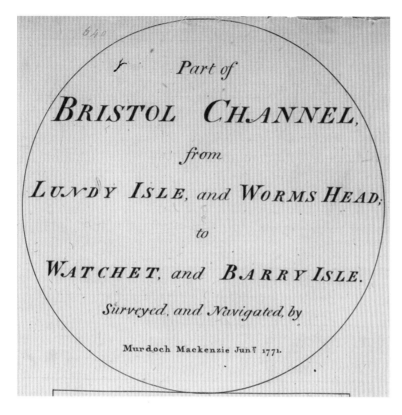

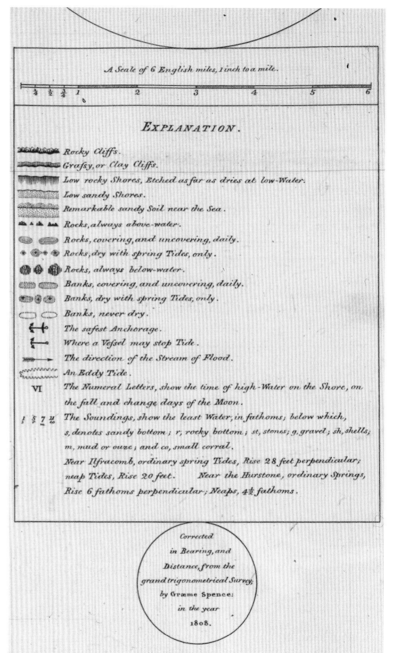

Above: The title from the Mackenzie-Spence survey. Underneath the title is a note that the survey had been 'Corrected in Bearing, and Distance, from the grand trigonometrical survey; by Graeme Spence: in the year 1808'. The Grand Trigonometrical Survey formed the basis of Ordnance Survey mapping.

Right: Although Mackenzie may have crudely drawn the topographic detail he surveyed, the hydrographic information was classified and a key drawn up to explain to mariners what each of the symbols stood for.

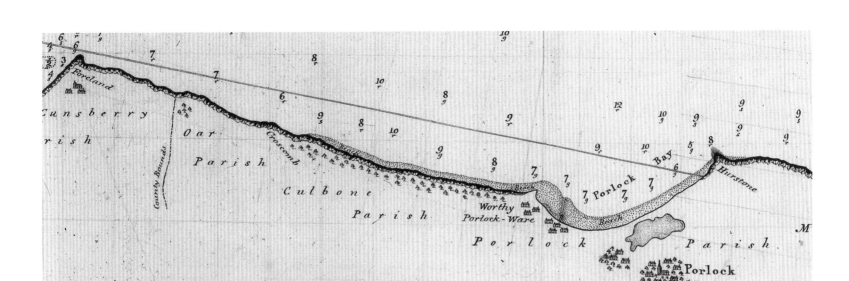

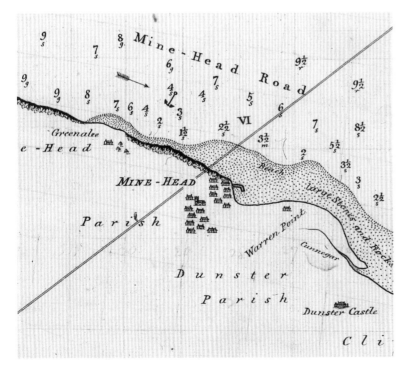

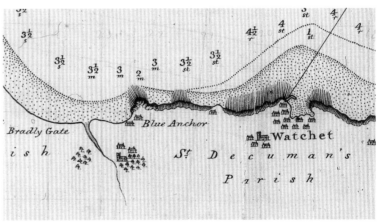

Three close-up images of the main towns and villages drawn by Mackenzie on the Somerset coast. Just off the coast at 'Mine-head' (left) he drew an anchor to symbolise a good place for ships to safely wait at anchor.

County of Somerset surveyed by Day and Masters
William Day and Charles Harcourt Masters
1782

The survey of Somerset by William Day (d.1798) and Charles Harcourt Masters (1759-*c*.1840) marked the start of a new age in the mapping of the county. Until the publication of their survey in 1782, nearly all maps of the county had been based on the work of Saxton, Speed or Strachey. The new survey formed the basis for all subsequent maps of the county until the Ordnance Survey maps were published from 1809.

Little is known about the life and career of William Day. However, it is known that by the time the survey of Somerset was complete until his death in 1798, he was resident at Blagdon near Taunton. Only three other local surveys by Day are known to exist, suggesting that he may have had another occupation besides surveying. Slightly more is known about his associate, Charles Harcourt Masters. He originated in Bath and was apprentice surveyor to Day. Although achieving recognition as a surveyor, Masters was later better known as an architect, becoming city architect and surveyor of Bath in 1787.

Map-making could be a costly business, but there were incentives for Day and Masters. In 1759 the Society of Arts announced:

> The Society proposes to give a Sum not exceeding 100L as a Gratuity to any Person or Persons, who shall make an accurate actual survey of any County.

Rewards were given by the Society throughout the following decades. Day and Masters submitted their survey for one such award in December 1782, but it was not fully considered until the following year. Day eventually received twenty guineas and a silver medal for his efforts, while Masters was awarded a silver pallet for his contribution to the survey. Their map became one of only thirteen county surveys to be recognised by the Society between 1765 and 1809.

It took Day and Masters seven years to complete their survey and Day claimed that 'the Map cost me more than a thousand Guineas, exclusive of my great labour and trouble'. When it was eventually published it was produced on nine sheets and sold for three guineas. Copies were sold by Day from his home at Blagdon, by Masters from Wade's Passage, Bath, and by John Wallis at his Map Warehouse, Ludgate Street, London. Day pleaded with subscribers to send for their copies and Masters used this opportunity to advertise for work as an estate surveyor. Masters went on to survey the navigation from Ilchester to Langport in 1794.

In some respects the detail of the survey is somewhat sparse. There is little focus on land use, including woodland and rural industry, which is interesting as the map was produced at a time of industrial revolution. The survey also neglects to depict ornamental parks in any detail, which became very popular during the eighteenth century. Part of the survey reproduced opposite depicts Barwick Park, near Yeovil; but the park is shown as little more than woodland. This is all the more curious as it is likely that Day and Masters would have relied on financial support from the gentry who owned such estates.

However, the survey does show mansions and notable houses, perhaps as an acknowledgment for the support of local landowners who subscribed to the publication. Details of ancient battlefields and encampments are frequently marked. Although lacking in the representation of some features, Day and Masters chose to depict the dense network of minor roads such as those in south Somerset, which are not shown in all the parishes.

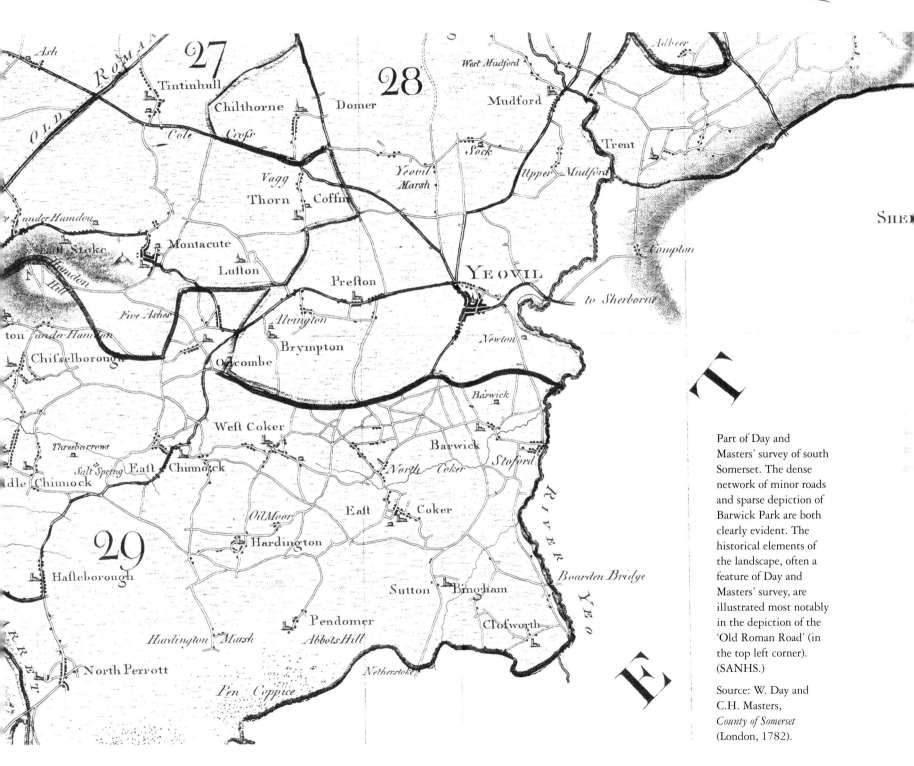

Part of Day and Masters' survey of south Somerset. The dense network of minor roads and sparse depiction of Barwick Park are both clearly evident. The historical elements of the landscape, often a feature of Day and Masters' survey, are illustrated most notably in the depiction of the 'Old Roman Road' (in the top left corner). (SANHS.)

Source: W. Day and C.H. Masters, *County of Somerset* (London, 1782).

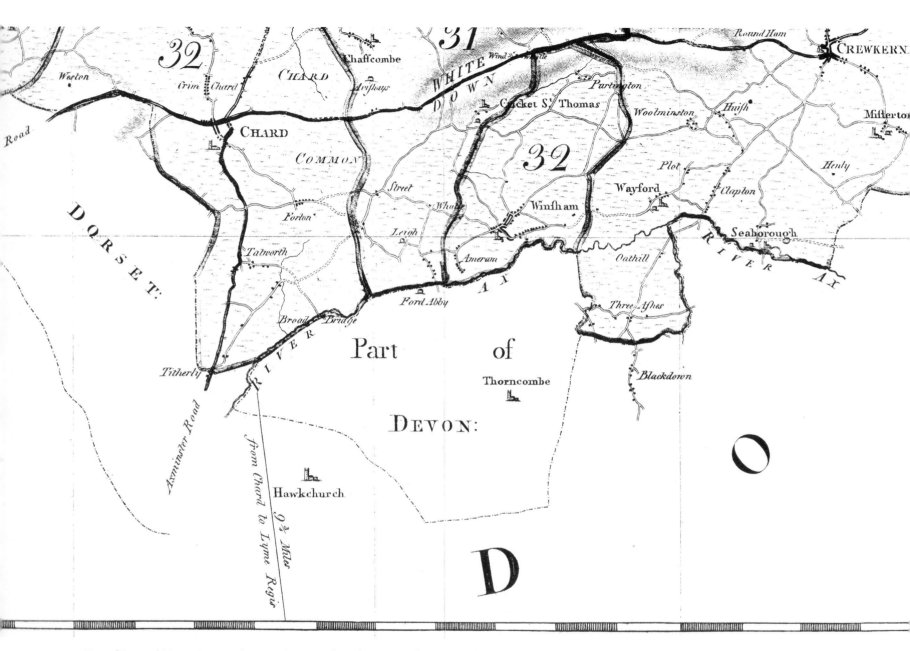

Part of Day and Masters' survey showing the county boundary, some of which is defined by the River Axe, between south Somerset and part of Devon and Dorset. The notable houses of Cricket St Thomas and Forde Abbey are depicted but, as with Barwick Park, the parkland is given little attention.

The distance from Chard to Lyme Regis, in Dorset, is given as 9¾ miles and the longitude from Greenwich is also shown. (SANHS.)

The magnificent cartouche on Day and Masters' map was designed and drawn by Coplestone Warre Bampfylde (1720–1791). Bampfylde was an amateur artist and architect from Hestercombe House, near Taunton. He exhibited landscape works at the Royal Academy of Arts and the Society of Artists from 1763 onwards, and designed the Market House in Taunton. He also served as Treasurer to Day and Masters' scheme.

The cartouche drawn by Bampfylde for Day and Masters was not created for aesthetic purposes alone. It was designed to make a statement about the county. The image of Neptune on the fountain and the ship in the background represents the county's maritime connections and the economic prosperity associated with it, especially through the woollen trade. The fountain from which the woman is filling a cup to give to the crippled man is symbolic of the healing properties associated with the springs at Bath, a reminder of the importance of the county within the nation. (SANHS.)

A *map of the Western Circuit of England*
Benjamin Donne and Son
1784

The Donne family were prolific map makers of their day. This rare map reproduced opposite, of the Western Circuit was prepared by father and son, Benjamin (1729-1798) and Henry and published in 1784 when the family were in the ascendency. It carries the elaborate title of 'A map of the Western Circuit of England Containing the Counties of Cornwal, Devon, Dorset, Somerset, Wilts & Hants, Geo-hydrographically Delineated on a scale of a Quarter of an Inch to a Mile'.

Producing maps such as this was an expensive business. To help make such a publication financially viable, the Donnes obtained assistance from local benefactors, sold advance copies by subscription and had a select network of retail outlets in London. In Bristol they received support from local merchants and aldermen, Thomas Harris esquire, William Blake, John Garnet esquire, Mr Clayfield and Mr Aldridge. In Exeter, John Baring esquire and Mr John Rowe assisted Donne, as did Messers Fox's, merchants in Falmouth, as well as Weres & Co. of Wellington. The Were family of Wellington were leading manufactures of cloth in south Somerset and married into the Fox family of Falmouth. Thomas Were moved to Wellington from Devon and was so successful in business that between 1754 and 1771 his business assets quadrupled, mainly thanks to sales in Italy, Switzerland, Holland and Germany. They later expanded their sales network as far as China, shipping cloth through Topsham, as well as by river to London.

In London, Donne used Mr Phillips of George Yard, Lombard Street, Mr Wilkinson of Cornhill and Mr William Faden of Charing Cross to sell his map. Even though map sellers such as Faden produced their own maps and were in many respects rivals of Donne & Son, Donne knew that just selling his maps to his customers in

Bristol would not have been financially viable. He also used Collins and Johnson, and Mr Easton in Salisbury, Mr L. Nicholson on the Isle of Wight, and numerous 'principal booksellers' around the country as outlets.

In early June 1784 he announced to subscribers that the map would be delivered to them 'in a few days', blaming the delay in publication on the engraver. He described it as

> well engraved on four sheets and half of imperial paper, on a scale sufficiently large, to shew distinctly the principal roads, position, distances of the several towns, parish churches, &c.

He also pointed out to gentlemen readers that it was not too late to subscribe to this enterprise.

As for the content of the map, this was also unique. Donne combined topographic and hydrographic information onto a grid which showed both latitude and longitude. He included insets of Plymouth, Portsmouth and the Scilly Islands, along with topographical information covering roads, towns, encampments, distances between towns, times of High Water, anchorages, buoys and tidal stream arrows. All this was under the unique description of being a 'Geo-hydrographically Delineated' map.

Opposite: A reduced reproduction of the area covering the county of Somerset, extracted from four individual sheets of the six printed in 1784.

Source: Private collection. Original size: 1422 x 840mm.

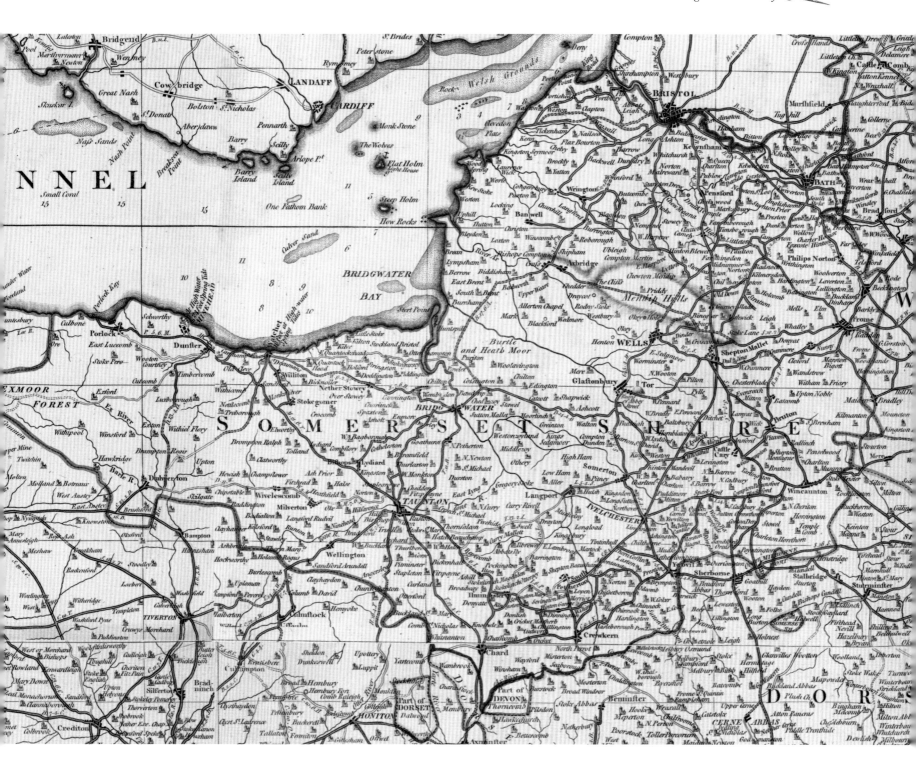

A *map of the country seven miles round Taunton*
Joshua Toulmin
1791

The Reverend Joshua Toulmin A.M. (1740-1815) was born in London and was a theologian and Dissenting minister of Presbyterian (1761-1764), Baptist (1765-1803), and then Unitarian (1804-1815) congregations. He came to Taunton in 1765 to serve as a Baptist minister and, in 1790, carried out a census of the town and 'counted nearly five and a half thousand people living within the area ringed by the turnpike gates'.

Shortly afterwards, in 1791, whilst employed as a schoolmaster, his book on *The history of Taunton in the county of Somerset* was published. This was the first detailed history of the town and Toulmin included a map of the country seven miles round Taunton. The concept of this circular map was not new in Somerset, as both Thorpe and Donne had produced similar works, and Toulmin based his version mostly on the recently published county mapping by Day and Masters. However, Toulmin was able to use his local knowledge to improve on Day and Masters, as well as to produce a detailed plan of Taunton reproduced opposite.

As he did not acknowledge the source of the map of Taunton it is thought he was its author. Despite his radicalism his *History* was dedicated to Sir Benjamin Hammet M.P. and was widely supported by some 400 subscribers, including the Reverend John Collinson, nine members of the Noble family, Mr Thomas Poole of Stowey, General Simcoe, Governor of Canada and Sir John Trevelyan M.P.. Toulmin was a radical and sympathized with both the Americans and the French during their revolutions. Subsequently, in 1794, he received his Doctor of Divinity diploma from Harvard University, America's leading university. He died in Birmingham in 1815.

REFERENCES

1 *Parade* .	19 *Paul's Meeting* .
2 *Castle Green* .	20 *Baptist's Meeting* .
3 *Hunt's Court* .	21 *New Meeting* .
4 *Jermin's Court* .	22 *Quaker's Meeting* .
5 *Carpenter's Lane* .	23 *Octagon Chapel* .
6 *Mount Lane* .	24 *Castle* .
7 *Gwyn Lane* .	25 *Market House* .
8 *Holway Lane* .	26 *Hospital* .
9 *Little Magdalen Lane* .	27 *Free School* .
10 *Willment's Square* .	28 *Theatre* .
11 *Black Boy Lane* .	29 *County Goal* .
12 *Whirligig Lane* .	30 *Gray's Almshouse* .
13 *Back Lane* .	31 *Pope's Almshouse* .
14 *Mill Lane* .	32 *Huish's Almshouse* .
15 *Rosemary Lane* .	33 *Henley's Almshouse* .
16 *Chip Lane* .	34 *Spital Almshouse* .
17 *St Mary Magdalen's Church* .	35 *Magdalen Workhouse* .
18 *St James's Church* .	36 *St James's Workhouse* .

Above: A key was included in the opposite corner to the map showing the numbers on the plan of Taunton. Toulmin called this list of places 'References'.

Opposite: An enlargement of Toulmin's plan of Taunton, showing a great deal more detail than any other place shown on his map (reproduced overleaf) published to accompany his *History of Taunton*.

Source: Revd J. Toulmin, *The history of Taunton in the county of Somerset* (Taunton, 1791).

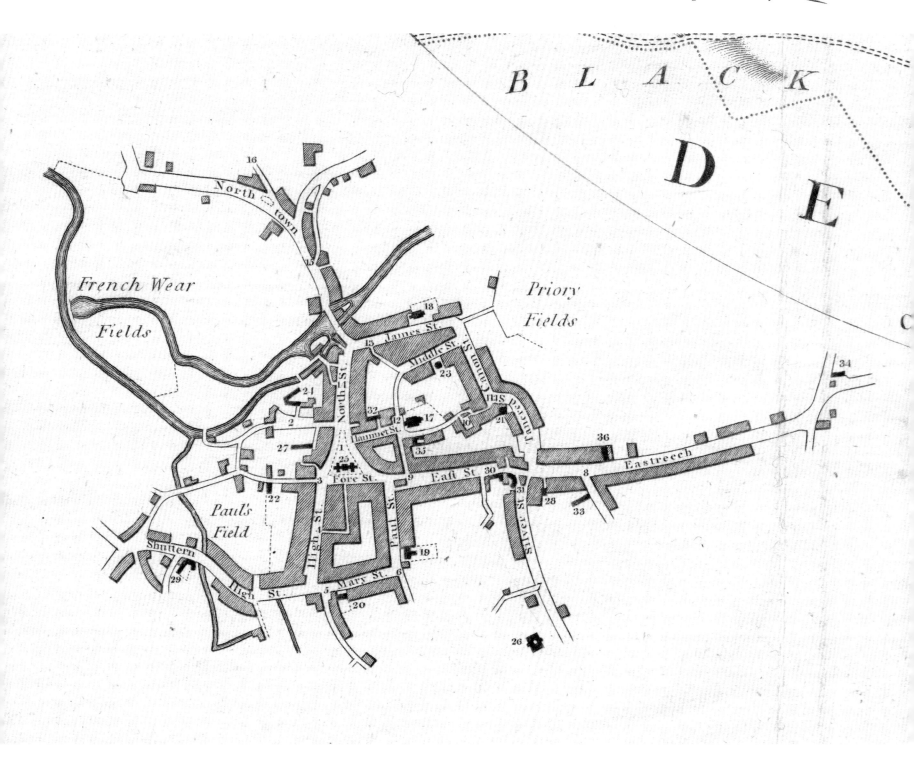

B L A C K

D E

French Wear

Fields

Priory

Fields

North town

16

15

18

13 James St.

Middle St.

23

North St.

24

32

17

2

Hammet St.

10 21

27

35

25

22

Fore St.

East St.

30

Silver St.

Eastreech

36

3

9

8

28

33

Paul's
Field

High St.

Paul St.

31

26

Shuttern

19

29

High St.

Mary St.

6

5

20

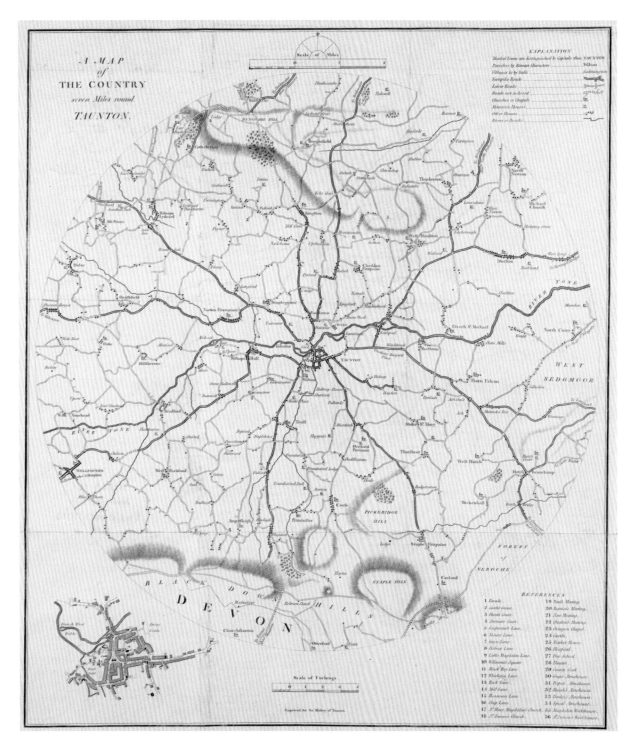

A MAP
of
THE COUNTRY
seven Miles round
TAUNTON.

Left: A reduced image of Toulmin's map. The main roads are shown as thicker double lines. In 1791 the main road from Taunton to Exeter used to run through the village of Bishops Hull, which was diverted and today avoids this narrow route.

Original size: 379 x 555mm.

Opposite: An extract from the map showing the course of the River Tone from Nynehead ('Ninehead') to 'Gibraltar' (between Bishops Hull and Taunton) and the streams running into it.

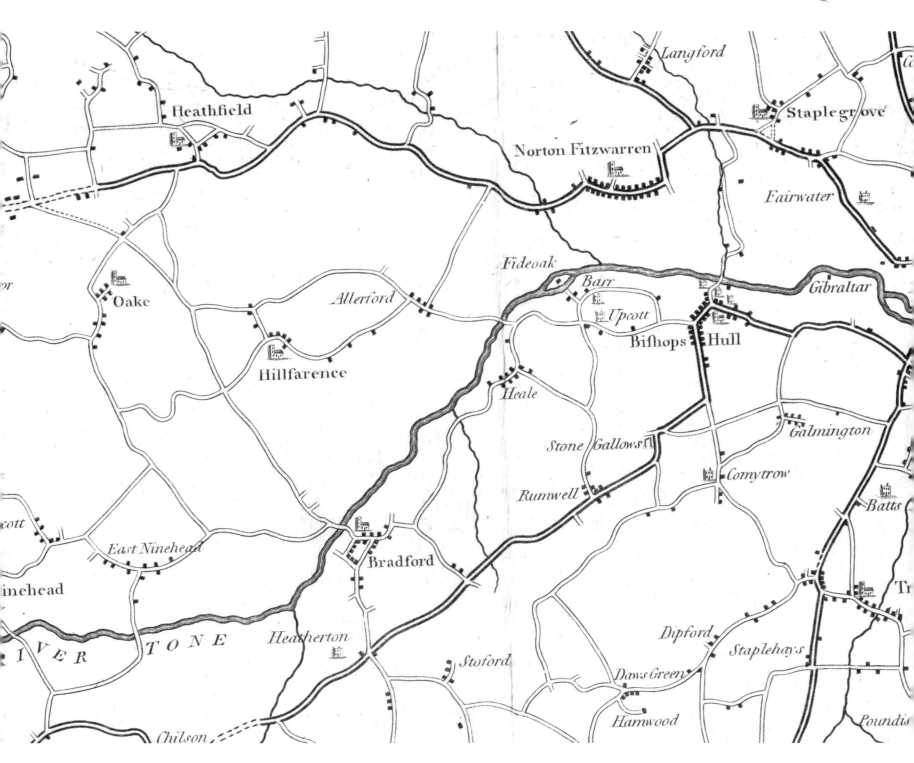

A new map of the Western Circuit of England
William Tunnicliff
1791

William Tunnicliff, land surveyor and publisher of Salisbury, produced a *Topographical survey of the counties of Hants, Wilts, Dorset, Somerset, Devon, and Cornwall, commonly called the Western Circuit* publishing it in Salisbury in 1791. His survey was not an antiquarian one, nor similar to that by Edmund Rack that had been partially published by the Reverend Collinson in the same year. Tunnicliff produced a description of the principal and direct cross roads, claiming to have described the situation of 'all the towns, village's, noblemen's and gentlemen's seats, navigable rivers, canals, &c upon and in the vicinity of each road'.

The volume contained individual maps of all the counties, as well as a general one showing the extent of the Western Circuit, reproduced opposite. Chubb described the map of Somerset as 'clearly engraved, but somewhat bare looking'. Tunnicliff was able to publish such a volume by obtaining subscribers and, in return, he published the coats of arms of those men who supplied them. It also contained a distance table for each county. This was not an original idea but one that helped to make this a useful volume of maps, itineraries and distance tables for the whole of the south west peninsula.

Tunnicliff also included a 'Travelling index of the great roads in Somersetshire' showing the distances from place to place and what great houses could be found on either side of the road. His alphabetical list of the principal nobility and gentry included their place of abode, as well as the road on which their seats could be found.

A

S U R V E Y

OF THE

C O U N T Y

OF

S O M E R S E T.

THE

DIRECTION and SURVEY of the GREAT ROAD

FROM

BATH TO SHERBORNE,

THROUGH

SHEPTON MALLETT, AND BY ANSFORD INN.

THIRTY-SEVEN MILES.

AT four miles from *Bath*, on the left, near one mile distance, is *Combhay*, the feat of *John Smith*, Efq.; at five miles enter *Dunkerton*; at fix miles, on the right, near half a mile diftance, is *Camerton Houfe*, the feat of *James Stephens*, Efq.; oppofite, on the left, near half a mile diftance, is *Woodborough*, the feat of the late *Richard Lanfdown*, Efq.; at feven miles enter *Radftock*; at ten miles, on the right, near one mile diftance, is *Midfummer Norton*, the feats of *William Kelftone*, Efq. and —— *Savage*, Efq.; at eleven miles, on the left, near one mile diftance, is *Charlton*, the feat of *Thomas*

I 4   *Samuel*

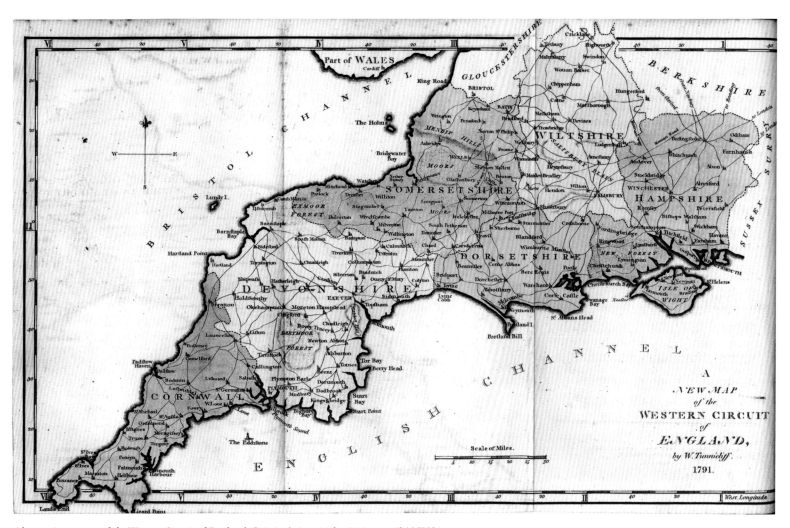

Above: *A new map of the Western Circuit of England*. Original size: 336 x 202mm. (SANHS.)

Opposite: The Somerset title page from Tunnicliff's *Survey*, 119. (SANHS.)

AN

INDEX TABLE

OF THE

DISTANCES FROM TOWN TO TOWN,

One and all from each Other,

IN THE COUNTY OF

SOMERSET,

AND ADDITIONALLY EXTENDED TO

Oxford, Portsmouth, Southampton, Plymouth, Weymouth, Falmouth, and LONDON.

Axbridge.																																		
28	Bath.																																	
21	24	Bruton.																																
18	40	27	Bridgewater.																															
23	26	3	24	Castle-Cary.																														
44	50	30	23	27	Chard.																													
37	42	23	31	23	8	Crewkerne.																												
46	68	54	28	51	32	40	Dulverton.																											
41	63	15	23	47	35	44	14	Dunster.																										
26	12	12	36	16	40	36	64	59	Frome.																									
15	24	17	16	14	29	22	44	39	20	Glastonbury.																								
27	33	15	20	10	17	10	45	43	24	12	Ivelchester.																							
29	45	27	25	22	5	8	33	35	36	24	12	Ilminster.																						
28	36	18	12	15	14	13	36	35	29	13	8	9	Langport.																					
33	36	10	31	10	26	18	56	54	25	22	12	23	20	Milborne Port.																				
33	55	41	15	38	18	26	15	18	51	31	32	20	23	43	Milverton.																			
43	65	52	25	48	37	46	15	2	61	41	45	37	37	56	20	Minehead.																		
16	10	21	34	22	46	39	62	57	18	20	29	41	32	32	49	59	Pensford.																	
34	40	22	27	19	10	5	38	40	33	19	7	5	8	18	25	42	36	Petherton, South.																
14	18	7	27	8	32	25	54	50	10	11	15	27	18	18	41	52	14	18	Shepton Mallet.															
23	31	13	17	10	20	14	41	43	24	8	4	16	5	14	28	45	27	11	13	Somerton.														
29	51	33	11	30	16	20	24	23	45	27	24	12	12	35	8	25	47	17	33	17	Taunton.													
36	58	40	18	37	14	22	18	22	52	34	31	19	22	42	4	24	52	24	40	27	7	Wellington.												
10	19	12	21	13	34	27	49	44	15	5	17	29	18	23	36	46	15	24	6	13	32	39	Wells.											
27	29	5	30	6	32	24	57	53	17	20	13	25	21	8	44	55	26	24	12	16	36	42	17	Wincanton.										
34	56	43	16	41	23	32	12	16	52	32	32	23	26	46	3	18	50	28	44	31	11	6	37	46	Wivelifcombe.									
32	38	15	25	14	17	9	47	48	28	17	5	14	12	9	34	50	34	9	16	26	33	22	15	37		Yeovil.								
18	12	27	35	28	52	45	67	58	24	26	35	47	38	38	50	60	6	42	20	33	46	53	21	32	51	40	Bristol.								
84	67	93	102	94	116	105	129	125	68	91	96	100	112	116	103	104	116	128	72	107	85	95	110	117	81	96	118	105	66	Oxford.				
120	88	80	109	81	103	95	136	132	77	97	92	98	100	77	118	133	96	96	87	93	110	117	94	79	121	87	102	79		Portsmouth.				
84	62	53	88	54	76	68	115	111	58	78	65	77	73	51	95	112	73	69	68	72	87	96	73	50	98	60	79	68	21		Southampton.			
67	65	40	54	39	36	28	60	59	54	49	37	35	41	28	55	74	69	33	41	42	47	43	56	36	58	32	75	103	81	60		Weymouth.		
101	122	103	85	100	74	82	71	85	117	101	91	79	91	100	70	83	116	84	112	91	74	67	103	106	70	91	122	189	176	155	96	Plymouth.		
150	172	152	134	149	123	131	123	137	166	150	140	128	140	149	119	133	165	133	161	140	123	116	152	155	119	140	171	238	225	204	145	55	Falmouth.	
131	108	110	137	113	141	132	164	160	108	132	123	135	128	114	151	162	118	132	117	123	143	150	122	108	154	123	115	54	72	76	128	216	268	London.

Note, Quarter Seffions for this County are held as follows:

The Firft Week after Epiphany, } at Wells. The Firft Week after the Clofe of Eafter,	The Firft Week after the Tranflation of Thomas a Becket, or July 7, at Bridgewater. And the Firft Week after Michaelmas-Day, at Taunton.

A reproduction of the distance table of the towns in Somerset in 1791. Note how the table was mounted in the book on a guard that was too long and hence the edge was too closely cropped. (SANHS.)

Source: Tunnicliff's *Topographical Survey*. Original size: 229 x 147mm.

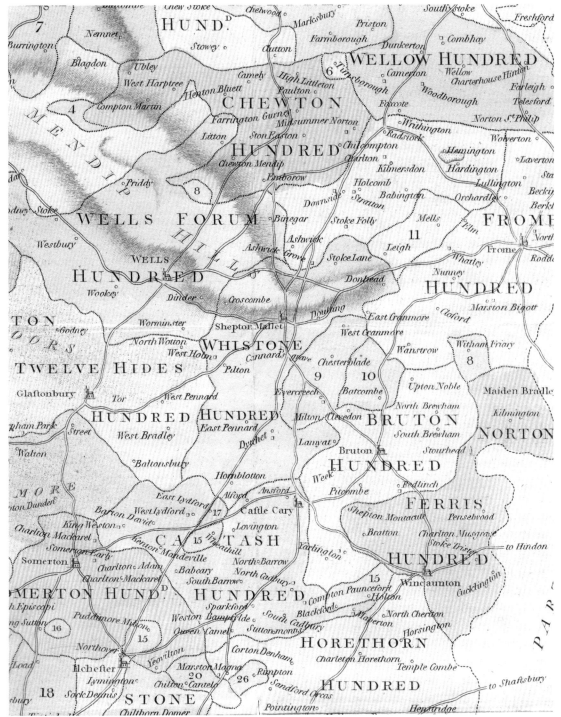

Extracts from Tunnicliff's 'New map of Somersetshire', 1791, showing the title, key to the point and line symbols, as well as an extract showing eastern Somerset, with the market towns marked as churches and the different hundreds brightly coloured. (SANHS.)

Source: *Topographical survey of the counties of Hants, Wilts, Dorset, Somerset, Devon, and Cornwall, commonly called the Western Circuit* (Salisbury, 1791). Original size: 562 x 429mm.

Plan of the proposed deviations of the Somersetshire Coal Canal
William Smith
1793

The map of the Somersetshire Coal Canal by William Smith (1769-1839) is a rare item. Smith worked for the Canal Company and lodged at Rugbourne Farm in High Littleton from 1792 to 1795, which can be seen marked on his map. Some information relating to the map's production is known. Smith recorded in his diary on 30 January 1794 how he had 'finished drawing canal plans on vellum & inking the lines'. It was only three days later that he spent time examining the impressions pulled from the copper plate. It was used by engineers during the construction of the canal.

The map was engraved by John Cary of The Strand, London. One of the main purposes of the map was to show the proposed deviations in the canal. A list of six deviations was included on the map.

The full title of the map reads: 'Plan of the Proposed Deviations of the / Somersetshire Coal Canal / (With proper Rail Roads to communicate therewith) / in the counties of Somerset and Wilts to join the proposed Kennet and Avon Canal; at, or near / Limpley Stoke. / Whereby a Communication will be opened between the districts through which the said Canal is intended to pass, / and / The extensive Coal Works in the Parishes of / Dunkerton, Camerton, Paulton, Timsbury, High-Littleton, Farmborough, Clutton, Writhlington, Radstock & Midsummer-Norton. Surveyed 1793'.

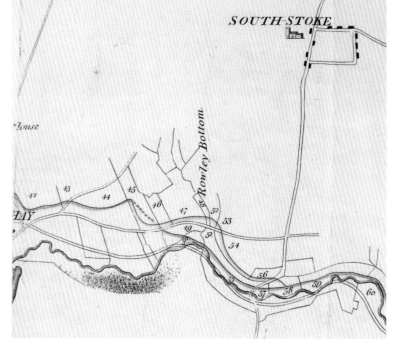

Above: A close-up of Rowley Bottom in the parish of Combe Hay. Smith found examples of fossils at Rowley Bottom and the parish was also the site of the lift or caisson, in the field marked number 45. Smith went on to become known as the 'Father of English Geology'. The printed version contains more information than the deposited version in the papers of the Clerk of Quarter Sessions.

Opposite: A reproduction of a section of the map showing Rugbourne in High Littleton where William Smith lived in the 1790s.

Source: SANHS, Tite Collection. Original size: 930 x 480mm.

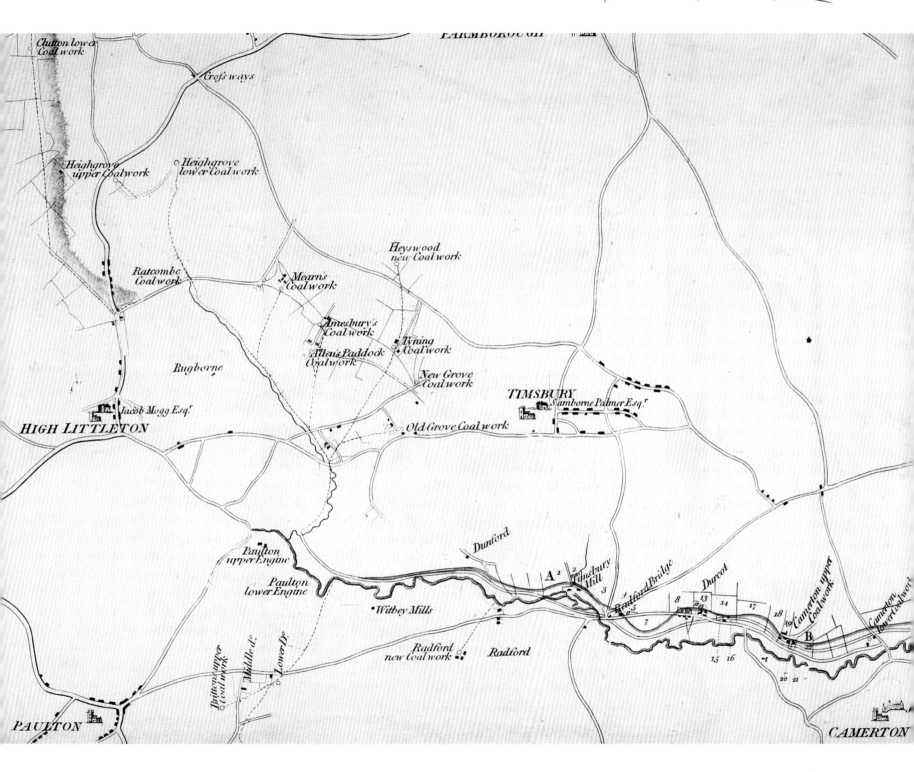

Plan of the proposed Grand Western Canal from Topsham in the county of Devon to Taunton in the county of Somerset
John Rennie
1794

The Grand Western Canal was a 'grand' scheme in the engineering world during the age of canal mania to canalise a route from Topsham, in Devon, to Taunton, which was connected to the rivers Tone then Parrett and on to the Bristol Channel. John Rennie F.R.S.E. F.R.S. (1761-1821) was an eminent civil engineer who also worked on projects involving bridges and docks. The Act of Parliament to build the Grand Western Canal was passed in 1796, two years after the map was published, with Rennie supervising the construction work until 1814.

A section from Tiverton to Lowdells, near Burlescombe, was opened in 1814 and an extension from Lodwells to Taunton commenced in 1830 and was completed in 1838. After leaving Taunton the canal snaked its way through Bishops Hull, Bradford, Nynehead, Hillfarrance, Wellington, Langford Budville, Kittisford and Ashbrittle before reaching Devon. However, the grand scheme to join the two channels never materialised.

The map was issued in two sheets and engraved by John Cary of The Strand, London. An elaborate cartouche on the map contained a variety of different fonts and styles. It showed a table of the branch lines to Cullompton and Tiverton, giving their distances and the fall of the water levels. Another table showed technical information concerning the line from Topsham to Taunton.

Above: John Rennie (Ian Coleby Collection).

Opposite: A reproduction of the section of the map showing the area from Bathealton to Langford Budville, including the proposed new channel marked in red.

Source: SANHS. Tite Collection. Original size: 1206 x 444mm (printed in two sheets).

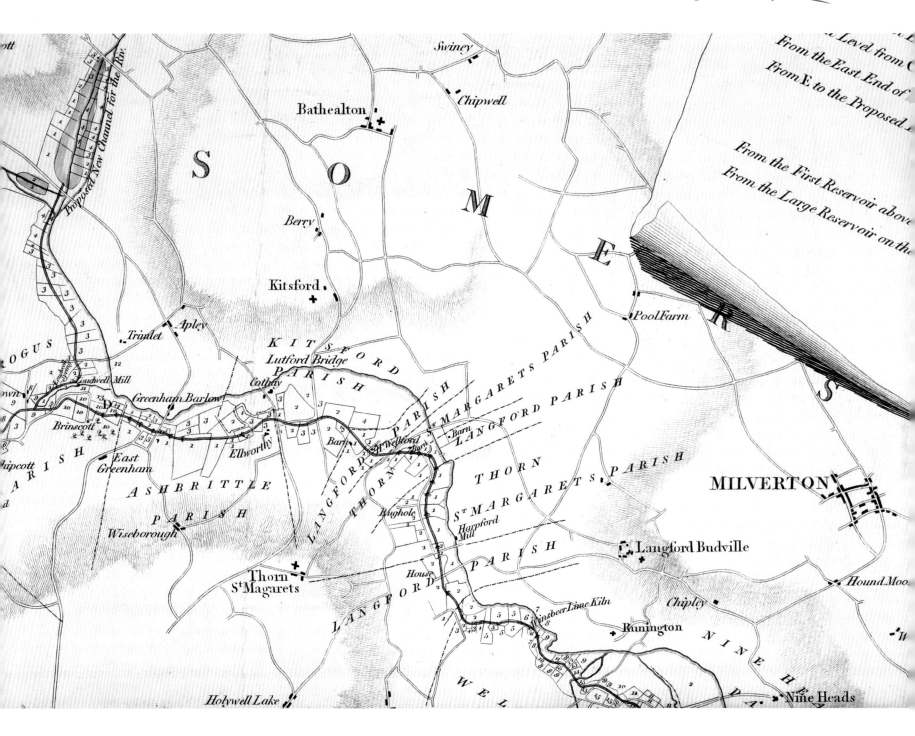

Swiney

Chipwell

Bathealton

S   O

M

E

Berry

Kitsford

Pool Farm

R

Proposed New Channel for the Riv.

Apley
Trunet

K I T S F O R D

Lutford Bridge
Cothay

PARISH

St MARGARETS PARISH

Langford PARISH

ROGUS

Loudwell Mill
Greenham Barlow
Ellworthy
Barn
H Welford
Barn
Barn

LANGFORD PARISH

MILVERTON

Brinscott
East
Greenham

PARISH

ASHBRITTLE

PARISH

Wiseborough

Bughole

THORN
St MARGARETS PARISH

THORN

Harpford
Mill

Langford Budville

Hound Moo

Thorn
St Magarets

House

LANGFORD PARISH

Winsbeer Lime Kiln

Chipley

Runington

NINE HEA

Holywell Lake

WEL

Nine Heads

From the East End of

From the Proposed

From the First Reservoir above

From the Large Reservoir on the

141

Somerset for the agricultural survey
William White
1794-1797

A man ahead of his time was John Billingsley (1747-1811) of Ashwick Grove. His grandfather, a Presbyterian, served as minister at Ashwick from 1699 to 1729 and John was thought to have lived at Ashwick Grove for the whole of his life. He acquired a small manor in Chewton Mendip and lands in Ubley following its enclosure in the 1770s. He invested in brewing, was involved with turnpike trusts, canals, drainage, the Somerset coalfield, water-meadows, enclosures, and served as vice-president of the Bath and West of England Agricultural Society. He wrote extensively on a range of agricultural subjects, and conducted a survey, for the Board of Agriculture, of the county's agriculture.

Through his drainage work he became associated with a land surveyor, William White of Sand, who lived in a grand house in the parish of Wedmore. White drew the *Plan for more effectively draining the turf bogs and flooded lands, near the Rivers Brue and Axe, in the County of Somerset* in 1794 (reproduced overleaf), which Billingsley included in his *General view of the Agriculture in the county of Somerset; with observations on the means of its improvement*, published in London in 1794.

White also undertook at least 15 other surveys between 1777 and 1806.

Above: John Billingsley by Joseph Hutchinson (1747-1830). From a contemporary engraving. (SANHS.)

Opposite: A reduced reproduction of Billingsley's map of 1797. Source: Billingsley, *General view* (1797). Original size: 266 x 223mm.

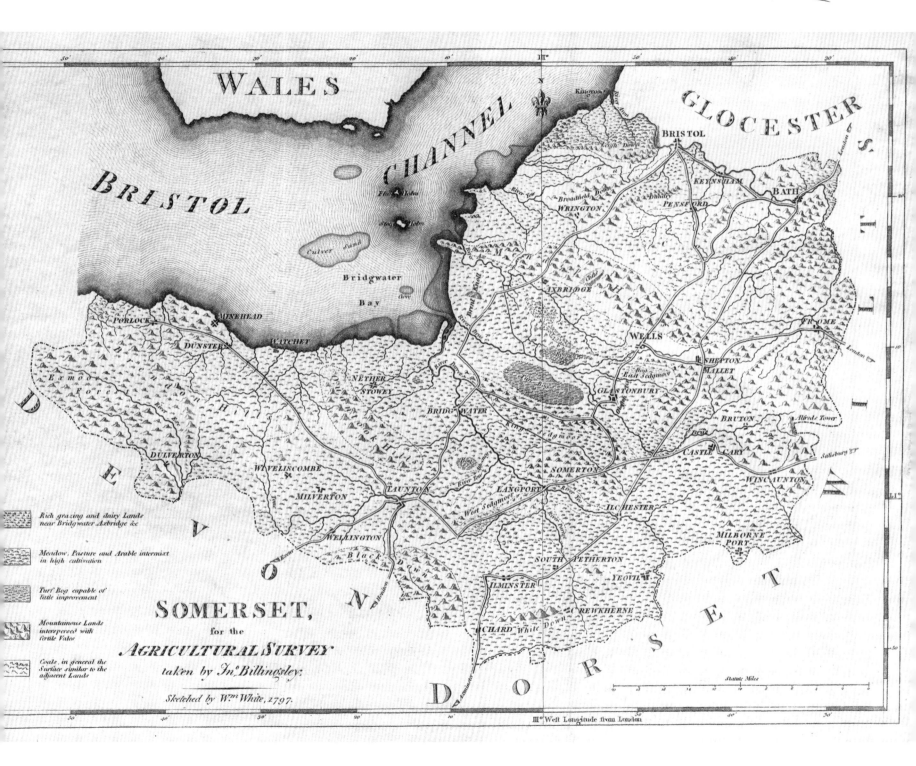

WALES

BRISTOL

CHANNEL

GLOCESTER

Culver Sand

Bridgwater

Bay

KEYNSHAM

BRISTOL

BATH

WRINGTON PENSFORD

AXBRIDGE

WELLS

FROME

PORLOCK MINEHEAD

DUNSTER WATCHET

SHEPTON
MALLET

Exmoor
Forest

NETHER
STOWEY

BRIDGWATER

GLASTONBURY

East Sedgmoor

BRUTON

Alfreds Tower

DULVERTON

CASTLE CARY

Salisbury 27

WIVELISCOMBE

SOMERTON

WINCAUNTON

MILVERTON

TAUNTON

LANGPORT

ILCHESTER

West Sedgmoor

WELLINGTON

Black Down

MILBORNE
PORT

SOUTH PETHERTON

D E V O N

ILMINSTER

YEOVIL

CREWKHERNE

CHARD *White Down*

W I L T S

D O R S E T

Legend

Rich grazing and dairy Lands
near Bridgwater Axbridge &c

Meadow, Pasture and Arable intermixt
in high cultivation

Turf Bog capable of
little improvement

Mountainous Lands
interspersed with
fertile Vales

Coale, in general the
Surface similar to the
adjacent Lands

SOMERSET,
for the
AGRICULTURAL SURVEY
taken by Jn.º Billingsley.

Sketched by Wm. White, 1797.

III° West Longitude from London

Statute Miles

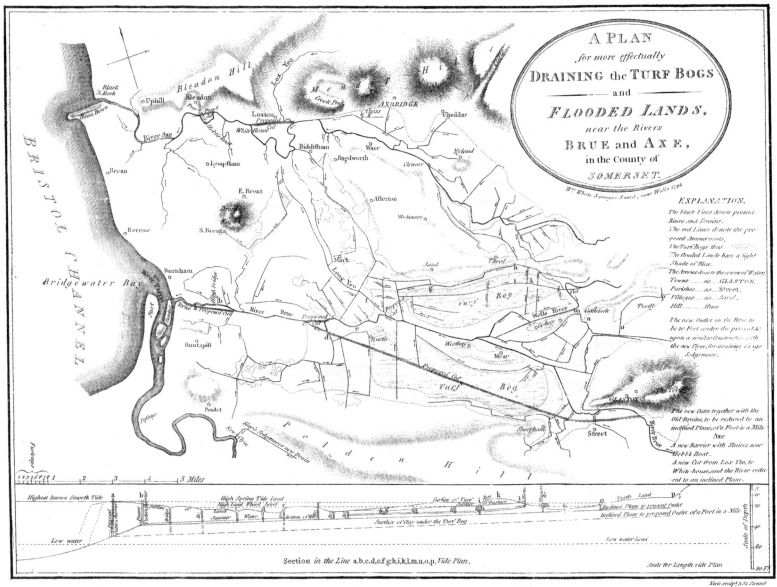

White's 'Plan' of 1794.   Source: Billingsley, *General view* (1794). Original size: 238 x 173mm.

CHAPTER FIVE

The Nineteenth Century

Tour Through the County of Somerset. A Geographical Game
Robert Rowe
1805

The idea of using a map as a game was not a new one in 1805, but the map reproduced opposite is thought to be the first to cover a county. Fortunately Rowe chose Somerset. The game was printed in London for Robert Rowe (*c.*1775-1843) of Gough Square, Fleet Street, and Champante & Whitroe of Jewry Street, Aldgate. Rowe was an engraver, publisher and geographer. The game, coloured by hand, was issued along with an eight page printed booklet which contained the rules printed by J.H. Hart of 23 Warwick Square. The map, which was folded and the rule book came in a slip case (right).

Starting at Yeovil participants travel around the county, ending up in Bath. Using pillars to represent each player, the participants could jump ahead by more than one place at a time depending on where they landed. To add an element of danger, Culver Sand (number 48) was added but if the player landed on it he was 'wrecked' and had to pay one counter to escape to Keynsham.

Although claiming to be a tour through the county, there are two oddities, the first being number 50 Flat Holm which is in Wales, and the other number 68 Longleat which is in Wiltshire. As for the map, this is based upon the engraver John Cary's *New map of Somersetshire divided into hundreds exhibiting its roads, rivers, parks, etc* published in 1805. The game was a shortlived publication as it was republished in 1807 by John Wallis senior of 13 Warwick Square, London and John Wallis junior of 188 Strand, but no surviving example is known.

Opposite: A reduced reproduction of the exceptionally rare map.

Source: Private collection. Original size: 610 x 480mm.

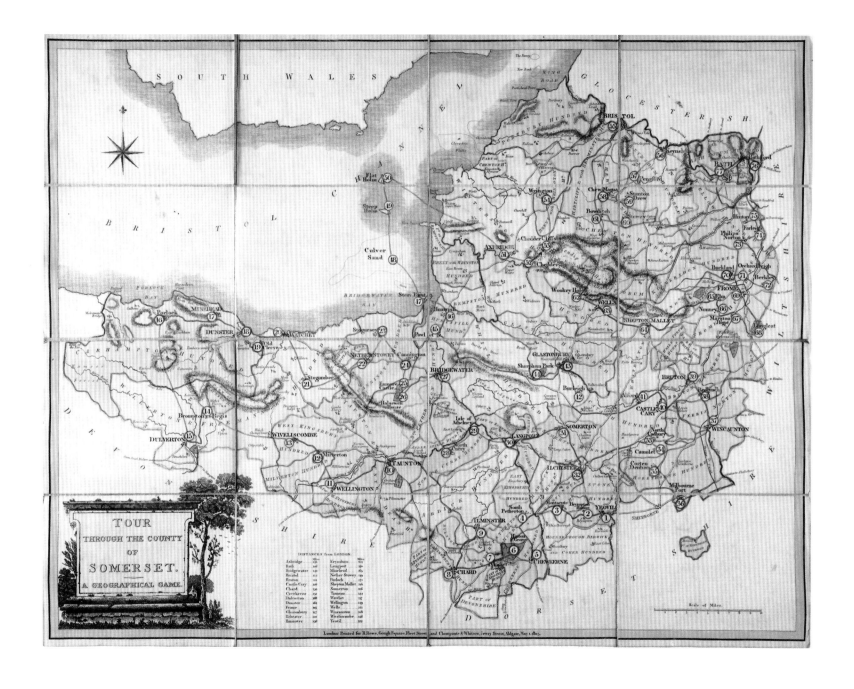

Sheet XX
Ordnance Survey
11 October 1809

The Grand Trigonometrical Survey of Great Britain was the first systematic attempt by the Government to map the whole country. Using the expertise of the Royal Engineers the earliest part of the West Country to be surveyed was the Plymouth area, between 1784 and 1786, the first part of Somerset was not surveyed until the years 1802, 1803 and 1804. The Ordnance Surveyors' manuscript drawings, which were used as the basis for the printed editions, are now housed at the British Library.

The first area of Somerset to be published by the Ordnance Survey was the western part of the county, including the vast majority of the county's coastline. Published in sheets in 1809, sheet 20 stretched from Oare Hill in the west to Westonzoyland in the east, and from Wick St Lawrence in the north to Cothelstone in the south. Sheets 21 and 27 covering the remainder of the west of the county were also published in 1809, with sheet 18 (covering the south-east) in 1811, sheet 19 (Bath and east Somerset) in 1817 and sheet 35 (the area to the south of Bristol) in 1830.

Precisely dating the early states of maps in this series can be undertaken by consulting volume two of *The Old Series Ordnance Survey maps of England and Wales* (Lympne Castle, 1977). For sheet 20, reproduced opposite, early states have the place name 'Sampford Bret' with only one letter 't'. However, the addition of the adjacent sheet number, just above the scale, shows the map reproduced here is state seven and was issued some time after 1823 but before the proposed line of the Bristol and Exeter Railway was added after 1835.

This particular sheet is in a private collection and was cut up and mounted onto linen so it could be folded. Once folded it was placed in a contemporary leather-bound case. The case was designed to be carried and it has a flap which securely covers the map protecting it from damage. When not in use it was kept on a library shelf as it has the word 'BRIDGWATER' tooled on to the spine to identify it from other maps in the series.

Sheet 20 and its protective case, slightly open to reveal the map.
Original size: 230 x 141 x 13mm. Source: David Worthy collection.

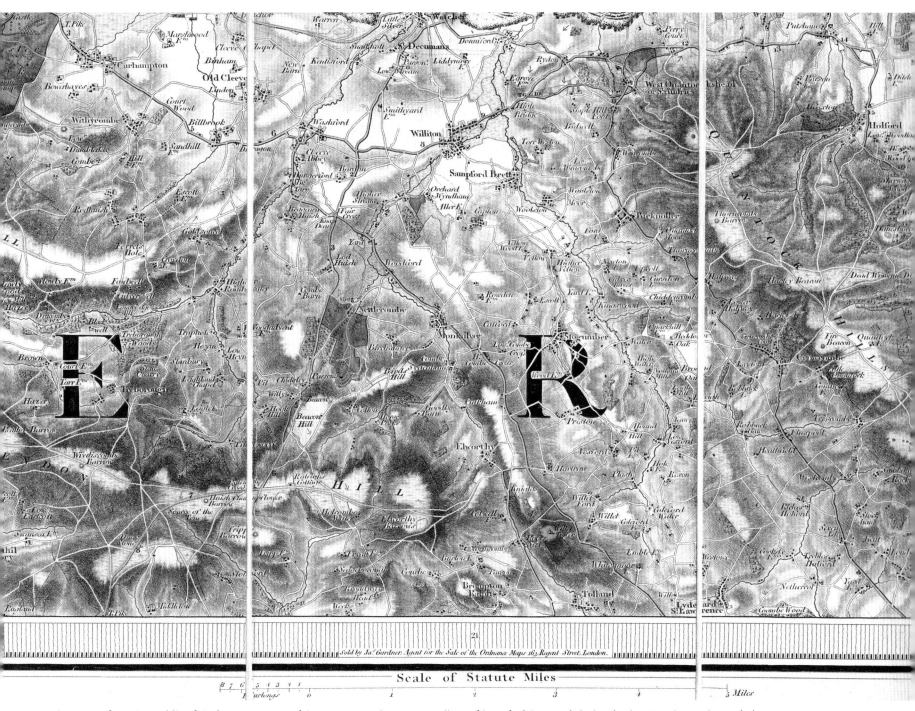

An extract from the middle of the bottom section of sheet 20. Note the correct spelling of Sampford Brett and the hand colouring. Original size: 624 x 935mm.

149

Fossilogical map of the country five miles round Bath
William Smith
1811

William Smith (1769-1839), engineer and mineral surveyor, described as the 'Father of English Geology', produced a ground-breaking map in 1815 known as, *A delineation of the strata of England and Wales, with part of Scotland*. Although the map carries a date of the 1st of August 1815, most of the maps were not issued until after the 2nd of November 1815, when Smith began signing and numbering them. There were 410 subscribers for his 1815 map, although not all subscribers took their copies and some maps went to non-subscribers.

Smith's map revolutionised the way in which people studied geology and is described in Simon Winchester's book as 'The map that changed the World'. At the time it was published the term 'geological map' was only used by a handful of people. The base map was produced by John Cary (*c*.1754-1835), an engraver based in London, and the colour was laboriously added by hand.

However, Smith also produced other maps which, although not as ground-breaking as his geological maps are worthy of inclusion in this volume. He produced a survey of High Littleton in 1793. But four years before Smith's *Delineation* appeared, the Revered Richard Warner (1763–1857), curate of St James's parish, Bath included a fascinating map of the country five miles around the city which he described as a 'Fossilogical Map'. The map accompanied a section in Warner's guide book called 'Fossilogical Phœnomena' and was engraved by William Gingell (d.1820), Engraver of Lyncombe and Widcombe. It shows 12 different types of samples at 51 different locations and shows the Somerset Coal Canal.

Portrait of William Smith, aged 69 (Horace B. Woodward, *The history of the Geological Society of London* (London, 1907)).

Warner included this memoir in his guide book as it was 'not so much for the information of the scientific, as for the gratification of the curious, and the amusement of the idle'. By publishing his 12-page memoir he hoped that 'some taste for that branch of natural history might be created among those numerous visitors and inhabitants of our city who have much time upon their hands, and are, now and then, at a loss in what manner to occupy it'.

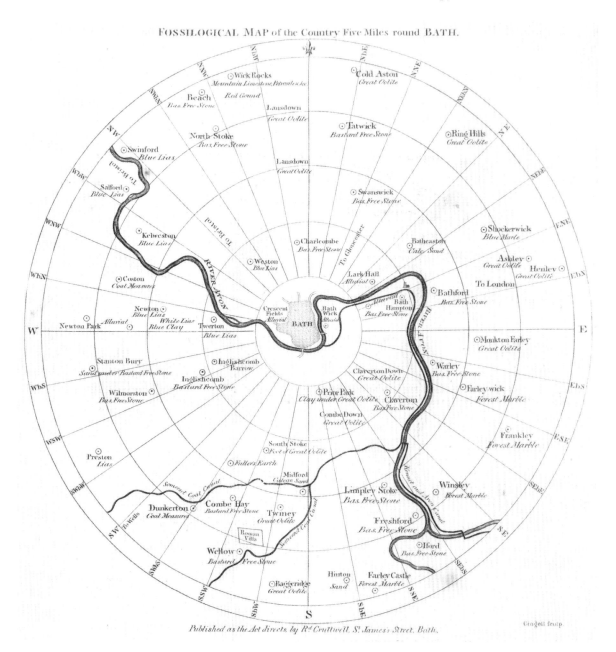

FOSSILOGICAL MAP of the Country Five Miles round BATH.

Published as the Act directs, by R.ᵈ Cruttwell, St. James's Street, Bath.

Gingell sculp

At the very end of the memoir, when discussing coal mining, Warner stated how 'Mr. W. Smith, the celebrated geologist and mechanic, and his able assistant Mr. Hill' had just been engaged by the Batheaston Company. It was hoped that Smith and Hill would be able to increase the company's output and therefore the price of coal in Bath would 'be materially diminished'.

Although the accompanying map is not credited by Warner to Smith, it is generally accepted that it is based on Smith's observations. Smith himself recorded in 1818 that Warner was one of the first five 'scientific gentlemen in the West of England who became acquainted with Smith's view on stratigraphy and fossils'.

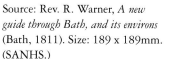

Source: Rev. R. Warner, *A new guide through Bath, and its environs* (Bath, 1811). Size: 189 x 189mm. (SANHS.)

Somersetshire
C. & J. Greenwood
1822

Described by Chubb in his introduction to his *Maps of Somersetshire* as part of a 'magnificent series of county maps', the Greenwoods' map of Somerset is certainly that. Christopher Greenwood (1786-1855) and his brother John (d.1840) were from Yorkshire; Christopher moved to London in 1818. They took advantage of a gap in the market to produce a popular series of more geographically accurate maps than had been available for the scale at which he published them.

By February 1819 Greenwood had acquired 16 subscribers for his Somerset map, including the Marquis of Bath, Earl Waldegrave, and Lord Arundell, as well as those who wanted complete sets of all the counties. This was no small expenditure as Somerset cost £3 3s and a complete set just over £140. It is thought Somerset was surveyed in 1820 and 1821, but surely such a task was impossible to complete in two years. Most of the data is based on the work of the Ordnance Survey, which for Somerset had been published by the time the Greenwoods issued this map in October 1822. The cartographic skill shown in the design and layout of their maps made them highly attractive.

The brothers produced a final work in 1834 called an *Atlas of the counties of England*, which contained less detailed small scale maps, although they were still very attractive. A facsimile of their 1822 *Somersetshire Delineated* and their map was reissued in 1980 and 1981 respectively.

Source: C. & J. Greenwood, *Somersetshire* (London, 1822).
(David Worthy collection.)

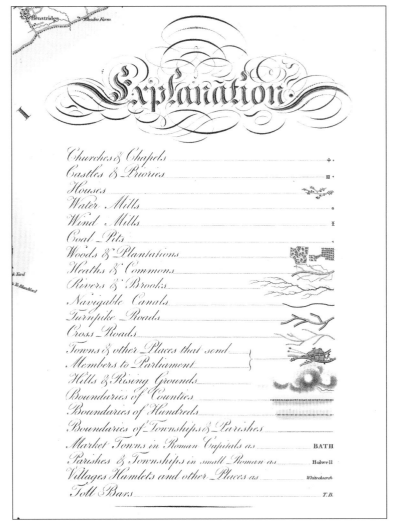

A reproduction of the key or 'Explanation'.

152

VIEW OF WELLS CATHEDRAL.

A reproduction of Wells Cathedral from Greenwoods' map of Somerset.

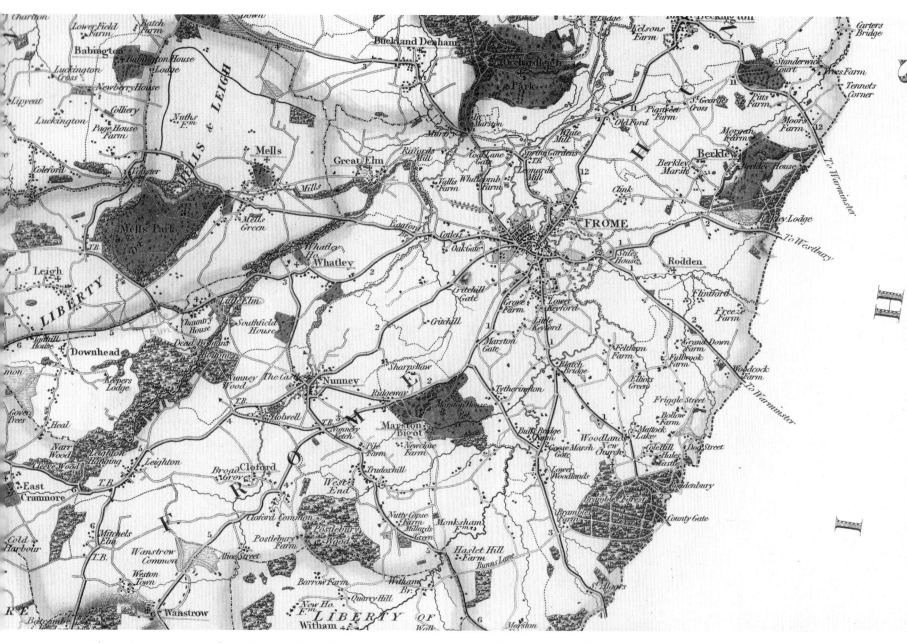

Above: An extract showing part of the Hundred of Frome and the town of that name. Note how all roads lead to Frome, showing how its importance as a cloth producing town had grown up since medieval times.

Opposite: In contrast to the area above, to the east of Bridgwater the Somerset Levels show relatively little urban development and how clearly the landscape is dominated by man-made drainage systems.

154

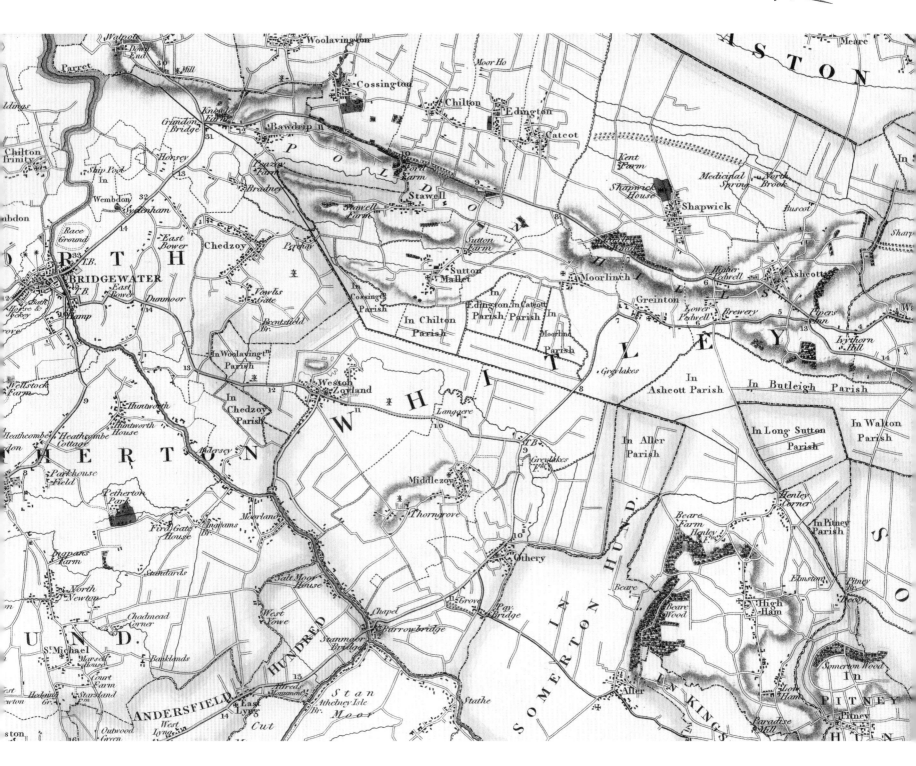

Line of the proposed English and Bristol Channels' ship canal
James Green
1824

The adventurous scheme to build a canal to join the English and Bristol Channels was raised in 1768 but it was not until 1825 that an Act of Parliament was passed for the scheme to go ahead. The route for the scheme was surveyed by James Green (1781-1849) under the supervision of Thomas Telford F.R.S. F.R.S.E (1757-1834) in 1824 and the resulting map is reproduced opposite.

A similar idea had been put forward in 1810 under John Rennie, resulting in the Bristol and Taunton Canal Act of 1811, but neither Telford's 1823 proposal, which Green worked on whilst still involved with the Bude Canal in 1824, nor the 1811 scheme managed to make it to the shores of the Somerset coast. If Telford's scheme been completed new docks and harbours at Stolford and at Beer, in south Devon, would have been needed. The estimated cost of the scheme was £1,712,844 and by 1828 the company announced they had failed in raising the necessary money to get the project off the ground, despite attracting around 600 subscribers.

Green went on to work upon the Grand Western Canal, and the Kidwelly and Llanelly Canal. He acted as a consultant engineer for the Bristol Docks, Newport Docks, and the South Devon Railway. He made a sizeable contribution to civil engineering in the south west of England.

Thomas Telford who supervised James Green's survey of the proposed canal. Telford enlisted Captain George Nicholls, who worked for the Honourable East India Company, to advise on the maritime side of the scheme.
(Ian Coleby collection.)

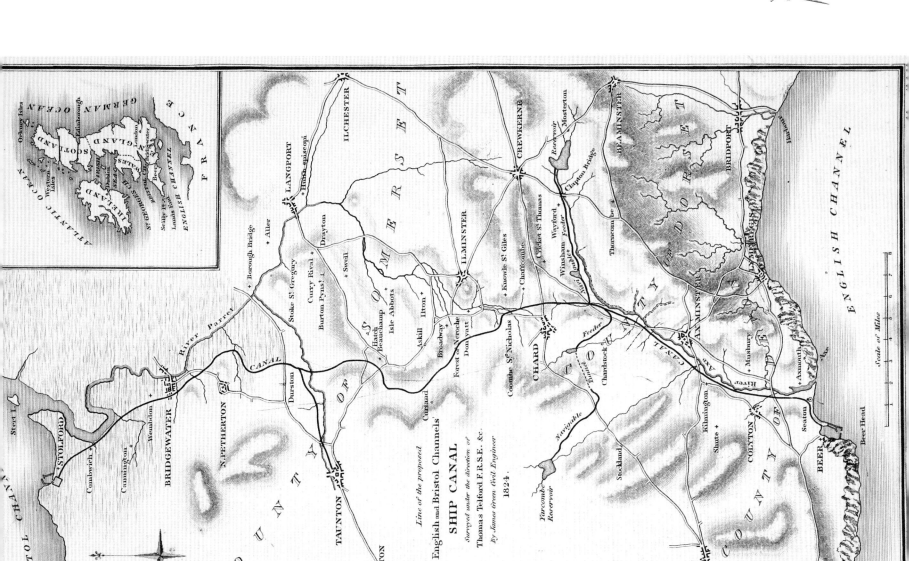

A reproduction of Green's map surveyed under the direction of Thomas Telford, 1824.

Source: SANHS, Tite Collection. Original size: 152 x 263mm.

Map of the north western district of Somersetshire
Samuel Stephens
1829

The map opposite was produced to accompany Appendix A of John Rutter's *Delineations of the north western division of the county of Somerset, and of its antediluvian bone caverns, with a geological sketch of the district* (London, 1829). This appendix is a geological sketch of the district and is classified with ten different types of rock marked on the accompanying map. The map was prepared by S. Stephens, a land surveyor of Shaftesbury, Dorset, and was printed using lithography. Despite this map's title it also includes five types of antiquities.

Rutter's *Delineations*, because of his multi-disciplinary approach to local history, was a landmark volume. His interest was much wider than other antiquarians. He wrote about many subjects including architecture, geology, archaeology, paleontology, the landscape, memorials, fonts, Roman roads and ecclesiastical antiquities. He used primary sources, such as the churchwardens' accounts of Banwell, suggesting that the copies made by George Bennett of Rolston 'would form a most interesting antiquarian publication' if only he could find enough subscribers willing to pay 5 shillings each.

Rutter's volume is relatively well illustrated. Many of the larger illustrations were based on the drawings of J.C. Buckler and the vignettes were supplied by William Barnes of Chantry House, Mere. Rutter was a Shaftesbury printer and publisher of *The Shastonian*, who also wrote a history of Shaftesbury and of Dorsetshire. The mapmaker Stephens had moved to Southampton by 1837.

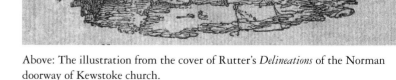

Above: The illustration from the cover of Rutter's *Delineations* of the Norman doorway of Kewstoke church.

Source: John Rutter's *Delineations of the north western division of the county of Somerset, and of its antediluvian bone caverns, with a geological sketch of the district* (London, 1829), plate 12. Original size: 253 x 176mm.

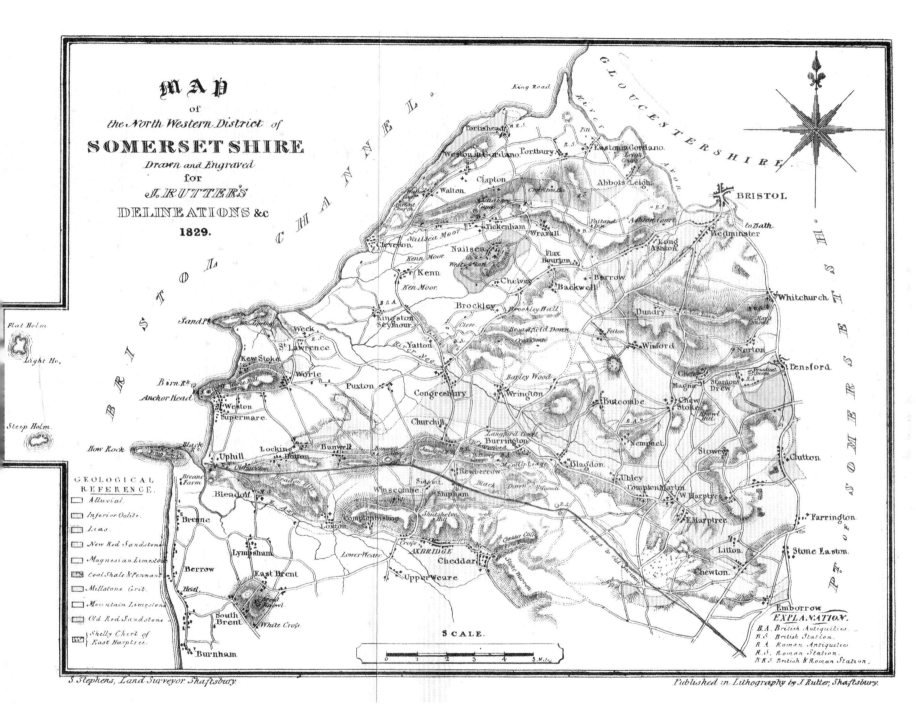

MAP

of

the North Western District of

SOMERSETSHIRE

Drawn and Engraved

for

J. RUTTER'S

DELINEATIONS &c

1829.

GEOLOGICAL REFERENCE.

Alluvial.
Inferior Oolite.
Lias.
New Red Sandstone.
Magnesian Limestone.
Coal Shale & Pennant.
Millstone Grit.
Mountain Limestone.
Old Red Sandstone.
Shelly Chert of East Harptree.

SCALE.

EXPLANATION.
B.A. British Antiquities.
B.S. British Station.
R.A. Roman Antiquities.
R.S. Roman Station.
B.R.S. British & Roman Station.

S. Stephens, Land Surveyor Shaftsbury.

Published in Lithography by J. Rutter, Shaftsbury.

County of Somerset Showing the sub-divisions for Petty Sessions, as arranged by the Quarter Sessions in 1829
G.T.S.
1834

This map of the county of Somerset is unusual and ground-breaking for two reasons. The first is because of its thematic content, and the second is its statistical content. It was printed not from the traditional copper plate but by lithography.

The thematic and statistical content arose due to the escalating cost of county rates. Reducing the cost was a cause championed by Sir John Lethbridge of Sandhill Park. In December 1833, at the Quarter Sessions for the county, Lethbridge presented a table of county rates from 1762 when the figure was only £1,077 to 1832 when the figure had risen to £22,226. He proposed that a petition, signed by all the magistrates, should be presented to both Houses of Parliament, 'complaining of the great burden laid on the Proprietors of Land and Houses, in their having to defray the present enormous expenses of the County-Rate'. At the same Sessions a committee of 12 magistrates was appointed to consider how the rate could be reduced 'to divide the county for judicial as well as political purposes'. The map opposite was the cartographic result of the committee's findings, carrying the lengthy title of 'County of Somerset Showing the sub-divisions for Petty Sessions, as arranged by the Quarter Sessions in 1829 – also the population, the number of committals, and the number of prisoners for trial, in 1831, and the proportion paid to the County Rate, by each sub-division, when the sum of £542.18.7¾ is to be raised'.

Not only does this map carry information on county rates, but it shows prisons, the political boundary of east and west Somerset, places where courts of Petty and Quarter Sessions were held, the number of cases brought before those courts and the number

committed, how much it cost to commit prisoners and the cost of transporting them, along with distances travelled, as well as population figures for the county, all arranged by hundreds. This was the first time such a mass of information had been brought together and portrayed in cartographic form.

But who was 'G.T.S.' the author of this map? Captain George Treweeke Scobell R.N. (1785-1869) of Kingwell near Hallatrow, a J.P. who attended Quarter Sessions in the 1830s. As a naval officer he would have had experience of map making. The lithographer, Joseph Hollway of 10 Union Street, Bath, who produced the map, also lithographed illustrations for sale catalogues, as well as maps for part of the estate sold 'by the direction of the trustees acting under the will of the late Sir John Palmer Acland, Bart.' in 1824. Hollway, who was also described as an engraver, produced scenes of Bath for the local and tourist market.

But why was this map printed from the relatively new technology of transfering the image from stone to paper and not from copper to paper? Lithography was known to be cheaper than copper plate printing, so as this map came into being thanks to the desire by a group of magistrates who wanted to save money, was this also a money-saving exercise? Unfortunately the standard of some lithographic work at this time lacked the quality of the work that had been produced by generations of copper engravers. This work is no exception.

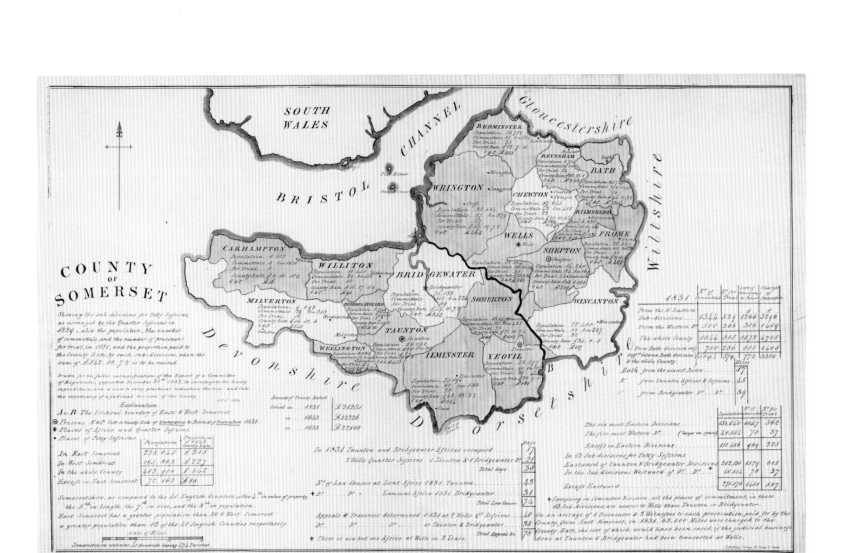

A reduced reproduction of the map by 'G.T.S.'.

Source: Adrian Webb collection. Original size: 462 x 278mm.

Tithe Commutation maps
1836

To replace the centuries old payment to the church of one tenth of a landowner's or tenant's produce, the Tithe Commutation Act of 1836 converted the levy into a payment. One consequence was the creation of very detailed parish maps which, along with their apportionments, have proved invaluable as a resource for historians. The Act put into place a national survey of land holdings which resulted in the production of a detailed map for almost every parish. There were 501 tithe districts in Somerset resulting in 482 maps of which 40 were printed. Most apportionments were written by hand but 19 were printed. There were 11 districts apportioned by holding rather than field, 252 maps give the name of the mapmaker or surveyor, drawn at one of four different scales. These maps were highly functional and mostly lack decoration as only five have cartouches.

When the 1836 Act was amended in the following year, a provision was inserted to the effect that, while every tithe map should be signed by the Tithe Commissioners, a map or plan should not be deemed evidence of the quantity of the land, or treated as accurate, unless it was sealed as well as signed. The official process of such map-making continued in Somerset into the mid 1850s.

There were some exceptions to the common notion that each parish had a new map detailing every parcel of land. Because local landowners were responsible for paying for the surveys, some parishes recycled existing maps. For example, the parish version of Aisholt's tithe map is dated 1833, Crowcombe's was surveyed in 1806 but updated in 1842 and Queen Charlton's was 'copied from a plan and survey taken by John Hinde AD 1760 by J P Sturge and son, Bristol, 1848'. Other tithe maps simply showed very little

detail as the whole parish was owned by one person, an example of which is the tithe map for Orchard Portman prepared by George Parsons, valuer, in 1837. One of the most attractive tithe maps in the county is that for the parish of Dunster, completed in 1842. Included on the map is an inset of the heart of the village, drawn at a scale of three chains to one inch and shown within an oval. Also shown is the historic castle, with the hill on which it sits shown in great detail. A copy was made by Robert Page, Assistant Tithe Commissioner, on the 2nd of May 1843.

A view of Dunster village drawn by John Buckler and published in 1830 (J. Savage, *History of the Hundred of Carhampton* (Bristol, 1830)).

Source: SHC, D/D/rt/m/397.

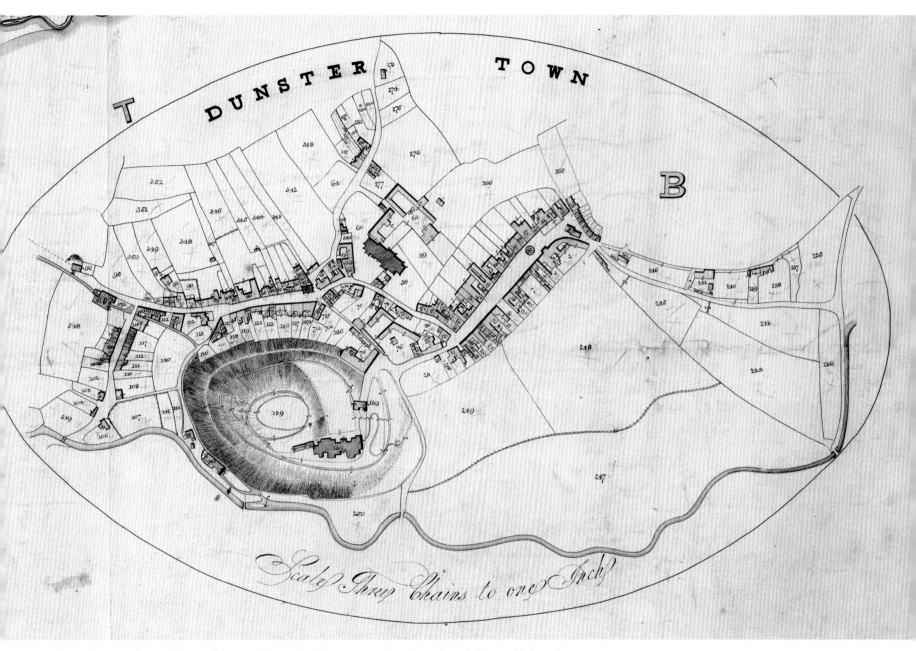

A reproduction of part of the much larger tithe map for Dunster, showing the castle and village with boundaries, water features, buildings, roads and paths depicted in great detail. (SHC.)

Wallis's picturesque round game of the produce and manufactures of the counties of England and Wales
Edward Wallis
c.1840

Edward Wallis, the manufacturer of the *Picturesque round game of the produce and manufactures of the counties of England and Wales*, reproduced to the right, operated from premises at 42 Skinner Street, Snow Hill, London between 1811 and 1844. He produced a great number of educational games, as well as dabbling in other lines of business, such as book publishing.

When it came to the Somerset section of the game (opposite) Wallis picked six geographical locations. Number 106 represented Bath where if the player landed there he would 'draw again'. 107 is Bristol, which he deemed was in Gloucestershire. 108 he called 'Clifton Bridge' being 'a magnificent structure, across St Vincent's Rocks, beneath which flows the Avon', building of which started in 1829. 109 marked the River Severn, 110 is Glastonbury which he noted as once having the 'grandest abbey in all England. The kitchen still remains'. 111 is the Mendip Hills, which he drew to resemble the Alps and described as 'A chain of limestone hills, rich in mineral treasures, and having several caverns, where bones of Tigers, Buffaloes, Hyenas, Wolves, and Bears, have been found'. 112 took the game player to Salisbury (in neighbouring Wiltshire) with the last remaining number in Somerset being 113 for Bridgwater, which he described as 'a town of great trade'. The depiction of Bridgwater as an industrial hub within the county portrays it as a centre of commerce. As the county's main port Wallis managed to show the River Parrett connecting it to the Bristol Channel.

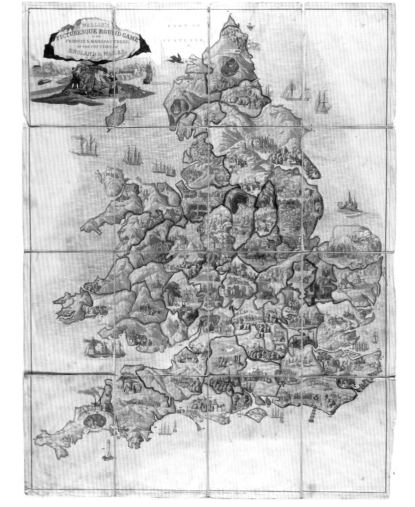

A reduced reproduction of a *Picturesque round game of the produce and manufactures of the counties of England and Wales*.

Source: Private collection. Original size: 495 x 650mm.

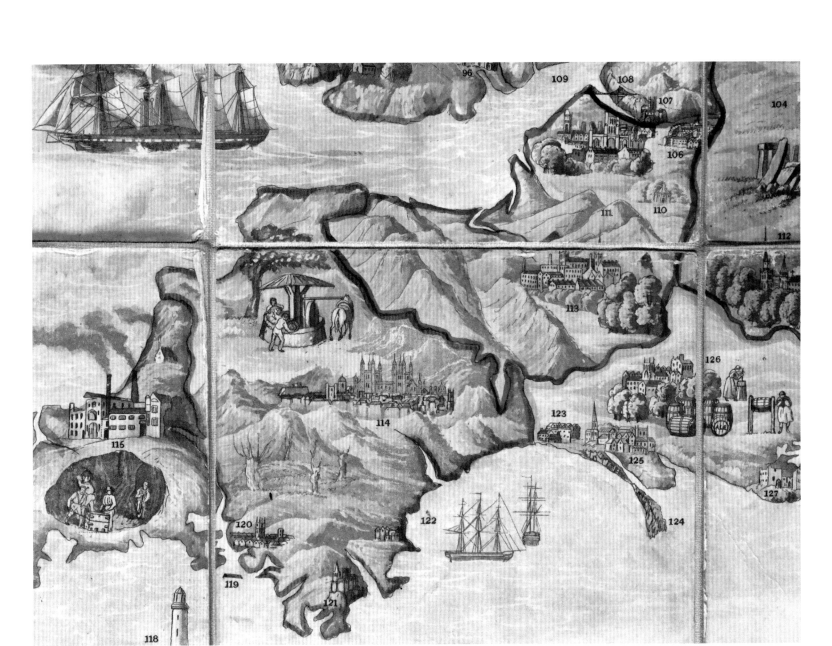

This section covering the South West of England, with west Somerset shown as an area of hills of no interest to game players, unlike Glastonbury and Bridgwater. Note how the map was mounted in sections onto linen so it could be folded away.

Map of the meets of Mr. Tudway's Hounds
1842

The Mendip Hunt was started as a private pack around the middle of the eighteenth century, and known as the Wells Subscription Harriers. Mr Tudway, who succeeded Mr Hall in 1837, was a wealthy landowner who, in 1842, was described as a 'good sportsman, and very popular as a master of hounds'. His huntsman was Joseph Mitchell, who was 'quiet and clever at his work', and Henry Jackson was whip. The hunt took place three times a week, for example in October 1842, it met on a Saturday at Hardington Pillars, on the following Tuesday at the kennels and on the Thursday at Hedgestocks Gate.

To mark the hunt's activities a map was published in *The Sporting Review* on 1st May 1842, for the proprietor by I. Mitchell, 33 Bond Street. *The Sporting Review* was a magazine popular with the field sports fraternity. It included a number of maps showing the areas covered by hunts, some with added vignettes, though the majority were fairly plain. The names of the meets are shown by the use of a St Andrew's cross, next to which is a number. The number signifies the number of miles from the kennels at Wallcombe, to the north of Wells, where the hounds were based. Such was the popularity of hunting that in the year the map was published Millard's Hill House, near Witham Friary, was offered for sale as being 'especially inviting to those whose inclinations may be diverted to the Sports of the Field, as it is abundant in Game, and regularly hunted by Mr. Tudway's Fox Hounds.'

List of Mr. Tudway's Meets, and their distances from the kennel:—

	Distance from kennel.		Distance from kennel.
Butleigh Wooton	9	Hardway	16
Butleigh Hillcross	11	Hardington Pillars	16
Bunn's Lane	18	High Ham	14
Camerton Court	14	Houndstreet Park	15
Chewton Gate	7	Hick's Park	15
Charlton Mackrel	14	Kingston Turnpike	15
Chilcompton	8	Leighton	12
Cheddar	8	Lottisham Green	8
Charlton Musgrove	17	Long Cross	8
Cross Keys, Lydford	12	Leigh upon Mendip	10
Clutton	12	Mell's Park	12
Cranmore Gate	9	Marden Bradley	20
Cucklington	19	Masbury Castle	4
Downhead	9	Nettlebridge	8
Evererench	9	Old Down	6
Farrington Gurney	9	Pennard House	7
Forefoot Inn	10	Postlebury	14
Gear Hill	18		

Fixtures in the country hunted by Mr. Tudway:—

Alfred's Tower	18	Slab House	4
Alford	14	Stourton Inn	20
Babington	13	Somerton Gate	15
Babcomb Lodge	11	Stratton on the Top	9
Beacon	6	Stoke Lane	8
Berkeley Lodge	18	Tadhill House	9
Brewham Common	15	Trudox Hill	14
Buckland Down	15	Tucker's Grave Gate	16
Radstock	12	Vobster	11
Redlynch Gate	14	Wanstrow	12
Rodney Stoke	4	Witham Friary	14
Stavordale	16	White Post, Norton Down	9
Soho Gate	11	Yarnfield Gate	17

Above: A list of the places visited by Mr Tudway and his hounds which was printed to accompany the map. Mr Tudway provided the information contained in the map.

Opposite: *A reproduction of a Map of the meets of Mr. Tudway's Hounds.*

Source: J.W. Carleton, ed, *The Sporting Review* (London, 1842). Original size (limit of information): 114 x 196mm.

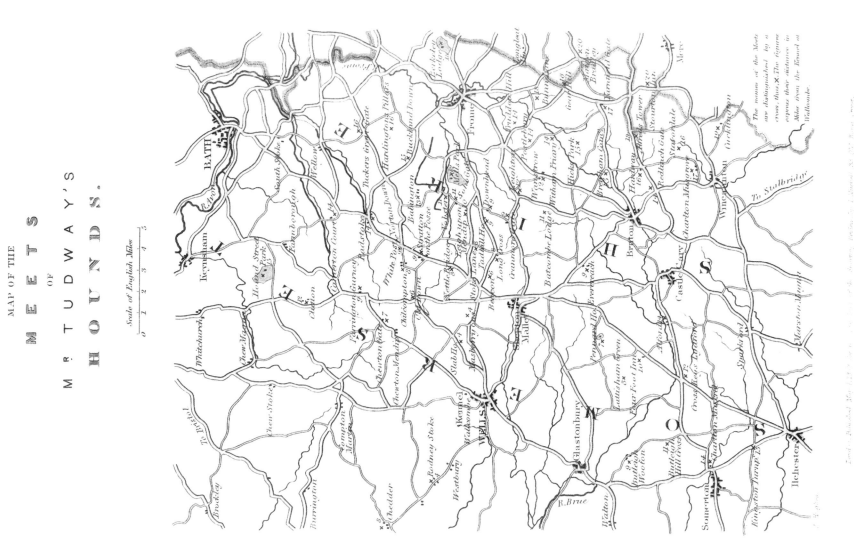

MAP OF THE

M E E T S

OF

M R TUDWAY'S

H O U N D S.

Scale of English Miles
0 1 2 3 4 5

Outline of the geology of Somersetshire
Thomas Dyke Acland, junior, and William Sturge
1851

Thomas Dyke Acland, junior, F.R.S. (1809-1898) and William Sturge (1820-1905), before being joint authors of *The farming of Somersetshire*, were, in fact, competitors. In a competition for £50 offered by the Royal Agricultural Society, both men entered rival reports, with Acland coming out on top. The winning report was subsequently printed in volume eleven part two of the *Journal of the Royal Agricultural Society*.

The two men came from very different backgrounds. Acland was the son of Sir Thomas Dyke Acland, 10th Baronet, and his wife Lydia Elizabeth Hoare, daughter of Henry Hoare, a partner in the banking firm. Educated at Harrow and Christ Church, Oxford, he was friends with William Ewart Gladstone and Lord Elgin, among others. He was a major in the Royal Devonshire Yeomanry Cavalry and in 1839 he was made a Fellow of the Royal Society. In 1837, he entered Parliament for West Somerset as a Tory but did not stand in the 1847 election, and remained out of the House of Commons for nearly twenty years.

Sturge was from a Quaker family, the son of Jacob Player Sturge of Bristol, a surveyor by profession. He worked in the family firm from the age of 14 and was involved making parish surveys under the Tithe Commutation Act of 1836. His surveying expertise led to his involvement with the enclosure of commons, the purchase of land for railways and waterworks, and his appointment to the office of Land Steward to the Corporation of Bristol in 1857. He took a leading role in the formation of the Surveyors' Institution in 1868, serving the office of president in 1878 and 1879. He also gave evidence to the Royal Commission on Agriculture.

(continued over)

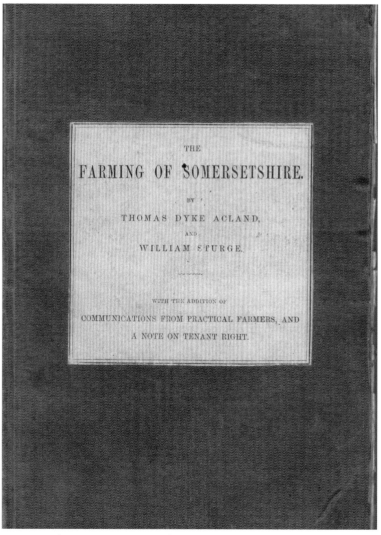

The cover of Acland and Sturge's *The farming of Somersetshire*, with the original paste down label and green cloth binding. (Adrian Webb collection.)

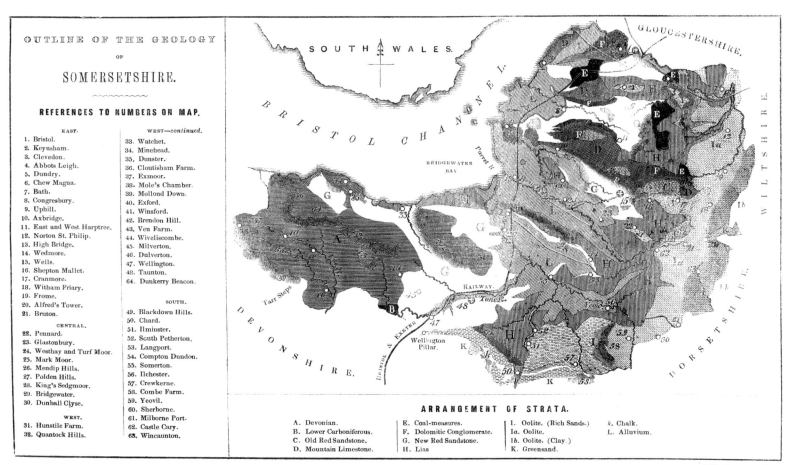

OUTLINE OF THE GEOLOGY
OF
SOMERSETSHIRE.

REFERENCES TO NUMBERS ON MAP.

EAST.

1. Bristol.
2. Keynsham.
3. Clevedon.
4. Abbots Leigh.
5. Dundry.
6. Chew Magna.
7. Bath.
8. Congresbury.
9. Uphill.
10. Axbridge.
11. East and West Harptree.
12. Norton St. Philip.
13. High Bridge.
14. Wedmore.
15. Wells.
16. Shepton Mallet.
17. Cranmore.
18. Witham Friary.
19. Frome.
20. Alfred's Tower.
21. Bruton.

CENTRAL.

22. Pennard.
23. Glastonbury.
24. Westhay and Turf Moor.
25. Mark Moor.
26. Mendip Hills.
27. Polden Hills.
28. King's Sedgmoor.
29. Bridgewater.
30. Dunball Clyse.

WEST.

31. Hunstile Farm.
32. Quantock Hills.

WEST—continued.

33. Watchet.
34. Minehead.
35. Dunster.
36. Cloutisham Farm.
37. Exmoor.
38. Mole's Chamber.
39. Mollond Down.
40. Exford.
41. Winsford.
42. Brendon Hill.
43. Ven Farm.
44. Wiveliscombe.
45. Milverton.
46. Dulverton.
47. Wellington.
48. Taunton.
64. Dunkerry Beacon.

SOUTH.

49. Blackdown Hills.
50. Chard.
51. Ilminster.
52. South Petherton.
53. Langport.
54. Compton Dundon.
55. Somerton.
56. Ilchester.
57. Crewkerne.
58. Combe Farm.
59. Yeovil.
60. Sherborne.
61. Milborne Port.
62. Castle Cary.
63. Wincaunton.

ARRANGEMENT OF STRATA.

A. Devonian.
B. Lower Carboniferous.
C. Old Red Sandstone.
D. Mountain Limestone.
E. Coal-measures.
F. Dolomitic Conglomerate.
G. New Red Sandstone.
H. Lias.
I. Oolite. (Rich Sands.)
Ia. Oolite.
Ib. Oolite. (Clay.)
K. Greensand.
k. Chalk.
L. Alluvium.

[To face page 1.

A reproduction of Acland and Sturge's map of the *Outline of the geology of Somersetshire*. Note how the map also includes the route of the Bristol and Exeter Railway and the 'Wellington Pillar', or as it is known today the Wellington Monument. Size: 198 x 110mm.

(*continued*)

Sturge was able to draw upon his greater knowledge of the east of the county for his report. Subsequently Acland found his report lacking much of what Sturge had found. Acland also drew upon articles published in the *Somerset County Gazette* by a tenant farmer, as well as materials prepared by Mr Gabriel Poole, a farming solicitor of Bridgwater, who was actively involved with the Somersetshire Archaeological and Natural History Society and the British Archaeological Association.

It was Acland's hope that by publishing the two reports together they would 'do more good together than either could do singly'. The authors also took the opportunity to point out areas of agricultural management needing improvement in the county, including:

> marsh and peat moors, to the expediency of breaking up inferior grass-lands, to the need of enlarging enclosures, and of providing better accommodation for cattle . . . security to tenants able and willing to invest capital in durable improvements.

Sturge continued his interest in agriculture right up until the year before his death when he wrote a pamphlet on the proposals for the taxation of land values. He died a very wealthy man with an estate valued at £153,019 19s net.

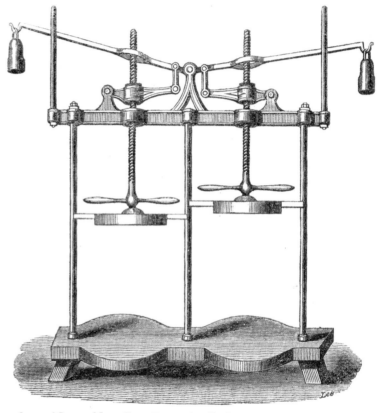

Improved Screw and Lever Cheese Press, used on Mr. Yeoman's Dairy Farm. *See page 54.*

Above: The illustration facing the title page of Sturge's report.

Opposite: A reproduction of the *Physical map of Somersetshire*, 1851.

Source: T.D. Acland and W. Sturge, *The farming of Somersetshire* (London, 1851). Original size: 198 x 110mm.

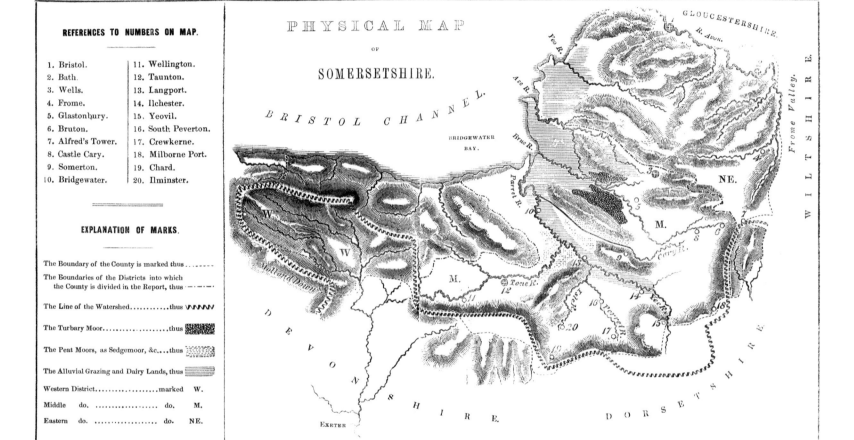

Map shewing the Langport, Somerton and Castle Cary turnpike roads
Anonymous
1857

The Langport, Somerton and Castle Cary Turnpike Trust was created in 1753. Its jurisdiction stretched from Castle Cary in the east across to the west of Langport, and from Street down to Somerton. In 1848 the Trust reported that it managed just over 70 miles of roads. By 1857, when the map opposite was produced, the debts accrued by the Trust were £17,590. This figure was lower than it had been as, in 1844, the Trust used its own surveyor to supervise the never-ending task of repairing roads. The surveyor invented a scraping machine and took out a patent on the invention saving the Trust several hundred pounds each year. The savings were used to pay off some of its debts.

A map was prepared in the year a detailed report was sent to the Secretary of State, Sir George Grey (1799-1882), asking for his support. Grey declined to interfere. A section of the map is reproduced opposite, showing the extent of the roads managed by the Trust, which are a combination of thick and thin lines.

The map was printed by John Waterlow & Sons. This company had printed lithographic copies of legal documents at Birchin Lane in London since 1810, and later began printing banknotes, postage stamps, traveller's checks, Treasury bills and bonds.

———— ∞ ————

Opposite: A reproduction of a section of the map showing the turnpike road from Chedzoy gate (in the top left corner) to the turnpike gate at Long Sutton (in the bottom right corner).

Source: SANHS, Tite Collection. Original size: 533 x 414mm.

Above: This roadside feature was recorded on the parish boundary of Kingsdon and Somerton in 1984 as part of the Somerset Roads Project. Historically it was along the route of the Langport, Somerton and Castle Cary Trust from Langport Bridge through Othery to Cobb Door. The road was turnpiked throughout under an Act of 1792. Although the stone may be original, the plate appears to be a replacement fixed before the trust wound up in 1879. (Brian Murless collection)

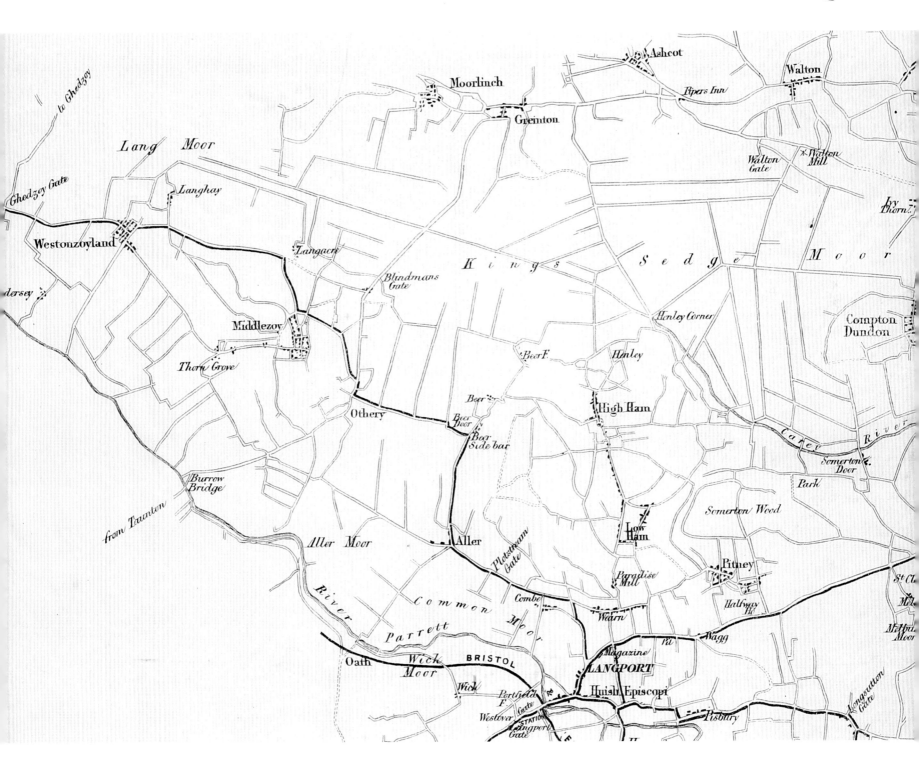

Great Western Railway &c. Sheet 3 Bristol to Exeter & Plymouth
Edward Weller F.R.G.S.
1863

To show the length of the Great Western Railway from Bristol to Plymouth on one sheet of an atlas in any detail was challenging, but Edward Weller F.R.G.S. (1819-1884) accomplished this challenge by creating four panels on his sheet. The first panel covered Bristol to Taunton, the next Taunton to Exeter, then Exeter to Plymouth, with a fourth showing the Yeovil branch line.

Weller was an engraver and cartographer. He produced maps for educational purposes and since 1856 he had been issuing them in the *Weekly Dispatch*. He gathered the maps together and issued them in atlas format in the *Weekly Dispatch Atlas*, with each map bearing the distinctive sign of a half globe with the figure of winged Mercury. The atlas was published in London in 1863 by Day & Son. Weller was a prolific cartographer who contributed maps to at least ten atlases.

Weller's *Dispatch Atlas* logo and winged Mercury.

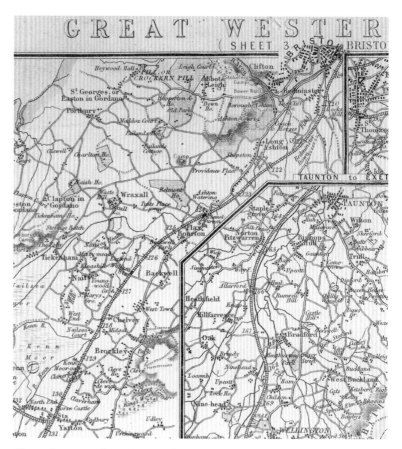

Above: An extract from the top of the map showing Bristol and the start of the mapping of the railway on this sheet. Underneath Bristol can be seen the panel where the railway ran from Taunton to Exeter and was included in one panel. (Adrian Webb collection.)

Source: E. Weller, *Weekly Dispatch Atlas* (London, 1863).
Original size: 312 x 456mm.

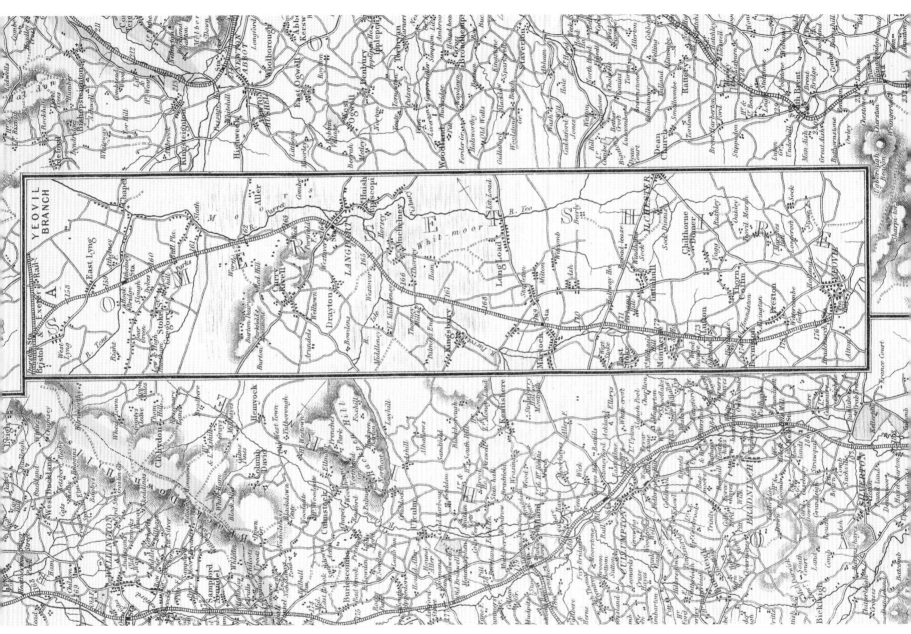

A reproduction of the middle section of the map showing the Yeovil branch line which left the main Bristol to Taunton line at Durston.
(Adrian Webb collection.)

Cruchley's reduced Ordnance map, Sheet 17
George Frederick Cruchley
1862, or later

George Frederick Cruchley (1797-1880) served his apprenticeship at the well known map-making firm of Arrowsmith. He set up his own business in the early 1820s. Like the Greenwoods he based his maps on those of the Ordnance Survey. The section reproduced opposite shows the Watchet to Minehead Railway that was opened in 1874 as an extension to the Taunton to Watchet line, which itself opened in 1862. Crutchley's Ordnance map, based on the Ordnance Survey maps, was issued some time between those two dates. In direct competition to the Ordnance Survey, Cruchley advertised his maps as being 'Half the scale and half the price of the Ordnance Map of England'.

His series of maps were issued at two miles to an inch and 65 sheets covered all of England, Wales and as far north as Perth. Those he produced for the county of Somerset were contained on five sheets, numbers 10, 11, 16, 17 and 18, the limits of which are shown below.

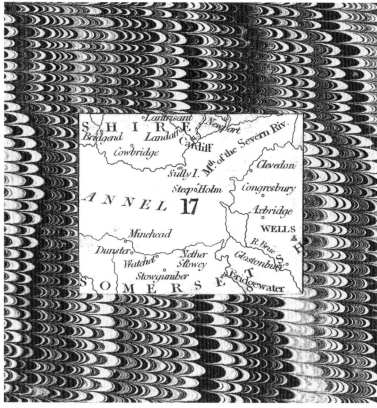

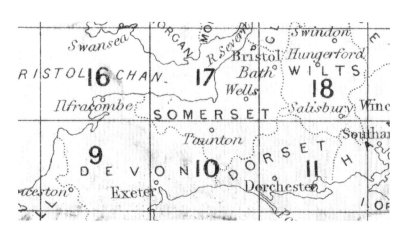

Above: Pasted on the inside cover is a small scale map of the area covered by the Ordnance map. Opposite: An extract showing the area of the West Somerset Railway.

Opposite: An extract from Cruchley's reduced Ordnance map. (Adrian Webb collection.)

Source: Cruchley's *Reduced Ordnance map*, Sheet 17. Original size divided into sections and mounted on linen: 659 x 503mm.

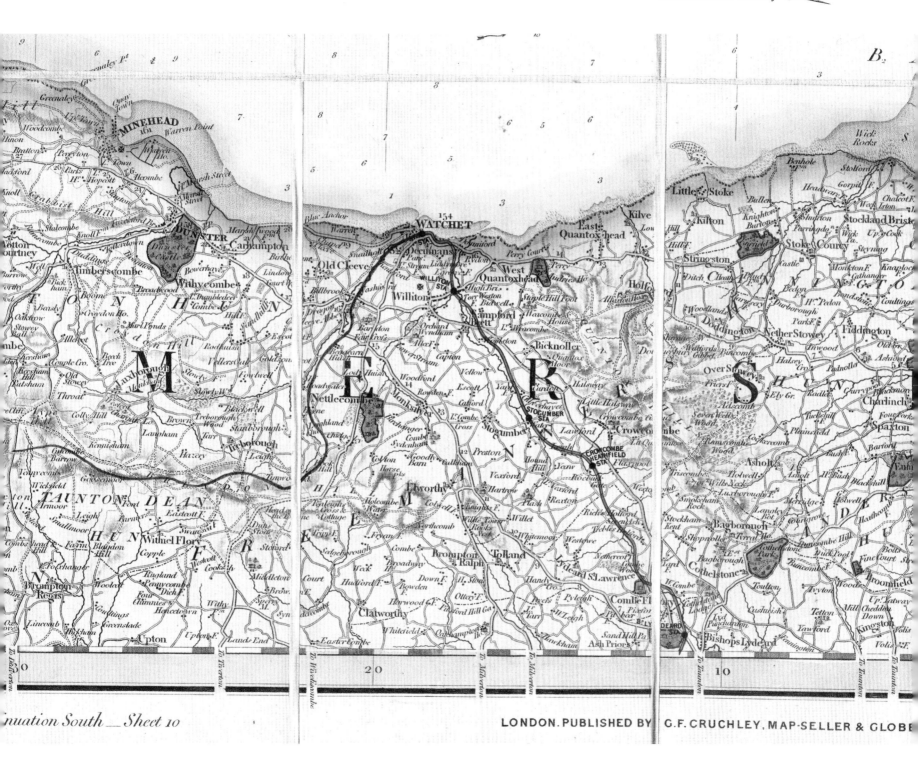

Somersetshire new divisions of county
Colonel Henry James
1868

The Second Reform Act, passed in 1867, granted the vote to all householders in the boroughs as well as lodgers who paid rent of £10 a year or more. At the same time it reduced the property threshold in the counties and gave the vote to agricultural landowners and tenants with very small amounts of land. Men in urban areas who met the property qualification were enfranchised and the Act roughly doubled the electorate in England and Wales from one to two million men.

In Somerset the Act brought about significant boundary changes, which came into effect at the 1868 general election. The major change was the introduction of a third county constituency. The southern end of East Somerset (including Glastonbury, Radstock, Shepton Mallet and Somerton as well as the area round Frome and Wells) was moved into the new Mid Somerset division. The revised East Somerset constituency was now defined as consisting of the Long Ashton, Axbridge, Keynsham, Temple Cloud and Weston Petty Sessional Divisions.

The temporary boundaries (shown in blue) of 1867 were different from the proposed boundaries of 1868. The extract printed opposite shows the change in east Somerset, where the areas around Frome, Mells and Kilmersdon became part of the East Division. The three divisions were East, West and Mid with Bath, Taunton and Wells being selected for the locations of the elections. For the West Division William Gore-Langton and the Hon. Arthur Hood were elected, for the East Division Ralph Shuttleworth Allen and Richard Bright and for the Mid Division Richard Horner Paget and Ralph Neville Grenville.

The map showing the new divisions, reproduced opposite, was published at a scale of four miles to one inch and zincographed at the Ordnance Survey Office, Southampton, under the super-intendence of Captain R.M. Parsons R.E. F.R.A.S. and Colonel Sir H. James R.E. F.R.S. Director of the Ordnance Survey. In each of the county maps the signature of Colonel James was reproduced, which appears above. The colours were overprinted on the map after the black line work had been printed.

The underlying information shown in black was generalised from existing Ordnance Survey mapping. No resurveying was involved in this map-making exercise.

Source: *Report of the Boundary Commissioners for England and Wales* (London, 1868). Original size: 483 x 330mm.

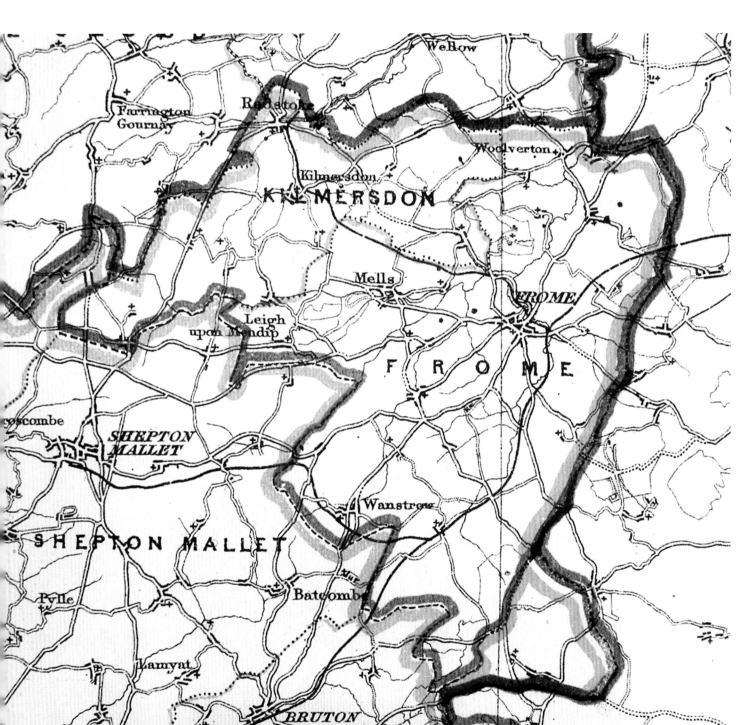

An extract from the map of the east side of the county showing the boundaries of the proposed parliamentary divisions of 1868 in red. The temporary boundaries proposed in the 1867 Act are shown in blue, the proposed sessional boundaries are shown in yellow and the proposed and temporary places of election in 1867 and 1868 are shown as red circles. (SANHS.)

Ordnance Survey
1880s

The six inch to the mile survey of the county of Somerset was the most detailed mapping of the county since the tithe surveys of the 1830s. The six inch mapping of England and Wales was prompted by the same mapping of Ireland, completed by 1846 and undertaken for land tax purposes. Prior to this, warfare, and the need for military intelligence, was often the catalyst for carrying out survey work.

In 1841 work began on the six inch survey in Lancashire, but progress was slow owing to the large amount of urban surveying required. By 1851 only a handful of counties had been completed, leading to debate as to the best scale to use. Eventually the 1:2500, or 25 inch, was adopted to replace the six inch scale. This was not due to popularity, but external influence. It was recommended by an International Statistical Conference held in Brussels in 1853 and was being used for mapping throughout Europe. Social factors also played a key part in defining the 25 inch map as the standard map scale. As towns grew rapidly and transport networks developed, large scale maps were needed to plan new industrial areas, urban development and railways.

The 1:2500 scale surveying began in the county of Durham in 1853, however it was not until the late 1850s that a model for mapping was finally agreed upon. Cultivated and settled areas were mapped at 1:2500, urban areas consisting of more than 4,000 people were mapped at 1:500, and unpopulated mountainous or moorland areas were mapped at a scale of six inches to one mile. The tithe maps are often considered the parent of the 1:2500 maps, which is why up until the 1870s the 25 inch maps were published

by parish and were often accompanied by a 'book of reference', giving information on the acreage of each piece of land and details on its use. After 1879 this information was included on the map, as shown on the example opposite.

Mapping in Somerset at a scale of 1:2500 did not begin until 1882. It showed great detail, including the names of roads and farms, as well as features such as orchards and public boundaries. Watercourses including rivers and streams were shown, along with fords and weirs as detailed on the map opposite. Public buildings were also named such as congregational chapels, and some maps even showed signal boxes and mills.

The Somerset 1:2500 map series went through a number of revisions throughout the twentieth century, including some revision of urban areas during the Second World War. Many maps used during the twentieth century for military purposes were derived from the six inch and 25 inch maps, including the 1:20,000 map used during the First World War and the 1:25,000 maps used during World War Two; the latter scale was later used for the modern Pathfinder and Explorer maps.

Opposite: An extract from a composite 25" Ordnance Survey map of sheet 79, parts of section 3 and 6. The map is made up of sheets which have been cut up and pasted together to form a non-standard size. (Adrian Webb collection.)

Source: SHC, DD/X/WBB/162, *c.*1886.

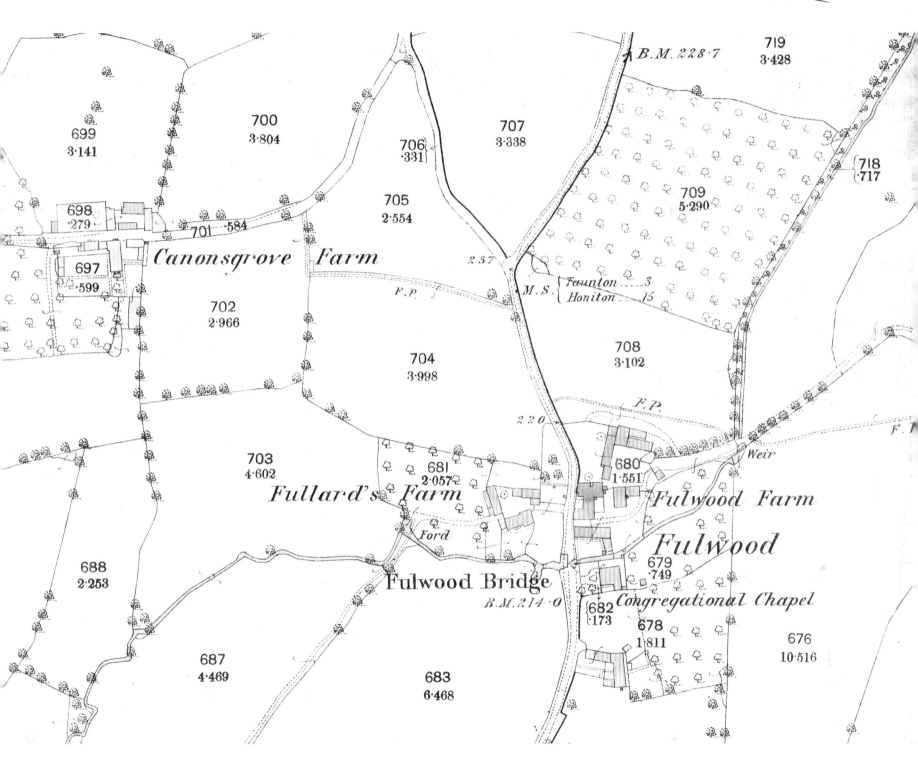

Geological map of the area between the Quantocks and the Mendips
W.A.E. Ussher
1891

William Augustus Edmond Ussher (1849-1920), was an officer of the Geological Survey and wrote extensively on geological matters. He spent much of his career working in South-West England and is best known for establishing the stratigraphical succession in the Devonian, Carboniferous and Permo-Triassic rocks of Devon and Cornwall. However, he had eight papers on Somerset subjects published by the Somersetshire Archaeological and Natural History Society over a 35 year period between 1880 and 1915.

His Somerset subjects included: the geology of West Somerset; geological features of Porlock valley; Triassic and Devonian rocks of West Somerset; Poole brickworks; British culm measures; Devonian, carboniferous and new red rocks; and a geological sketch of Brean Down. His 48-page paper relating to coal deposits 'on the probable nature and distribution of the palaeozoic strata beneath the secondary, etc., rocks of the southern counties, with special reference to the prospects of obtaining coal by boring south of the Mendips', published in 1891 contained two maps. His *Geological map of the area between the Quantocks and the Mendips* from that paper is reproduced opposite.

To commemorate Ussher's achievements The Ussher Society was founded in 1962 to promote the study of geology and geomorphology in South West England.

Opposite: Ussher's geological map.

Source: W.A.E. Ussher 'On the probable nature and distribution of the palaeozoic strata . . .' in the *Proceedings of the Somersetshire Archaeological and Natural History Society*, 36 (1891), 88-136. Original size (to the black border): 202 x 134mm.

Above: A photograph of W.A.E. Ussher.
(© Natural Environment Research Council.)

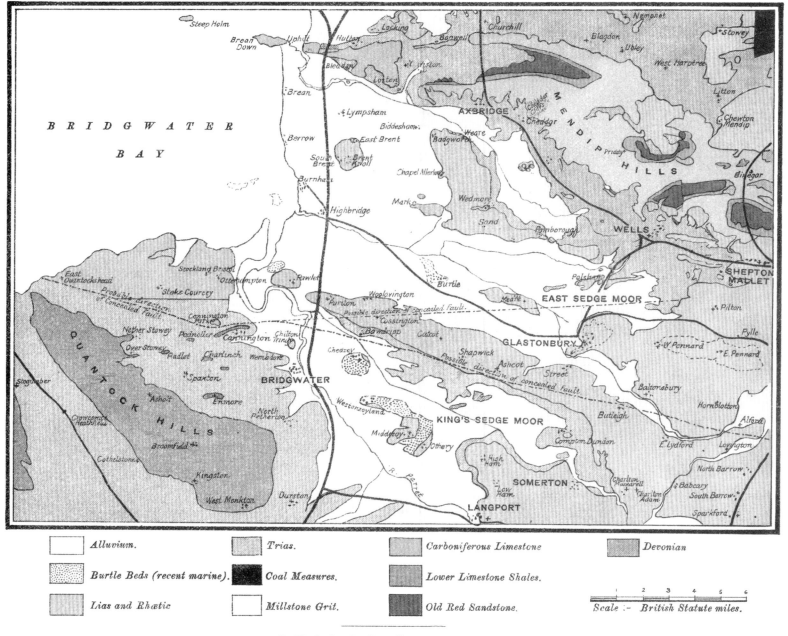

☐	Alluvium.		Trias.		Carboniferous Limestone	Devonian
⠿	Burtle Beds (recent marine).	■	Coal Measures.		Lower Limestone Shales.	
▦	Lias and Rhætic	☐	Millstone Grit.		Old Red Sandstone.	

Scale :— British Statute miles.

GEOLOGICAL MAP

OF THE AREA BETWEEN THE QUANTOCKS AND MENDIPS,

BY W. A. E. USSHER.

Bacon's county map guide {to} Somerset for cyclists & tourists
George Washington Bacon
1892, or later

George Washington Bacon F.R.G.S. (1830-1922) published his maps for cyclists from 1889 which were sold at 6 pence each in a cloth case, or for one shilling if the map was mounted on cloth. Bacon came to London in 1861 from America but went bankrupt in 1867. His fortunes improved and he eventually purchased Edward Weller's English county steel plates used in the *Weekly Dispatch Atlas*. Bacon & Company acquired James Wyld's map-making business which was eventually acquired by the Scottish firm of W.A. & K. Johnston. Maps using the Bacon brand were being produced as late as 1956.

His county map guide for Somerset was a slim but cleverly thought-through product. The front, reproduced right, showed two cyclists and stated how the publication was designed for both cyclists and tourists. Bacon was using the growing market for cycling to cash in on extra sales of what were Ordnance Survey maps, but he presented them in a folded format which could easily be carried in a cyclist's pocket. He sold space to Fry's, who advertised their 'pure concentrated Cocoa' that was 'recommended by the highest medical authorities' and ideal after a cycle ride in the colder months. He also ran an advert for Dr J. Collis Browne's Chlorodyne for coughs, colds, asthma, bronchitis and neuralgia. He included advertisements for his own *Pocket atlas and gazetteer of the World*, as well as his *Cycling road-map of England & Wales*, which he issued in seven sheets; sheet seven covered Somerset.

The map was accompanied by a small guide book and gazetteer.

(continued over)

Above: The front cover of the map.

Opposite: A reproduction of the top right corner of the map. (Adrian Webb collection.)

Source: Private collection. Original size: 632 x 437mm.

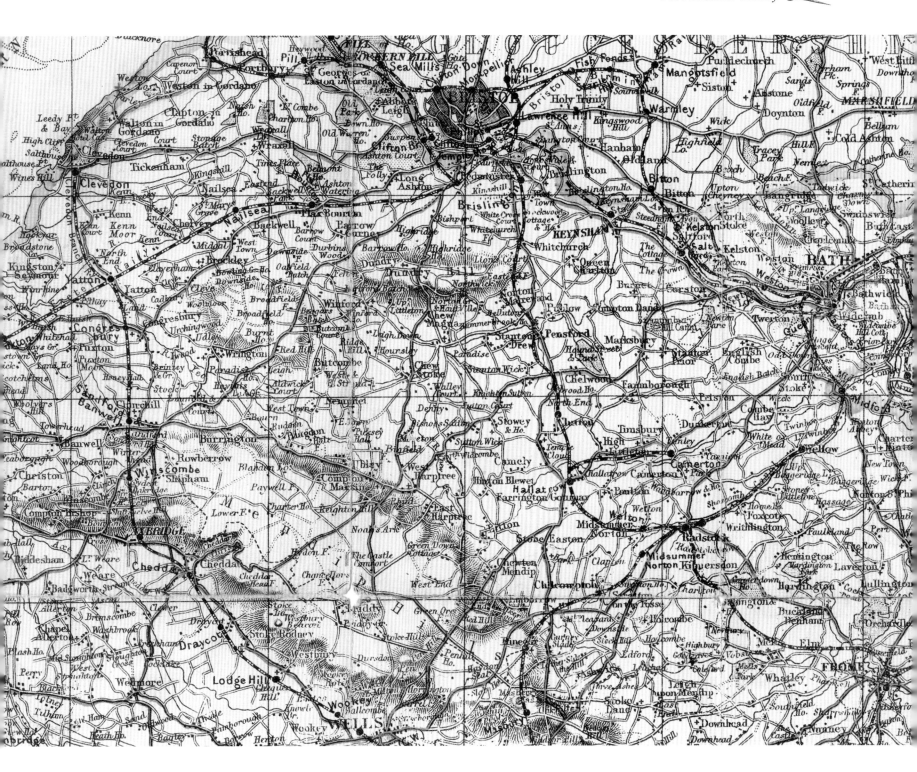

(continued)

The 1880s and 1890s saw a great increase in the popularity of cycling, not only domestically but for other purposes. Such was the versatility of bicycles that in September 1887 a meeting was held in Taunton to consider the 'desirability of forming a cyclists' corps' as part of the Somerset Light Infantry. To meet the demand for bicycles and tricycles in the county in 1889 there were seven manufacturers and nine 'warehouses and agents'.

However, cycling was not without its risks. In 1897 the Reverend C.H. Bousfield, rector of Bratton St Maur, whilst out cycling with a female companion, was thrown from his tricycle and died shortly afterward from injuries to his head before a doctor was able to attend to his injuries.

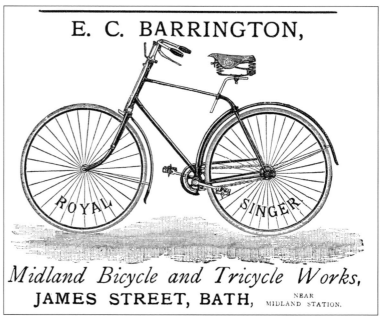

Above: A local advertisement for the Midland Bicycle and Tricycle Works at James Street, Bath, run by E.C. Barrington in 1894. The bicycle is a Royal Singer model (*The Post Office Bath Directory, 1894*).

Left: Edith Annie Cornish of Aginhills Farm, Bathpool, near Taunton, with her bicycle, *c.*1905. Note it had two bells on the handle bars (Margaret Webb collection).

CHAPTER SIX
1900–1958

[Fire Insurance Map of Bath]
Charles E. Goad
1902

The Charles E. Goad Company produced fire insurance maps from 1895 for most urban areas. The unparalleled urban growth in Victorian Britain meant the risk of fires breaking out increased, therefore information needed to be obtained on the usage of properties, whether commercial, residential, educational, etc for insurance purposes. As Somerset was thought of as a rural county only the Bath area was mapped. Details of the occupants of each commercial property for the area from south of the river as far north as the Assembly Rooms, containing information on properties in the parishes of Widcombe, Bath Abbey, Bath St Michael's Without, St Bartholomew's and Walcot, was mapped.

The example reproduced opposite includes Bath's famous Theatre Royal. Within the theatre can be seen two blue coloured circles which represent private hydrants or standpipes, which were essential. The use of almost every room is recorded and the locations of windows, iron doors, shutters and openings. Such information was used for fire prevention and to help fight fires. If this information had been available on Good Friday 1862 it might have helped avoid the total loss of one of the most attractive of all the provinical theatres in England. The building was insured in the West of England Insurance Office for about £600, but its value and contents was thought to be worth £25,000.

Above: The inside of the Theatre Royal following its renovation by architect C.J. Phipps F.S.A. (1835-1897) following the disastrous fire of 1862. The theatre received further improvements in 1892. Today it is a Grade II listed building with a seating capacity of 950. (*The Illustrated London News*, September 1864, SANHS.)

Opposite: A reduced reproduction of the plan showing the Theatre Royal, Monmouth Street, St John's Place, Sawclose and Beauford Square. (Bath in Time.)

Source: Bath in Time – Bath Central Library, Goad's fire insurance plans of Bath city centre. Original size: 590 x 630mm.

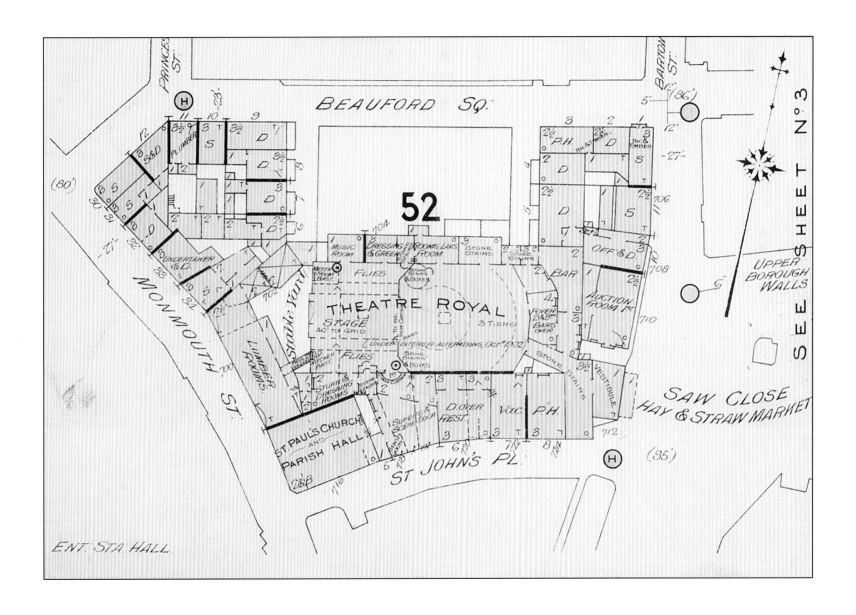

Pople's new touring, cycling, and driving road map of forty miles about Burnham
Blanche Jane Pople
1909 to 1924

By the time this map was published Burnham-on-Sea had become a thriving tourist venue. To take advantage of this, Pople & Churchill of 25 College Street, Burnham, a local firm of booksellers, stationers and printers, produced a map for the use of tourists, cyclists and motorists. Pople and Churchill also sold postcards, periodicals, magazines and operated a circulating library. Mr James Pople, senior partner in the firm formerly of J. & B. Pople, died in 1908 and the business was continued by his daughter Blanche Jane Pople.

The map was published in conjunction with one of the leading commercial map publishers of their time, Gall & Inglis. They advertised, on the reverse of the map, their 'Half Inch' map series of England, Scotland and Wales, as well as their 'Cycling Edition' mounted on cloth and folded ready for the cyclists pocket. They also promoted their 'Contour' road books containing 500 maps printed on India paper, and their plan of London.

The date this map was published was some time after 1909 when Gall & Inglis started operating from 31 Henrietta Street, London, and before 1924 when they operated from 12 Newington Road, Edinburgh. The 'Pople' whose map this name carries was Blanche Pople, making this a rare map indeed. Although it is well known that young ladies used to be paid to hand colour maps, the number of ladies who can be attributed as map-makers from this period is very small.

However, when it comes to dating this map more accurately the information shown on the map is misleading. The information on the land does not include the extension to the railway opened in 1907 and some of the information in the Bristol Channel was taken

from a chart that was first published in 1839. Similarly the use of the circles to show the distance from Burnham was an idea used by Thomas Thorpe in 1742 (see pages 116-119).

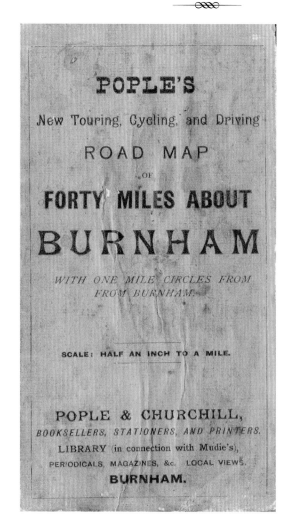

Left: A reproduction of the front cover of the map.

Opposite: A reproduction of Pople's map.

Source: Adrian Webb collection. Original size: 537 x 408mm.

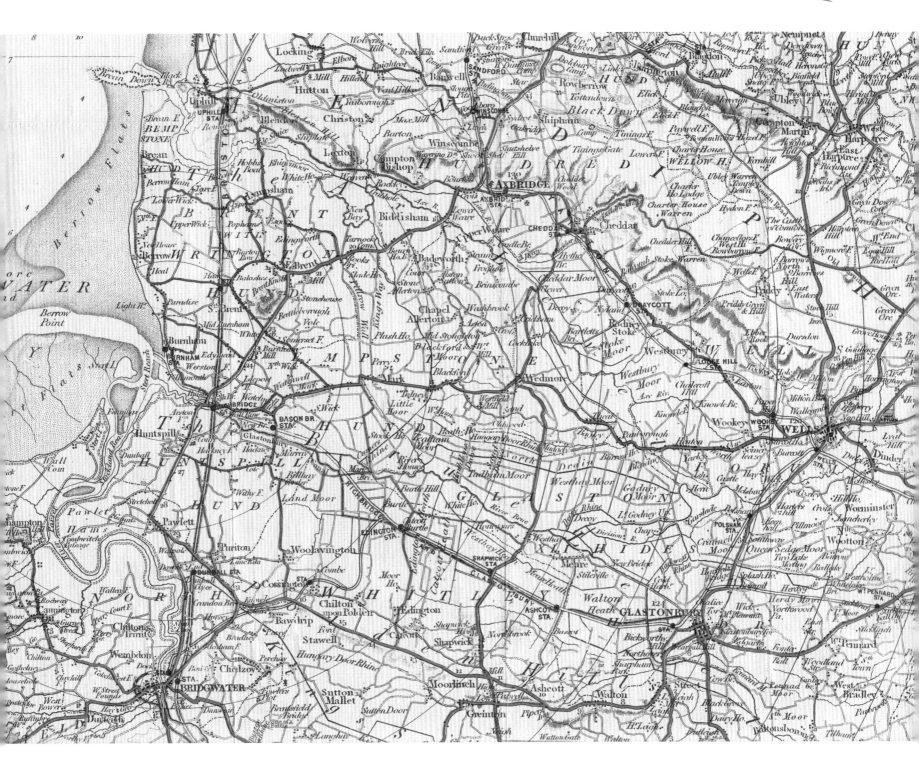

Domesday valuation books and maps
Inland Revenue Valuation Offices
1910

In 1910 a bill reached the statute book that became the Finance Act 1910. This Act outlined a number of duties on land, the main one being an increment value duty. Throughout the late nineteenth and early twentieth century, land had often increased in value as a result of state expenditure on infrastructure such as roads and water supply. The Finance Act 1910 aimed to make private landowners pay for part of the increased value in their land not attributable to their capital outlay. Subsequently a survey of landholdings was needed. For the purposes of the survey, England and Wales were divided into 14 divisions with 118 Valuation Districts which were sub-divided into Income Tax Parishes.

To create a datum line from which the increase in land value could be calculated, a valuation of all the land in the United Kingdom was made. The survey was dubbed a 'New Domesday'. There were some exemptions to the duty, including farm land that was not worth more than its agricultural market value, but the valuation included all property whether it was likely to be exempt or not. The valuation process began in the summer of 1910 when valuation books were drawn up from existing information in the rate books. Landowners and anyone in receipt of rent from land then had to complete and return a form known as 'form 4-land', after which a physical inspection was undertaken of the property. Details from both were transcribed into valuers' field books which were to become the official record of the valuation. The survey was completed by autumn 1915, only six months behind schedule.

Many landowners opposed the Act, and eventually incremental value duty was repealed by the Finance Act 1920. However, the information gathered between 1910 and 1915 provides a unique snapshot of the people of Britain and their homes before the social upheaval of the World War One.

The map opposite shows the village of Timsbury just outside Bath, best known for its coal mining in the eighteenth and nineteenth centuries. It is the working copy used by the valuers to carry out the survey. The maps act as an index to the field books. The extent and location of each property, or plot of land, is shown and given a number which relates to an entry in the field book.

Plot number 1571 is Timsbury House, which was the manor house of the village, and is recorded in the survey as belonging to John Stukley Palmer Samborne. Thought to have been built in the late fifteenth century, the house remained in the Sambourne family for a number of centuries. The gross value of the property was given as £3,500.

A detailed description of the rooms and their use is recorded: the panelled hall oak stairs, three large bedrooms, one with a bath, two bathrooms, two old bedrooms and a nursery with two bedrooms. Alongside the main house a walled garden, three glass houses and stables are also recorded. This description provides a glimpse into the lifestyle of the occupants at the time and is especially important as the house was demolished in 1961.

Opposite: A reduced reproduction of part of the map of the manor of Timsbury.

Source: SHC, DD/IR z 7/17. Original size: 620 x 490mm.

An extract from the Inland Revenue archive of mapping for the 1910 survey. In this instance this map of Timsbury was a lithograph (printed in 1900 by William Lewis & Son of Northgate, Bath) of the 1841 tithe map prepared by Messrs Cottrell and Cooper. The colours were added to show the owners in 1910: pink belonged to the Manor Company, light green to S.S.P. Samborne esq., Brown to Mrs Parish, light blue to Bissets, yellow to Messrs Mogg and purple to B. Smith esq. The annotation in blue pencil shows coal veins that were not being worked. (SHC.)

Contoured Road Map of Bridgwater and Quantock Hills
Ordnance Survey
1918

The turn of the twentieth century gave rise to a greater number of cyclists and motorists using the roads, increasingly for leisure purposes. The Director-General of Ordnance Survey, Colonel Charles Close K.B.E. C.B. C.M.G. F.R.S. (1865-1952), saw this as an opportunity to promote maps to the growing leisure industry. This was somewhat hindered by the First World War, when many surveyors and draughtsmen were posted abroad to aid the war effort. However, after the war the Ordnance Survey returned its attention to addressing the needs of those using maps for leisure.

The map opposite is a reprint of a map first produced in 1918. It depicts many ornamental parks and gardens, including Willett House, Norton Manor and Halswell House. Historic sites such as the battle of Sedgemoor are also labelled and youth hostels are identified, all of which would have been useful to those exploring the Somerset landscape.

In an attempt to appeal to the leisure industry Close appointed a professional artist, Ellis Martin (1881-1977), to create covers for the maps to help market them. The image produced on the front of the Bridgwater and Quantock Hills map was typical, showing a cyclist studying a map and planning his route across the countryside; exactly the type of person it was hoped would buy and use the map. The artwork achieved its desired purpose and sales of the maps reached record levels.

Right: The front cover designed by Ellis Martin. (Adrian Webb collection.)

Source: *Ordnance Survey Contoured Road Map of Bridgwater and Quantock Hills Popular Edition sheet 120*, corrected to 1936. Original size: 709 x 483mm.

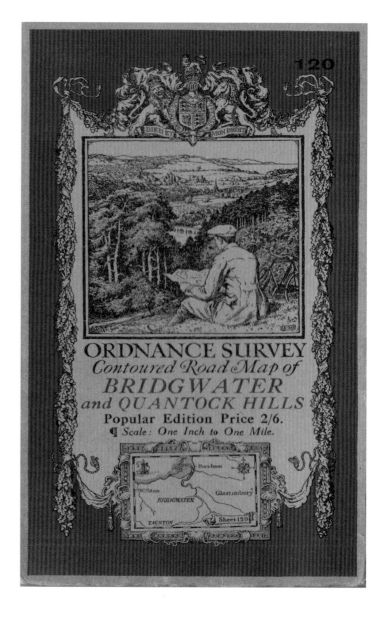

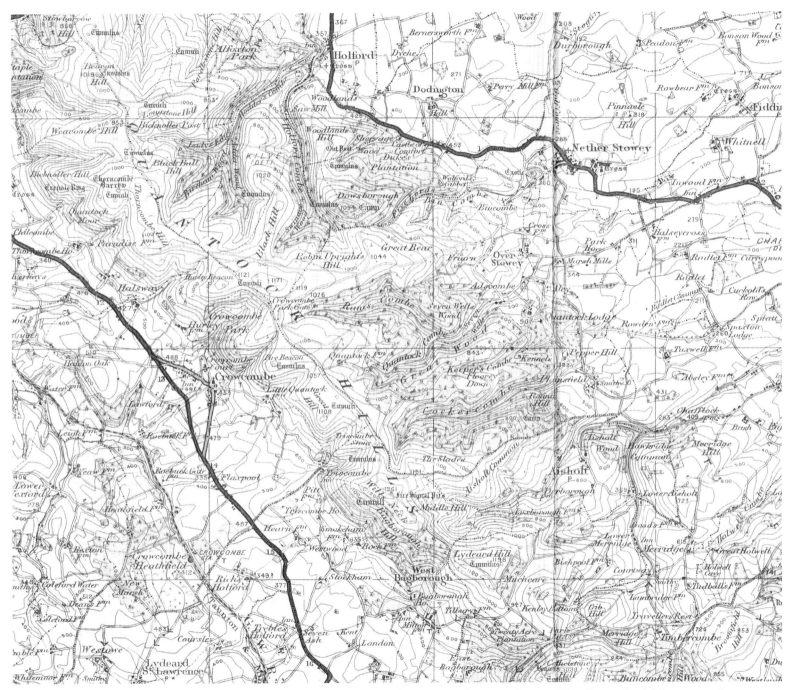

An extract from the map showing the closely contoured landscape of the Quantocks, stretching from Fyne Court to West Quantoxhead. The scarp on the western side is in contrast to the gently sloping rich arable lands on the eastern side. All were attractive sights for tourists venturing into Somerset.

Hardings' Guide map to the district of Taunton
J.W. Harding & Co.
c.1925

The idea of printing commercial maps with advertisements around the border started in the second half of the seventeenth century. A resurgence in the early twentieth century saw local examples produced in 1908 of the Wells, Frome, Shepton Mallet and Glastonbury district that was published and sold locally from Robert M. Fisher's musical warehouse in Highbridge. A *New Business Map of the Wells Parliamentary Division* was published in 1906 by Stephens and Mackintosh of Leicester, advertising contractors and publishers of maps for local guides, almanacks and directories. 1,240 copies of this map were printed by George Gibbins and Co. of Leicester from 1903, which included inset plans of the larger population centres of Weston-super-Mare, Burnham-on-Sea and Wells.

In the 1920s J.W. Harding and Co. of 39A Park Row, Nottingham produced 'guide maps' on a similar theme for places across the country. Their map covering the 'District of Taunton' was issued in 1926 but unlike the Wells map of 1908 Hardings sold copies of their maps through all of their advertisers. This meant the map was available from 14 outlets in Taunton and one in Norton Fitzwarren, Norton mills, and including Fisher and Sons Ltd, ironmongers; E. Williams, opticians; W.J. Coles saddlery and trunk depot; G. Hinton & Sons gun makers and sports depot; Marshalsea Brothers Ltd, motor engineers; A.H. Collard, grocer; John Broomfield, brush manufacturer; F. Adams Ltd, florists and fruit merchants and J. Venn & Co., butchers. The maps were sold folded with a standard design on the cover which was used for other towns and cities with only the name being changed, e.g. Bristol or Frome.

Above: A reproduction of the front cover.

Opposite: A reduced reproduction of the whole map. (Adrian Webb collection.)

Source: *Hardings' guide map to the District of Taunton*. Original size: 586 x 787mm.

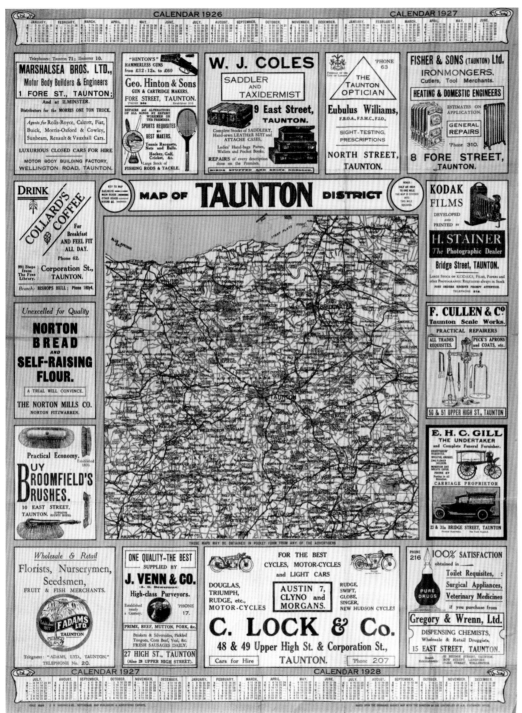

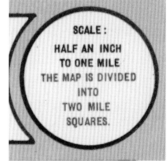

A reproduction of the whole map. Below: Enlargements of the two circles next to the title explaining the scale and the key to the symbols used on the map.

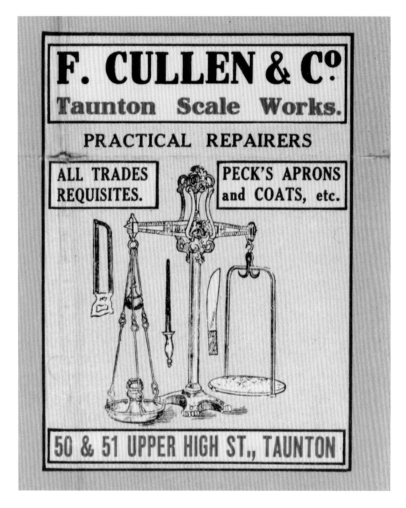

Above: Two adverts from the map showing the tools of the trade of scale makers and undertakers.

Opposite: An extract from the map published at half an inch to one mile, which was based on the Ordnance Survey.

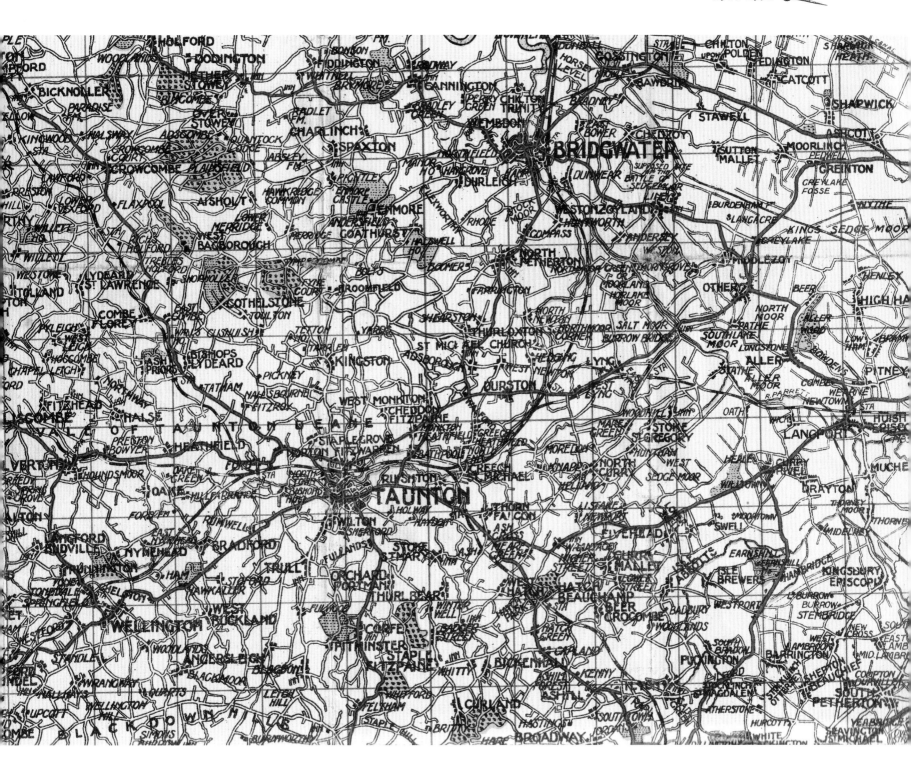

The rapid route indicator Taunton area
The Route Indicator
*c.*1930

The Rapid route indicator series of maps was published by 'The Route Indicator', whose proprietors were Geographia Limited of 55 Fleet Street, London E.C.4. The concept followed in the genre of road books and distance tables but it used a clever combination of factors to enable users to calculate the distance they needed to travel. The patent for a 'Means for indicating the direction, distance and route between starting point and destination in journeys' was taken out in 1928. The map in the centre of the sheet is very cluttered but to help users the main routes, or 'exit roads', were coloured red.

Folded copies of the map could be purchased for 2 shillings from Barnicott and Pearce, 44 Fore Street, Taunton, who also sold maps published by the Ordnance Survey, Bartholomew, Philip, Michelin, Bacon, Dunlop, Geographia and others. Barnicott and Pearce were best known for their book printing and advertised as 'The Wessex Printing, Stationery, Bookselling, Die Stamping, Bookbinding and Map Mounting House', using the map opposite to convince customers that all routes led to their premises. One advertiser on the map, G. Hinton & Sons, used a similar idea that 'All Routes Lead to Sport, Sport is the Zest of Life'. As a commercial map partly funded by advertisers it contains 13 advertisements for local businesses. Seven of the advertisers were involved in the motoring business (e.g. car sales or repairs) and the other six hospitality and leisure. The map can be dated to some time shortly after 1929 when Dyer & Crofts started using the telephone number Taunton 554.

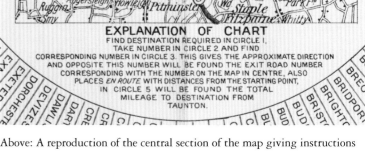

Above: A reproduction of the central section of the map giving instructions how to use the *Rapid route indicator* to calculate your distance between places.

Opposite: A reduced reproduction of the complete map.

Source: Private collection. Original size: 705 x 515mm.

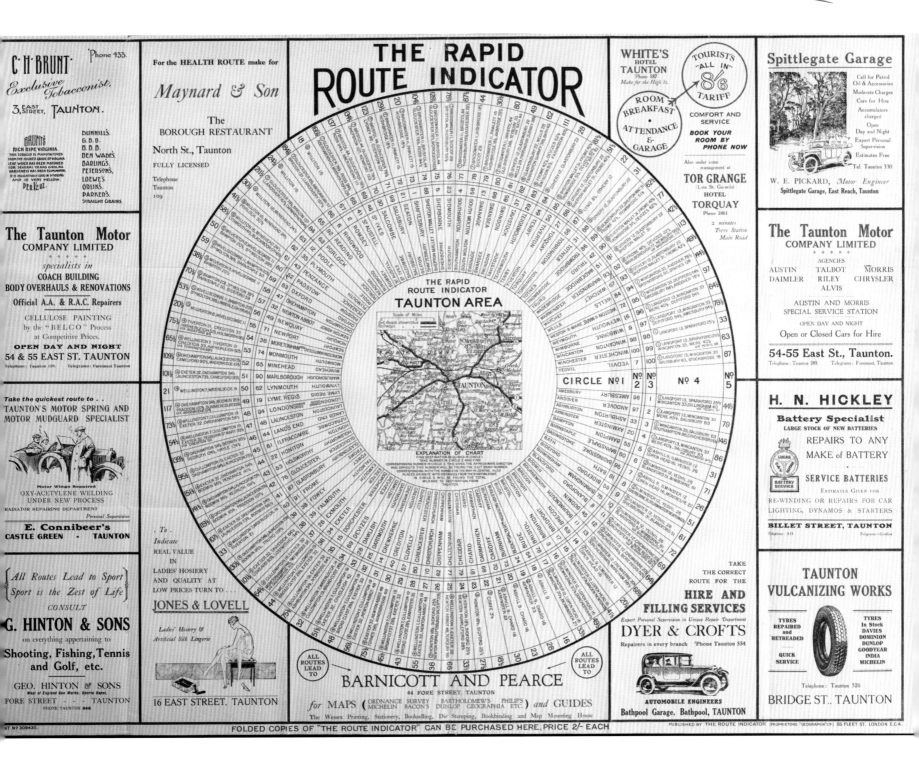

THE RAPID ROUTE INDICATOR

THE RAPID ROUTE INDICATOR
TAUNTON AREA

Bristol & Bath regional planning scheme
Patrick Abercrombie and Bertrand F. Brueton
1930

The concept of regional planning for north Somerset and Bath was the result of an initiative of the Bristol Town Planning Committee. Bristol had taken the lead was because its need was not confined to the limits of the city but was one that had to be considered in a regional context. Subsequently a conference for interested parties was held at the Council House in Bristol in 1923 and a Joint Committee was set up under the Town Planning Act.

Over 20 county and district surveyors were involved in the project. The resulting report and over 35 maps, which varied in size, were prepared by Professor Abercrombie and Mr Bertrand F. Brueton. The maps were a mixture of highly coloured fold-outs and black-and-white plans within the text. They were undoubtedly the most colourful maps that had ever been published for any part of the county of Somerset. The report covered a wealth of subjects.

The coloured fold-out maps began with a contour map of the region showing its physical and artificial features, followed by a geological map, then maps showing rainfall, archaeology, historic roads, road traffic, accessibility, industrial sites, landscape survey, drainage, water supply, electricity, a zoning plan, proposals for new roads and a map titled 'an open spaces diagram'.

The report was issued with a slip case containing nine large sheets, measuring 83 x 75 cms, of very colourful zoning maps. The zones depicted areas of residential, industrial, agricultural, special landscape reservation, rural and open spaces. The maps were printed by Partridge and Love Limited of Bristol and the colours were overprinted on Ordnance Survey mapping. The sheets also contain proposals for new roads and railways, as well as boundaries for coal, water and sewerage purposes. The report was published by the University Press of Liverpool and Hodder & Stoughton Limited of London in 1930.

Source: P. Abercrombie and B.F. Brueton, *Bristol & Bath regional planning scheme* (London, 1930).

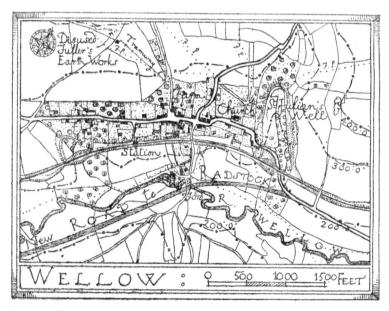

The map of Wellow contained with the text of the report, on page 60, published at 1¼ inches to 1500 feet.

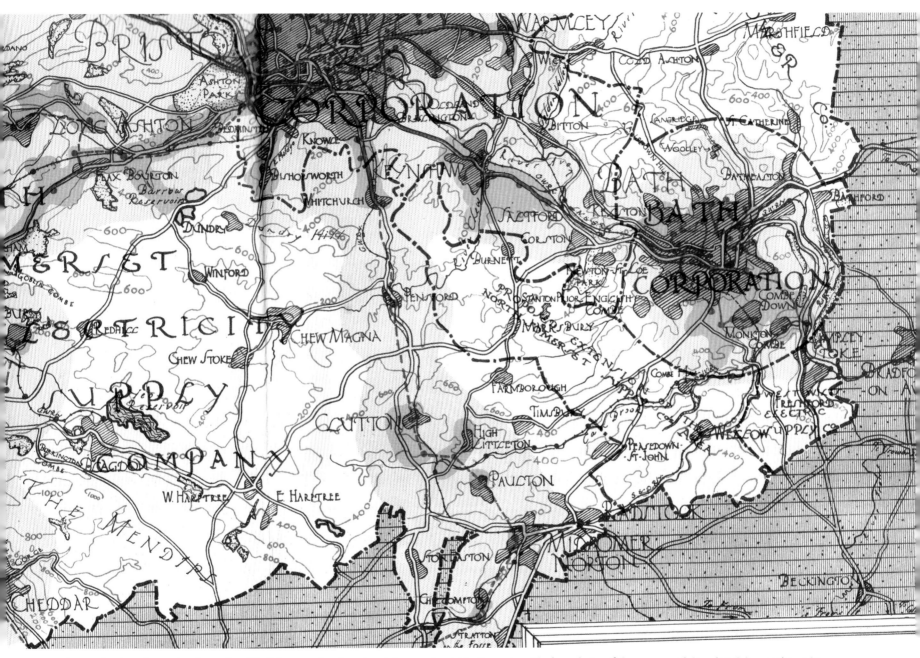

A reproduction of a section from plate 32 of the map showing electricity supply within the region. The boundaries of the areas supplying electricity are shown in blue dots and dashes, generating stations are shown as red squares, and high tension mains as red lines, sub-stations as red circles. The light orange area shows the extent of areas capable of being served by existing sub-stations, with the dark orange showing the area served in 1928. Original size: 430 x 413mm.

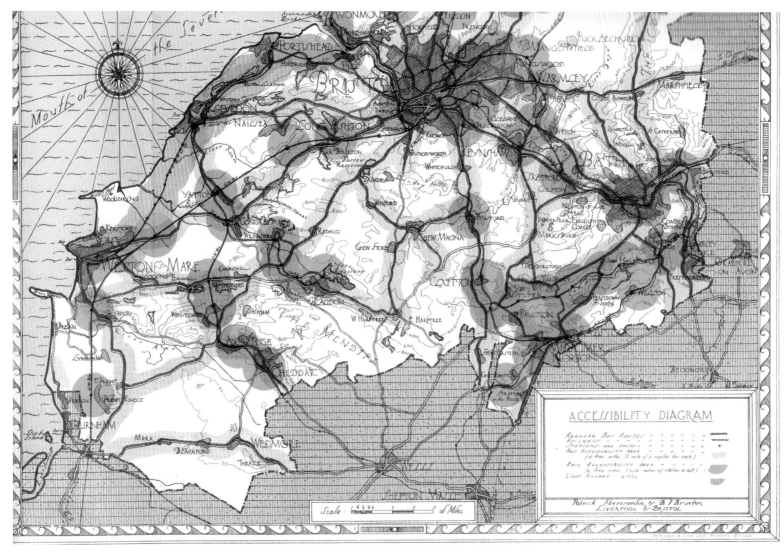

Above: A section from the map titled 'Accessibility Diagram'. The diagram, or map, was all about road and rail routes being used to show how accessible places were. Original size: 278 x 267mm.

Opposite: An extract from plate 33 of the character zoning map.
Original size: 430 x 415mm.

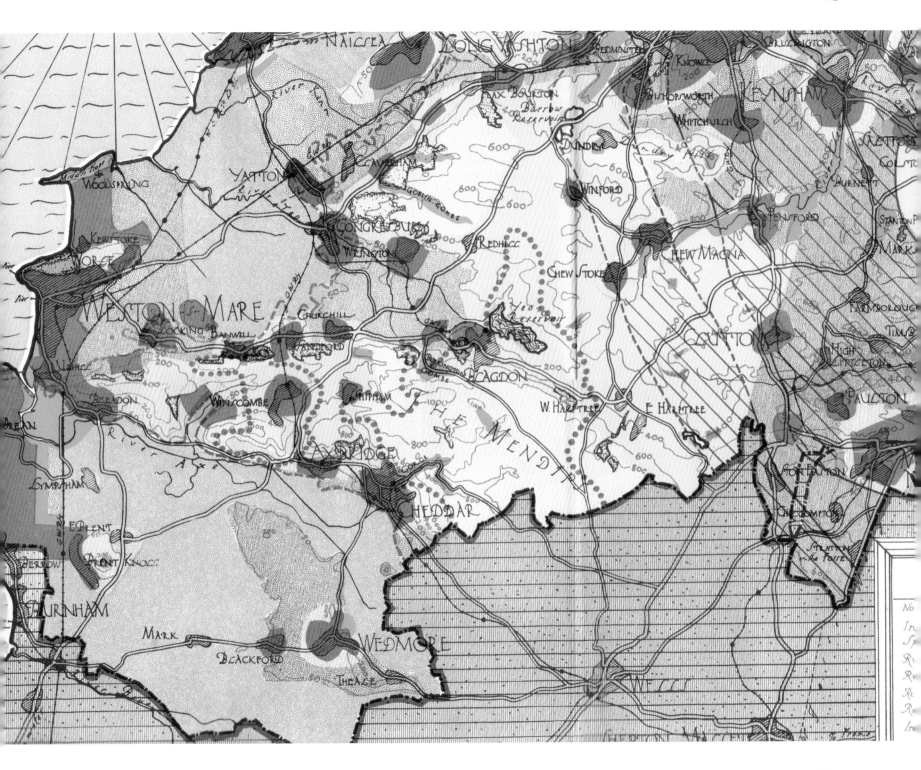

Somerset regional report: a survey and plan prepared for the Somerset County Council
W. Harding Thompson, F.R.I.B.A.
1934

The need for information for planning purposes resulted in two regional reports which together covered the whole of the ancient county of Somerset. The report for the southern part of the county was written by W. Harding Thompson, but he acknowledged that the creation of the maps was down to a group of people, principally Sir Frank Beauchamp, Mr Arthur Hobhouse and

> other members of the Committees appointed by the County Council for their careful consideration of the large scale maps.

He also thanked Mr Geoffrey Clark

> who, throughout the investigations and preparation of the maps and diagrams, has devoted his ability, experience and enthusiasm to the subject of this volume.

The volume contained 14 maps, of which ten were issued as loose sheets in a wallet at the back of the volume. These maps were of a much more attractive appearance than those produced for the neighbouring volume covering north Somerset, Bristol and southern Gloucestershire. Their content varied from physical geography, such as contours, geology and rainfall, to an analysis of the 1921 and 1931 census returns. Extracts from three of the maps can be found opposite and on the following two pages. The maps were based upon the Ordnance Survey and printed by Vincent Brooks, Day & Son Ltd, lithographers of London W.C.2.

Source: W. Harding Thompson, *Somerset regional report: a survey and plan prepared for the Somerset County Council* (London, 1934). Original size of folded maps: 608 x 333mm.

MAPS AND DIAGRAMS	
GENERAL SURVEY OF EXISTING CONDITIONS	
1. CONTOURS .	*End of book*
2. GEOLOGICAL	” ”
3. RAINFALL .	” ”
4. ROUTES OF NATIONAL IMPORTANCE	*Facing p.* 20
5. MAIN COMMUNICATIONS	*End of book*
6. TRAFFIC CENSUS .	” ”
7. PUBLIC TRANSPORT SERVICES	*Facing p.* 22
8A. DISTRIBUTION OF POPULATION	*Facing p.* 28
8B. CENSUS OF POPULATION, 1921 AND 1931 .	” ”
8C. ANALYSIS OF OCCUPATIONS .	” ”
9. AGRICULTURE	*End of book*
10. INDUSTRIES	” ”
11. DRAINAGE AND SEWAGE DISPOSAL	” ”
12. WATER SUPPLIES .	” ”
13. ELECTRICITY SUPPLY .	” ”
14. LANDSCAPE .	” ”
PLANNING PROPOSALS	
15. OUTLINE ZONING AND RESERVATIONS	*End of book*
16. PROPOSED STATUTORY REGIONS	*Facing p.* 102

With the exception of diagrams 4, 8A, 8B and 8C, the maps and diagrams are based upon the Ordnance Survey, with the sanction of H.M. Stationery Office.

xii

Above: A reproduction of the list of maps and diagrams included in the report.

Source: W. Harding Thompson, *Somerset regional report: a survey and plan prepared for the Somerset County Council* (London, 1934), xi.

Opposite: An extract from the 'Industrial' map showing the area to the south of the county. There were more factories in the Chard, Ilminster, Martock, Yeovil and Crewkerne area than in any other equivalent area covered by the report. This area also included factories at West Coker and North Coker. The quarries at Norton-sub-Hamdon and Whitestaunton are shown with a red square. Compared to a similar area stretching from Frome to Wells, the two quarries in the south of the county were dwarfed by the 18 on the Mendips. The title and key to the symbols have been extracted from a separate part of the map.

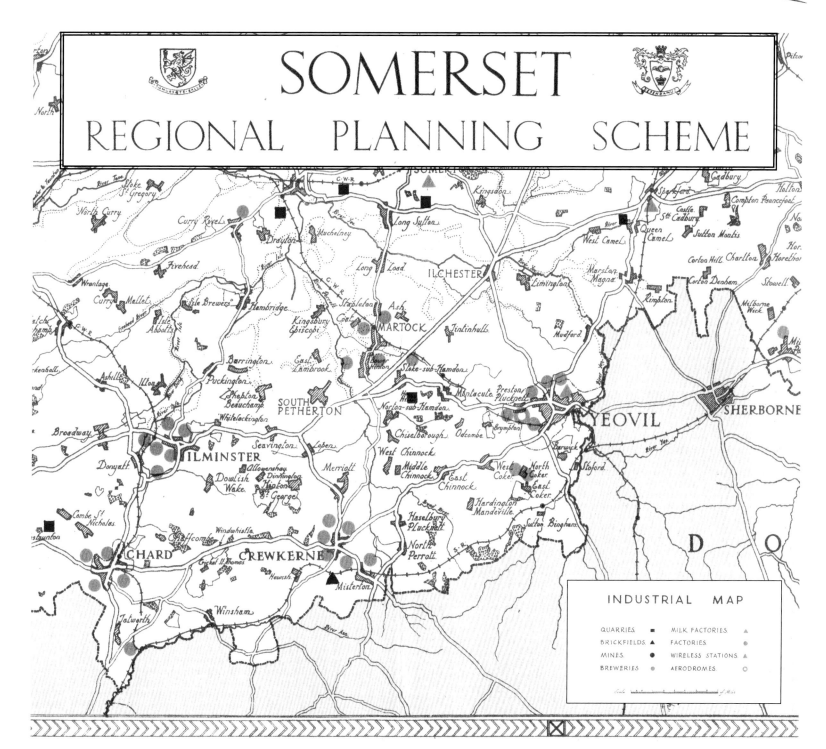

SOMERSET
REGIONAL PLANNING SCHEME

INDUSTRIAL MAP

QUARRIES	■	MILK FACTORIES	▲
BRICKFIELDS	▲	FACTORIES	●
MINES	●	WIRELESS STATIONS	▲
BREWERIES	●	AERODROMES	○

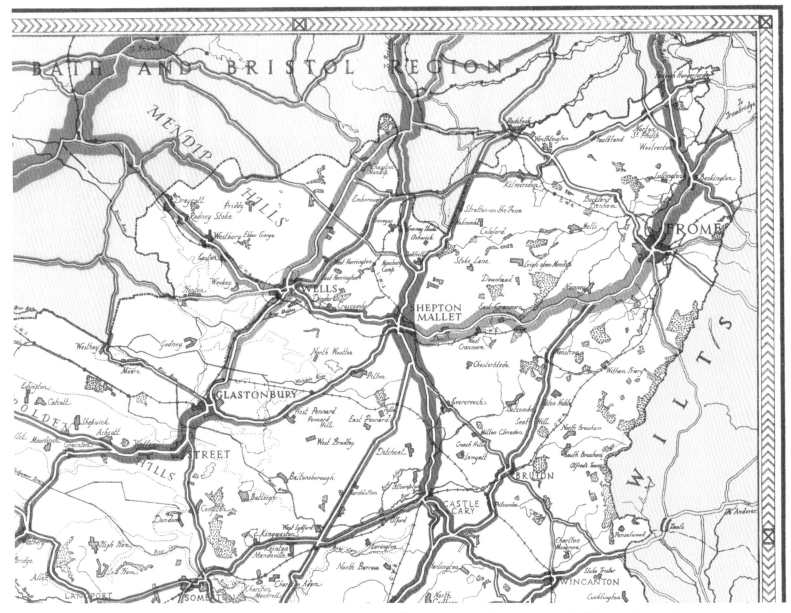

Above: Described as a 'Road traffic diagram', this map shows the tonnage on classified roads obtained from a census of traffic on 'A' class roads taken in 1931 and 'B' class roads taken in 1929. The red lines show an increase in traffic and the blue colours shows a decrease in use. The main increase in road traffic occurred in what was to become the 'M5 corridor'.

Opposite: The report made many recommendations for changes within the county. This is an extract from the map showing 'suggested' uses for all the land in the region and secondary zoning to be considered in all of the schemes. The key is superimposed in the top left corner.

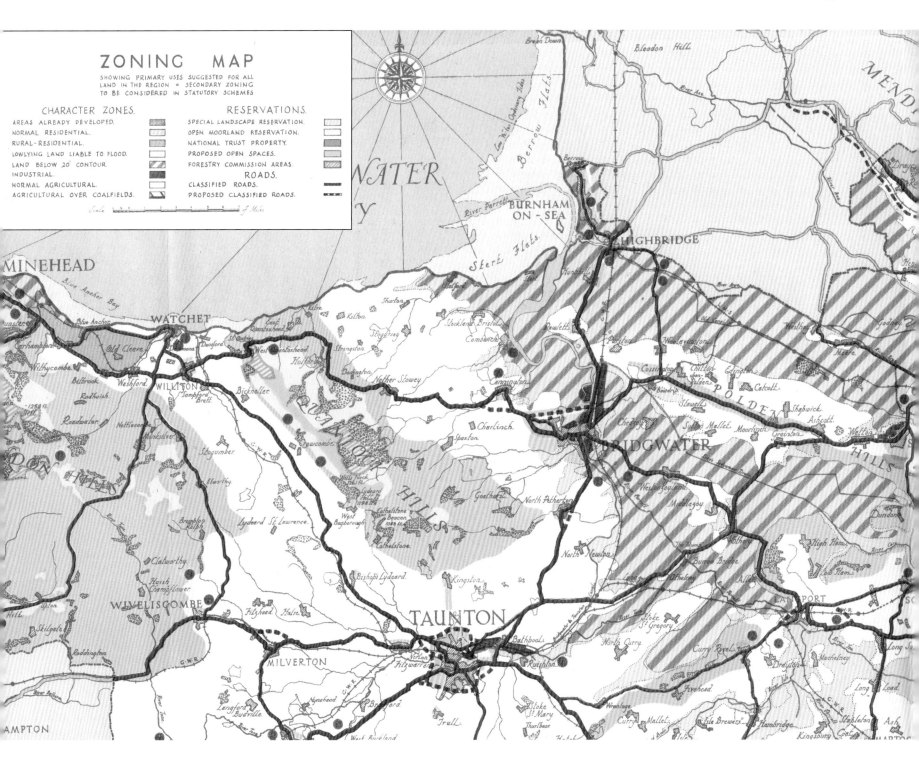

ZONING MAP

SHOWING PRIMARY USES SUGGESTED FOR ALL
LAND IN THE REGION • SECONDARY ZONING
TO BE CONSIDERED IN STATUTORY SCHEMES

CHARACTER ZONES.

AREAS ALREADY DEVELOPED.
NORMAL RESIDENTIAL.
RURAL-RESIDENTIAL.
LOWLYING LAND LIABLE TO FLOOD.
LAND BELOW 20' CONTOUR.
INDUSTRIAL.
NORMAL AGRICULTURAL.
AGRICULTURAL OVER COALFIELDS.

RESERVATIONS.

SPECIAL LANDSCAPE RESERVATION.
OPEN MOORLAND RESERVATION.
NATIONAL TRUST PROPERTY.
PROPOSED OPEN SPACES.
FORESTRY COMMISSION AREAS.

ROADS.

CLASSIFIED ROADS.
PROPOSED CLASSIFIED ROADS.

Scale of Miles

Route map of Somerset & East Devon area
Western National Omnibus Company Limited 1934 – 1948

In 1931 Tilling's bought into the Southern National Omnibus Company Limited and into the Western National Omnibus Company Limited. Southern National and Western National operated from 1929 and in 1934 they bought the Royal Blue business. Shortly after World War Two, in 1948, Tilling's bus business was nationalised. This map is thought to date between 1934 and 1948. Unfortunately the number plates on the front of the buses are indistinct, so their date of registration cannot be established.

The map is both functional and decorative. Bus routes are shown in different colours, with the map (based on the Ordnance Survey) surrounded by the arms of the towns, including those in Somerset for Bridgwater, Burnham-on-Sea, Chard, Glastonbury, Minehead, Shepton Mallet, Taunton, Wellington, Yeovil and those of the county of Somerset. Service numbers of the 'omnibus routes' are shown in the colour of the service they relate to, i.e. red numbers relate to services run by the Western National Omnibus Company Limited, blue for Royal Blue Express, and green for the Southern National Omnibus Company Limited.

The map was printed by the lithographic method in Exeter by Wheaton's. A. Wheaton and Company is one of the oldest, still trading companies in Exeter. It can be traced back to 1780, when James Penny opened a bookshop and printer in Southgate Street. William Wheaton purchased the business in 1835.

Source: Adrian Webb collection. Original size: 728 x 504.

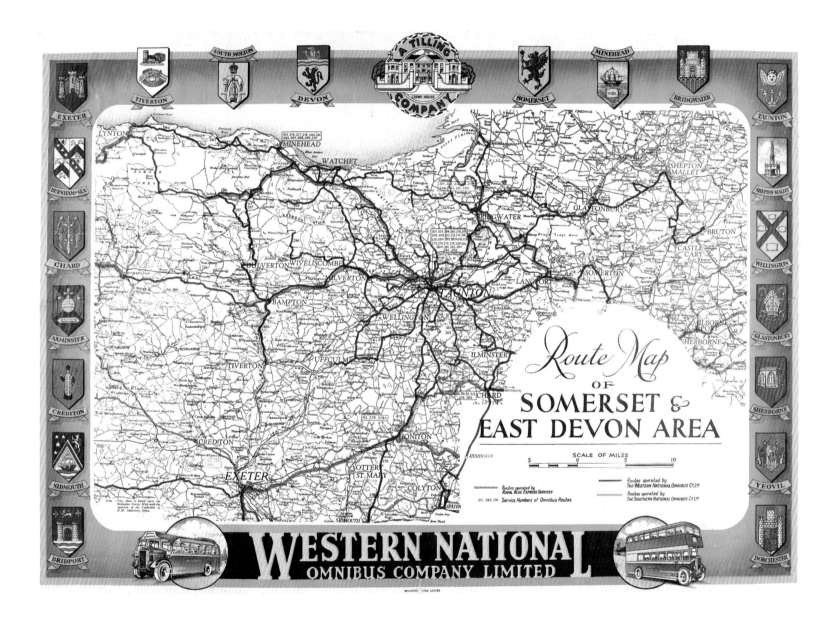

Sheet 121, *Wells & Frome*
Land Utilisation Survey of Britain
1938

In 1931, Mr F. Burkinshaw, County Education Secretary of Somerset, wrote to the Director of the Land Utilisation Survey informing him that approval had been given for the survey of the county to go ahead. Thus part 86 of the Land Utilisation Survey of Britain, which covered the county of Somerset, was underway, but a massive amount of data needed to be collected before the report could be completed. L. Dudley Stamp described the process of how the data was collected and how the maps were made:

The report that was compiled complemented the seven one inch to the mile Land Utilisation Survey sheets needed to cover the county.

The county is a large one and the set of 323 six-inch maps was purchased by the Education Committee. By June the maps had been allotted to schools and distributed. Although the headquarters of the Survey in London undertook to deal with all the enquiries from the surveyors, the County Education Secretary reported on July 31st that his office had also written over 250 letters on the subject! Completed maps began to come in from July onwards and by the end of 1931 a third of the county had been finished. But difficulties arose with the remoter areas and it soon became clear that the whole county could not be reached from the schools. The work, however, went on steadily during 1932. On March 7th, 1933, a conference was held at Weston-super-Mare and the completion of the field-work discussed. The assistance of new volunteers was sought: during 1933 Taunton was surveyed through the schools of the Municipality; a number of areas were surveyed by members of the Somerset Rural Community Council; a tract by Sidcot School (Winscombe); a considerable part of the

north by Professor S.H. Reynolds of the University of Bristol; and a large area by Mr. C.H. Puckett, B.A., of King's College, University of London. During 1934 many of the remaining tracts were surveyed by Mr. L.W.C. Maidment, B.A., of University College, Southampton.

On July 16th, 1935, through the kind offices of Mr. J.N.L. Baker, M.A., B.Litt., of the School of Geography of the University of Oxford, an offer was received from Mr. T. Stuart-Menteath (then attached to the School) to assist in the work of the Land Utilisation Survey. After discussing the matter on July 22nd, Mr. Stuart-Menteath agreed to be responsible for the completion of the field-work in Somerset, the revision of all work carried out, and the preparation of the Report. In the months which followed he travelled very extensively in the county, penetrating every corner, covering hundreds of miles, interviewing scores of farmers and getting in touch with the Somerset Farm Institute (Cannington) whose Principal, Mr. W.D. Hay, B.Sc. (Agr.), has afforded unstinted help and made available his own unique knowledge of the county and that of his colleagues, Messrs. D. Rowe, J.E. Forshaw and F.R. Wallbutton. By the end of 1935 the Bridgwater-Taunton one-inch sheet (No. 120) was ready for publication and once more the County Education Committee lent its support by a generous grant of £50 towards publication, the grant to be repaid in maps as published. Mr. S.C. Morland, the son of the Chairman of the Education Committee, has further contributed the historical chapter to the Report. The Report itself at the School of Rural Economy, University of Oxford, where Mr. Stuart-Menteath has had the advantage of the co-

(continued over)

Above left: An extract from an original survey. Note how a 1903 second edition Ordnance Survey sheet was used as a collector sheet. This covers part of the parish of Brompton Regis. (Source: SHC, A/BAZ/9/8/10.)

Above right: An extract from the published sheet for Wells and Frome. The area to the north of Wells is littered with yellow areas signifying heath and moorland. Green signifies forest and woodland, purple is gardens, red is 'land agriculturally unproductive', brown is arable and light green is meadowland and permanent grass. (Source: SHC, DD/SAS/c2631/4.)

(continued)

operation of his colleagues and especially the advice of Professor J.A. Scott-Watson, Mr. C.S. Orwin, Major G.D. Amery and Mr. J.N.L. Baker.

Today this mass gathering of information is referred to as 'crowd sourcing'. Back in the 1930s children and adults in Somerset clearly played a key role in gathering the data needed for these maps. To acknowledge this a list of all the individuals and schools who took part in this project in Somerset was printed as Appendix Two in the report.

The report acknowledges the final part of the map-making process that was undertaken:

> The reduction of the six-inch sheets to a convenient scale of one inch is the vital link between the collection and records, and the publishing of material, and this has been done by the staff of the Land Utilisation Survey.

The maps were available from the Land Utilisation Survey of Great Britain at the London School of Economics.

An example of one of the Ordnance Survey sheets used as a collector sheet is in the Sellick papers. A section is reproduced on the previous page showing Lyncombe in Brompton Regis. The sheet has been marked with capital letters to show how the land was being used. In the fields marked with a capital letter 'A' the person undertaking the survey has added the type of cultivation, such as oats.

At the top of the sheet the surveyor made some notes about the area: how roads and lanes had been worn down, the south sloping fields were meadow ('M') and arable ('A'), the woods, were mainly beech with some fir, were 'generally small and badly grown'. Many of the woods had 'patches cut down and not replanted'.

The reduction of the six-inch sheets to a convenient scale of one inch is the vital link between the collection and records, and the publishing of material, and this has been done by the staff of the Land Utilisation Survey.

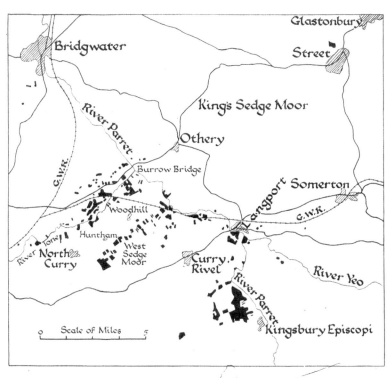

One of the maps from inside the text of the published report showing sites of 'Withy Beds' in central Somerset (from p.65 of the report, figure 12). Source: L. Dudley Stamp and T. Stuart-Menteath, *The land of Britain. Part 86 Somerset* (London, 1938). Original: 115 x 103mm.

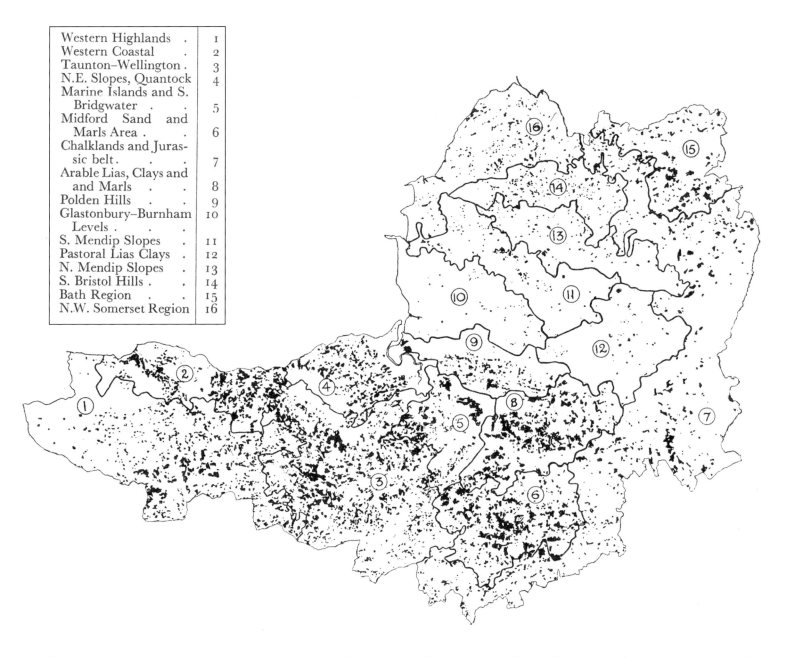

Western Highlands .	I
Western Coastal .	2
Taunton–Wellington .	3
N.E. Slopes, Quantock	4
Marine Islands and S. Bridgwater . .	5
Midford Sand and Marls Area . .	6
Chalklands and Jurassic belt . . .	7
Arable Lias, Clays and and Marls . .	8
Polden Hills . .	9
Glastonbury–Burnham Levels . . .	10
S. Mendip Slopes .	11
Pastoral Lias Clays .	12
N. Mendip Slopes .	13
S. Bristol Hills . .	14
Bath Region . .	15
N.W. Somerset Region	16

A map from the published report showing 'The Production Regions of Somerset'. Arable land is shown in black. The numbers refer to the regions given in the text of the report, which has been superimposed in the top left-hand corner in two columns. The scale is approximately 12 miles to 1 inch. Source: *The Land of Britain. Part 86 Somerset*, page 71. Original size: 150 x 115 mm.

British Isles. Sheet III. A.0103 [and] *A.103*
Hydrographic Department
1939 and 1944

Contemporary records in the UKHO Archive show that a few years before World War Two, a new section was formed in the Hydrographic Department in London to provide Air Charts for the use of the Fleet Air Arm. The Department had produced Air Charts in strip form in 1914 and in June 1917 a comprehensive scheme of charts of the British Isles and the North Sea was commenced. In 1935 some specimen charts were produced and shortly afterwards a series at a scale of 1:1 million and measured 17 inches by 17 inches came into being. They were given the prefix letter 'A' followed by the number '0' to signify their classification as being secret. A contemporary account describes how they were:

> Constructed on the Mercator Projection on scales of 1/1M and 1/2M to a standard size of 17" x 17" to fit the Bigsworth Board. Being devoid of soundings they were more in the nature of a map than a chart the topography consisting chiefly of contours layered in a graded blue tint with spot heights, main tows, roads, railways, boundaries, woods, lakes and marshes, Navigational aids such as lighthouses and light vessels, Air Beacons, Airfield and Seaplane Bases, Air Corridors and Prohibited Areas, and other information appertaining to Aircraft were shown. The charts were not border-graduated but showed a parallel of latitude and a sub-divided central meridian, a compass rose and lines of magnetic variation. They were schemed so that each chart in a series had a 50% overlap with adjacent sheets.

Two images of the facilities and bi-planes at Weston's airport prior to World War Two. (John Penny collection)

A comprehensive sheet of abbreviations (number A.2000) was produced to accompany the charts.

Source: UKHO, OCB A.0103 and A.103.
Size: 432 x 432mm.

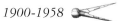

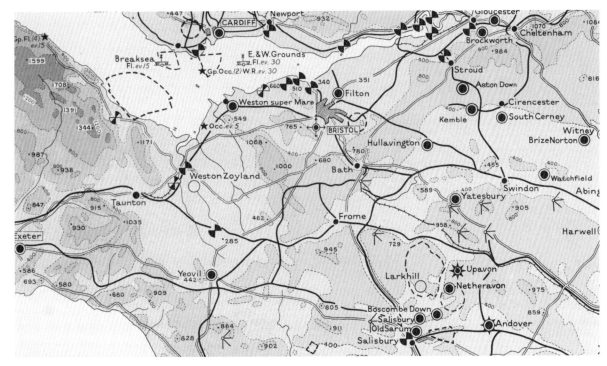

On 31 October 1939 a new chart in the Air Chart series covering southern England was published. The capacity within the county at the start of World War Two was only twelve sites of interest to aviators. When compared to the number of facilities available in 1944 (see the image below) the figure had risen to sixteen, including Church Stanton which was renamed in 1943 to RAF Culmhead.

Source: UKHO, OCB A.0103.

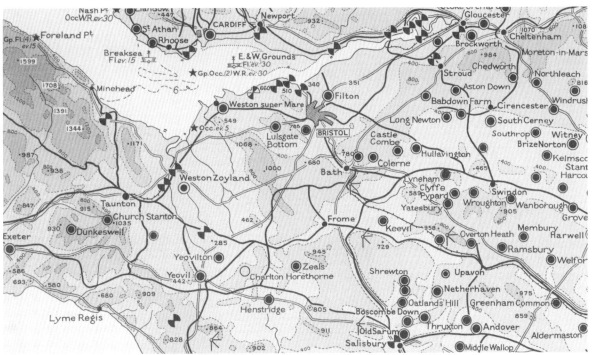

On 29 November 1944 a new edition of the Air Chart covering southern England was published. This new edition was an improved version from its predecessor as the linework was changed to black to improve its visibility.

Source: UKHO, OCB A.103.

World War Two Farm Survey
1941-1943

Dire food shortages during the Second World War meant there was a need to increase home food production, which in turn meant increasing the amount of land used for cultivation. Therefore the 'Farm Survey' was undertaken by the Ministry of Agriculture and Fisheries. County War Agricultural Executive Committees were set up which had the power to requisition derelict land, tell farmers what to grow and inspect property, all in an effort to ensure the land was being used efficiently and for maximum productivity.

Nearly all farms were surveyed between June 1940 and early 1941, and classified as either A, B or C, according to their productivity. Later, between spring 1941 and the end of 1943 a second survey was undertaken with the aim of informing post-war agricultural planning. That is what became known as The National Farm Survey.

The maps used to record the survey were Ordnance Survey 25 inch sheets reduced to half size, although some six-inch sheets were also used. The maps were annotated to show the boundaries of each farm, and each was assigned a unique farm code. The map opposite depicts the Farm Survey covering the Hankridge and Blackbrook areas to the east of Taunton. One of the largest farms in this area, Hankridge Farm, outlined in pink in the top centre of the map, was classified as an 'A' farm and it was owned by Mr Ling.

These maps provide a unique snapshot of the Somerset landscape during a significant moment in history. Today, this landscape is almost unrecognisable, transformed by a housing estate and the Hankridge retail park. One of the few remaining indications this farm existed is the farmhouse, which is now the Hankridge Arms public house.

Equally as interesting as the maps are the forms which accompany them. The survey comprised four forms, three of which were sent to the farmer and one which was completed by an inspector who visited the farm. In the general comments section relating to Hankridge Farm the inspector wrote 'Farmer has been in occupation 22 years. Outbuildings – suitable and adequate'. This section of the form was often contentious as some inspectors were less complimentary about the farmers.

The condition of the farm was described in detail. The water supply to the farmhouse was by means of a well, but there was no water supply to the farm buildings. The roads, buildings, fences, ditches were all recorded as 'good' or 'fair'. There was no infestation with pests, but a problem with weeds, in particular thistles, was noted. The farm had 45 head of cattle and calves, 10 sheep and lambs, 2 pigs, 3 horses and 63 poultry. The farm employed 3 workers: one regular worker aged between 18-21 and a regular worker over 21, as well as a casual worker also over the age of 21. The farm also had one Austin motor car.

Opposite: A reduced reproduction of a section of the sheet covering the Hankridge and Blackbook area, including parts of the parishes of Ruishton, Creech St Michael, West Monkton, and Taunton St Mary Magdalene Without.

Source: TNA, MAF73/36/71 sheet LXXI 9. Original size: 500 x 360mm.

England, South sheet 11, 2nd War revision military, ¼-inch to one mile: GSGS 3957 Geographical Section, General Staff, War Office and Ordnance Survey 1943

The War Office Geographical Section, General Staff used the existing Ordnance Survey mapping to produce a series of air maps for navigators. Earlier aviation maps had a Royal Air Force designation, rather than 'G.S.G.S.'. These maps formed part of the G.S.G.S. series and were compiled and photolithographed by the Ordnance Survey in 1943. They were based on the Ordnance Survey Fourth edition ¼-inch to one mile series.

Although a colour system was used with an accompanying key to show heights in both feet and metres, significant spot heights were included by a white tab to improve their legibility. This purple layering was designed for use in low light planes. One important aspect that the maps did not show were the areas that were considered dangerous to flying.

Each map has the War Office Cassini grid in purple and is overprinted with red aeronautical symbols showing information useful to pilots, such as aerodromes, airports, air lights, prohibited areas, etc. The air navigation map reproduced here shows many differents dangers and aids to navigators.

These sheets were issued to American forces for Operations Overlord and Neptune (the D-day landings) as part of a suite of maps and intelligence documents.

Source: Adrian Webb collection. Original size: 729 x 512mm.

Opposite An extract from G.S.G.S. 3597 sheet 11, of the north of the county.

Key to symbols   **Examples**

AERODROME
  HEIGHT IN FEET ABOVE MEAN SEA LEVEL   Lulsgate Bottom 682

AERONAUTICAL LANDMARK ....   Viaduct at Yeovil

AIRWAY OBSTRUCTION OR
OBSTRUCTION OVER 200 FEET
(60 METRES) ABOVE GROUND LEVEL:
  UNLIGHTED ....   North Petherton

EXPLOSIVES AREA ....   Bason Bridge

GOLF COURSE ....   Long Ashton

H.T. CABLES OF PARTICULAR
DANGER TO NAVIGATION ....   Easton in Gordano

MARINE LIGHT ....   Weston in Gordano

RACE COURSE .... R.C.   Crewkerne

Above: A reproduction of the red aeronautical symbols used on the map. Because the map was issued during the Second World War, a key to these symbols was not included on the map. The symbols shown above are taken from a pre-war issue of a GSGS series. Many other red symbols were used in this series but they do not appear within the county of Somerset.

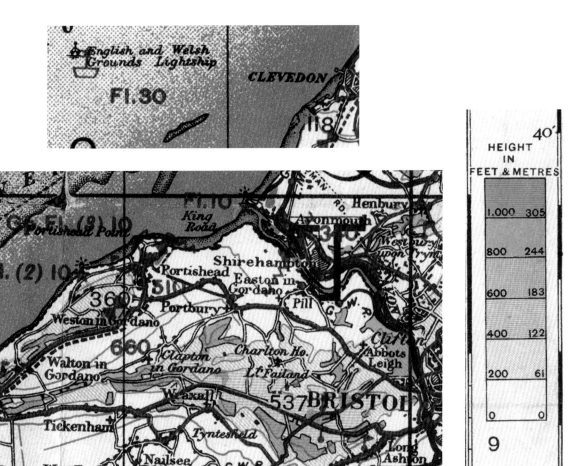

Top: The lightship situated on the English and Welsh Grounds, opposite Clevedon, is shown (enlarged) in red with the legend 'Fl.30' (flashing every 30 seconds).

Above: An extract showing the unusual symbols, in red, at Shirehampton, Weston in Gordano and Failand.

Right: The key to the colouring of the relief used in the map, with the darker colour being used for the higher ground, unlike the water areas where the darker blue is used for the shallower waters.

Opposite: An extract from the sheet covering the south of the county and the airfields on the Blackdown Hills.

The West Country revealed
Brian Walker
1958

The last map to appear in this volume was published in 1958 by the highly popular *Farmers Weekly* magazine and covered the whole of the South West of England. 1958 was Bristol's Royal Show Year that saw Queen Elizabeth the Second visit Bristol, where she made the first ever directly dialled long-distance phone call in the United Kingdom.

Its creator, Brian Walker, showed a range of aspects of the county, not just those that were stereo-typical of the farming community. He showed the locations of all the county's hunts, mortar boards for private schools, a man drinking from a flagon at the foot of Glastonbury Tor, Hinkley Point Nuclear Power Station, Long Ashton Research Station, and much more.

The location of the 'County Institute' at Cannington is shown as a mortar board within a laurel wreath. Established in 1921, Cannington College became the Cannington Centre for Land-based Studies. It is now part of Bridgwater College and its facilities include the Animal Management Centre, Equestrian Centre with indoor and outdoor arena, Activity Centre, a 180-hectare Farm, the historical 'Walled Gardens' and a nine-hole 18-tee golf course. It offers courses in animal care, agriculture, arboriculture, countryside, equine studies, fish management, floristry, game and wildlife, horticulture and sports turf.

A fine touch to this map is the inclusion of Hinton Blewett and the accompanying legend 'home of Brian Walker cartographer', along with a drawing of his pens, brushes and drawing paper. This is possibly the only time that the residence of a Somerset cartographer has been specifically named in this way on a published map of the ancient county.

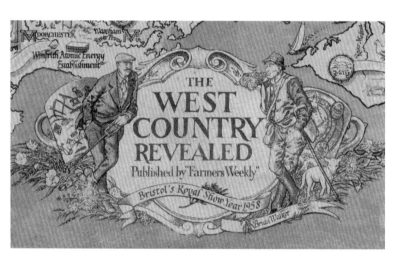

Above: The cartouche from the map including the statement about Bristol's Royal Show Year in 1958. Gone are the cherubs of the seventeenth century, to be replaced with two country gentlemen. Retained are traditional symbols of the countryside, a lamb and a mug, presumably to represent cider making and drinking. The mug is decorated with agricultural implements, such as a rake, fork, plough, hoe and shears.

Source: *The West Country revealed* (1958). (Adrian Webb collection.)
Original size of the map: 449 x 287mm. Original size of the depiction of Somerset (east to west x north to south): 198 x 112mm.

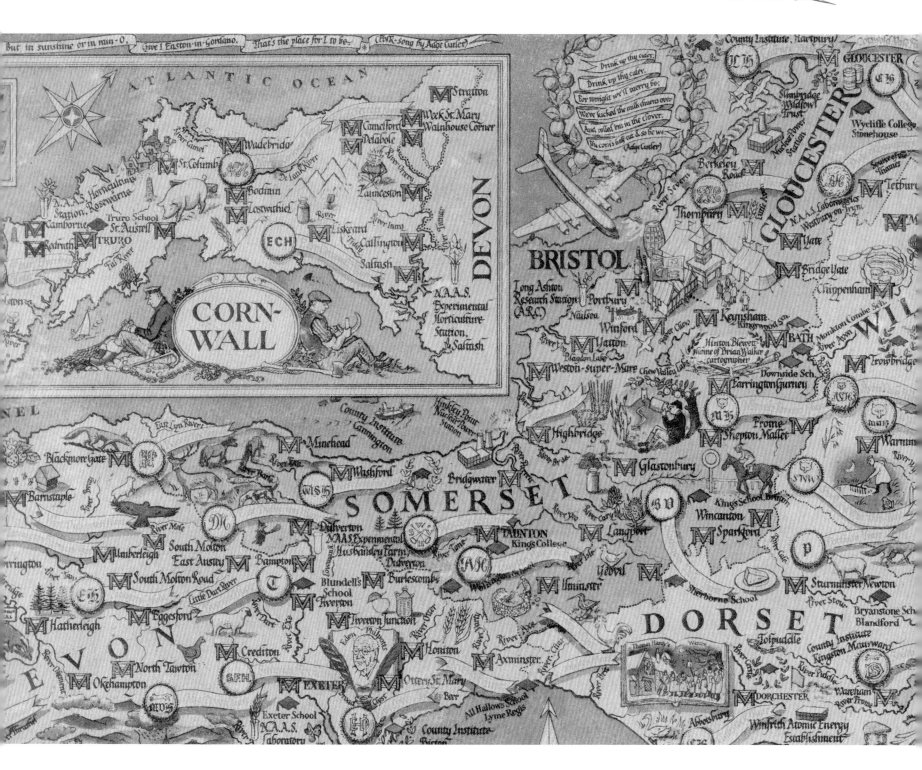

Index of personal names